T0326621

Knowledge Workers in Contemporary China

Knowledge Workers in Contemporary China

Reform and Resistance in the Publishing Industry

Jianhua Yao

LEXINGTON BOOKS
Lanham • Boulder • New York • London

Published by Lexington Books
An imprint of The Rowman & Littlefield Publishing Group, Inc.
4501 Forbes Boulevard, Suite 200, Lanham, Maryland 20706
www.rowman.com

16 Carlisle Street, London W1D 3BT, United Kingdom

British Library Cataloguing in Publication Information Available

Library of Congress Cataloging-in-Publication Data

Yao, Jianhua, 1982–
Knowledge workers in contemporary China : reform and resistance in the publishing industry / Jianhua Yao.
pages cm
Includes bibliographical references and index.
ISBN 978-0-7391-8664-0 (cloth : alk. paper)—ISBN 978-0-7391-8665-7 (electronic)
1. Publishers and publishing—China—Employees. 2. Publishers and publishing—Employees—Labor unions—China. 3. Publishers and publishing—China. 4. Editors—China. 5. Labor—China. 6. Labor unions—China. I. Title.
HD8039.P92C685 2014
331.7'6107050951—dc23
                        2014016196

Printed in the United States of America

Contents

List of Tables

Abbreviations

ACFTU	All-China Federation of Trade Unions
BIBF	Beijing International Book Fair
CCTV	China Central Television
CCYL	Chinese Communist Youth League
CLB	China Labor Bulletin
CNN	Cable News Network
CPC	Communist Party of China
CPD	Central Propaganda Department
CPI	Commercial Press International
CWWN	Chinese Working Women Network
GAPP	General Administration of Press and Publication of China
GDP	gross domestic product
ISBN	International Standard Book Number
MII	Ministry of Information Industry
PAC	Publishers Association of China
PAS	Publishers Association of Shanghai

SARFT	State Administration of Radio, Film, and Television
TVE	township and village enterprise
WTO	World Trade Organization

Preface and Acknowledgments

As Vincent Mosco (2006) remarks, despite a number of outstanding exceptions, media labor is a blind spot in communication studies. My work attempts to benefit the research community on media labor by advancing theory and research on knowledge workers—mainly editors—in the Chinese publishing industry with specific attention given to three different but interrelated processes: *commodification, structuration,* and *spatialization* of the political economy of communication.

To specify, this book will first analyze the ways in which the deepening of the media *commodification* process has forced Chinese editors to serve the political interests of the state and, at the same time, to generate profit for their companies and promote political and social reforms. Second, I will explore the *structuration* process by analyzing how fundamental social, technological, political, and economic changes—especially those in class relations and power dynamics—have produced five critical problems for Chinese editors. Third, I will explore the *spatialization* process by addressing its three indispensable components: globalization, neoliberalism, and the global division of labor. As China is increasingly integrated into the global political economy, most Chinese editors have faced great changes in their value systems and their daily work processes. As a result, the privileged existence of the working class, including editors, as the master of the Communist society has been transformed in many ways.

Most importantly, this book aims to suggest plausible solutions to the problems of Chinese editors (media workers in general), addressing the benefits of labor convergence, the basic functions and major limitations of worker organizations and trade unions, and how they can further help Chinese editors better deal with the challenges associated with current publishing reform when labor unrest is on the rise.

To conclude, this book will concentrate on the trajectories of the labor process transformation of Chinese editors; their changing social, economic, and political roles; and their dilemma, challenges, and opportunities in relation to current social reform and China's integration into the global political economy. Through the political economic analysis of knowledge workers in the Chinese publishing industry, I intend to better understand the broader social and economic transformations, particularly the network of power relations and institutional contexts in which Chinese editors are situated, that have been taking place in China since the late 1970s.

This book would not have been possible without the unwavering support of many people. To name a few, I want to express my deep gratitude to my supervisor, Dr. Vincent Mosco, for his constructive advice and thoughtful inspiration, both of which are precious for my doctoral program at Queen's University, Canada. I am also greatly indebted to Dr. Cao Jin, my former professor and lifelong friend at the School of Journalism, Fudan University, China. Without her organizational skills and personal connections, I would not have been able to conduct the field work involved in this research. Besides, a special thank you is owed to my parents for their unconditional love, as well as their trust and encouragement. I want to thank them for sharing every happiness and sorrow in my life, and I love them both.

Finally, I would like to take this book as a starting point for my future academic career as a young sociologist, and particularly a political economist of communication.

Introduction

The study of knowledge workers has raised a number of important questions for academics and policymakers. Daniel Bell (1999) maintains that with the rise of a society dependent on intellectual technology, particularly on the production and distribution of theoretical information, a new class of leaders—a genuine knowledge class of well-trained scientific and technical workers—was rising to prominence. With the emphasis on meritocracy based on education and skills in the production and distribution of information, knowledge workers have successfully become central figures in this new political and economic system.

Many political economists have supplemented this tradition, such as Herbert Schiller (1973), Harry Braverman (1974), Manuel Castells (1996), and Vincent Mosco (1998; 2004; 2009). Compared to industrial workers, knowledge workers—professional, skilled, and presumably middle-class—are playing a decisive role in the global market. Vincent Mosco and Catherine McKercher (2008) point out that with knowledge workers taking up an enormously large share of the jobs in the developed world, and their numbers growing dramatically in the poorer nations as well, they are becoming more and more active in the labor movement globally.

However, the decline in the power of labor worldwide, as a result of both technological convergence and corporate or institutional convergence, has turned much of the world's labor force, including knowledge workers, into precarious workers (Winseck 1998; Mosco and McKercher 2008; Ross 2009). As Andrew Ross maintains, no one, not even those in traditional professions, can any longer expect a fixed pattern of employment in the course of their lifetime. The rise of contingent employment is steady. For this reason, both industrial workers in low-end services and knowledge workers in high-wage occupations are under tremendous pressure to anticipate, and prepare for, a future in which they will still be able to compete in a changing marketplace. Knowledge workers are pressured by long hours, deadline speedups, and a division of labor that reduces employee autonomy. Worse still they are increasingly confronted with the radical uncertainty of their futures, the temporary nature of their work contracts, and their isolation from any protective framework of social insurance.

Contributing to the numerous studies on knowledge workers, my primary argument in this book is that *using the tool of a political economy analysis, especially through its three different but interrelated processes—commodification, structuration, and spatialization—gives us an important way in which to demonstrate the network of power relations and institutional contexts that knowledge workers in the Chinese publishing industry are situated in, as well as to conceptualize the challenges confronting them. These challenges are brought about by both media reform and social transformation, in the context of technological developments in the information age as well as China's increasing integration into the global political economy.* To be more concrete, I aim to examine the precarious condition of knowledge workers in the Chinese publishing industry, particularly editors, by analyzing their changing labor process and the decline of their social welfare benefits. What is more important, in this book, I also attempt to understand how editors are responding to the problems aforementioned, and to investigate whether worker organizations and trade unions are effectively representing their rights and interests.

KNOWLEDGE WORKERS IN
CHINA'S PUBLISHING INDUSTRY

Class analysis is of critical importance to this book. According to Braverman (1974), studying the class consciousness of knowledge workers is a key to understanding not only their common problems, interests, and prospects, but also their relations with other members of the working class. For this reason, this book specifically concentrates on Chinese editors, due to the following factors: the rapid growth of the Chinese publishing industry, the emergence of a large number of full-time editors, the change in the nature of publishing houses from public institutions to companies, rapid technological developments in the information age, and China's increasing integration into the global division of labor. This book also highlights the significance of establishing worker organizations and trade unions of editors, and of knowledge workers in the Chinese media industry in general, as an effective response to the challenges resulting from both social development and the global division of labor.

Class Consciousness of Knowledge Workers

As Zhao Yuezhi[1] and Robert Duffy (2007, 230) maintain, with the development of "authoritarian capitalism," the reconfiguration of class power serves as a constitutive dimension of China's market reform, and it becomes impossible to fully understand the characteristics of China's socioeconomic changes without clarifying China's social classes or conceptualizing China's class relations. In China, due to the massive privatization of the state-owned enterprises and the Party's embrace of information technologies, industrial workers are quickly losing control of the production and technological innovation process that they have gained under the "proletarian politics" of the pre-reform era. On the contrary, knowledge workers are usually well-educated, equipped with up-to-date technological skills, and are often situated in higher social hierarchy. In this situation, for a better understanding of the class consciousness of knowledge workers, this book pays special attention to their emergence as a leading class of the socialist state by analyzing their common problems, interests, and prospects, because any analysis of the configuration of class power in contemporary China will neither be complete nor accurate without considering knowledge workers as an important part of the working class. In addition, this book also addresses the opinions, feelings, sentiments, and changing moods of knowledge workers in the Chinese publishing industry, which are best interpreted in the examination of their relationships with other members of the working class, particularly industrial workers.

Chinese Media Workers and Editors

According to *The General Report on the Development of China's Media Industry 2010*, the gross output value of the Chinese media industry in 2010 reached 490.796 billion *yuan* (approximately eighty billion dollars), compared with 210.897 billion *yuan* in 2004 (Cui 2010). The media industry itself is fast developing, and the number of media workers has increased to about three million in 2010. Divided into different occupational sections, media workers in China include editors, journalists, photographers, broadcasters, and publication distributors in publishing, newspaper, broadcasting, television newspaper agencies, and distribution institutions. This book specifically examines editors in China's publishing industry based on the following reasons.

First, the Chinese publication industry is developing at an amazing speed. According to *China Statistical Yearbook 2008*, 256,000 different kinds of books were published in 2008, compared with 150,000 in 1978, with the total printed copies of books and sheets rising to 6.936 billion and 56.073 billion from 3.86 billion and 13.54 billion, respectively (China Statistical Yearbook

Editorial Department 2008). The central government has also planned key book publication projects and established prizes for excellent books to promote the development of China's publishing industry. Meanwhile, the number of newspapers, journals, and magazines rose from 1,098 different kinds (including 168 different kinds of newspapers and 930 different kinds of journals and magazines) in 1978 to 11,492 different kinds in 2008 (including 1,943 different kinds of newspapers and 9,549 different kinds of journals and magazines). It is also worth mentioning that along with the rapid development of the information industry, the electronic publication market has already taken shape with over two thousand different kinds of electronic publications coming out annually. At the same time, the number of editors has grown incredibly in the past few years. Currently, there are 579 publishing houses, 363 audio-visual publishing units, and 228 electronic publishers in China, with 60,906 full-time editors altogether. They constitute the major component of Chinese media workers.

Second, one of the most important impacts of the Chinese media reform, especially the media conglomeration process since 2002, is to introduce marketization into the media sector, which has changed the nature of publishing houses from public institutions to companies. In China, the intense competition in the media market has resulted in more diverse and autonomous media, and the spectrum of media products has been expanded, ranging from serious news journalism to purely entertainment stories. However, for editors, marketization has come with less protection from the central government, and more exposure to market competition because the central government still controls and regulates the publishing industry with strict rules and censorship, but has unloaded its responsibilities to either improve the working conditions of editors or increase their social welfare benefits (Li 1995; Cao 1998; He 2003; Zhou 2005a).

Critically, media reform is accompanied by the changing labor process of editors. Questions, such as "Do editors work overtime?" "Do editors still need to take daily attendance since much of their work now can be done at home?" and "For editors, does editing still remain as the main task?" might sound simple, but the examination of their labor process, along with the analysis of employment relations, reward systems, and union organizations, becomes a key element to understanding how consent has been manufactured among editors. According to Michael Burawoy (1979), these elements are so important that they provide a clear vision of the broader political and economic conditions, as well as social patterns of class formation and class reconstitution of editors, both of which are crucial to a political economic analysis.

Third, it is interesting to observe the twofold impacts on editors as a result of rapid technological developments. On the one hand, editors are constantly pressured to pick up new knowledge updated quickly in the information age.

Therefore, their work pressure has substantially increased, and concurrently, their work process is altered in pursuit of effectiveness and efficiency instead of high quality (Wang 2008a). On the other hand, new media have emerged on a remarkable scale in China, and they have greatly challenged the editors who are mainly working on printed media, including books, journals, magazines, and newspapers. Development in China's Internet industry and mobile media industry has made electronic publications increasingly acceptable to readers of all ages, especially to the young generation. Compared with traditional ones, electronic publications are much cheaper and more convenient and environmentally friendly. Even though more positions for the editors who provide online readings and mobile texts might be available, most of the editors, who work on traditional publications, are faced with the problem of contingent employment, declining social welfare benefits, and intense work pressure because less and less profit can be generated by publishing traditional reading materials (Zhang and Peng 2001a; Li 2003; Bi 2005).

Fourth, with China's increasing integration into the global political economy, it is essential to examine editors in the context of the global production of communication and information technologies, focusing on the global division of labor. In recent years, most of the major foreign publishing companies have established branches in China, specializing in copyright trade, business cooperation, as well as market research and development. Cao Jin and Han Shaowei (2008) point out that China's copyright trade has enjoyed a boom, and over ten thousand different kinds of books were imported and 1,300 were exported in 2007. At the same time, foreign companies are also involved in the production of audiovisual and electronic publications in the form of joint ventures in most of the large cities in China. One good example is that in addition to expanding book clubs, Bertelsmann AG has strategically invested in printing, e-commerce, radio and television, cooperated with the Chinese central government, and more importantly, in co-publishing books and magazines with local Chinese publishing houses. Therefore, it needs to be acknowledged that China has become more engaged with the informational global economy, with its economy being continuously reshaped by a broader transnational production network. For this reason, the political economic analysis of Chinese editors needs to highlight the transformation of a wide range of social institutions, as a response to global capitalism. Such transformation includes the rapid construction of labor markets, the restructuring of established labor forces, new state policies for regulating social reproduction, dramatic changes within household relations, and the creation of new cultural values (Taylor 2008).

Responses and Unions

In this context, how are Chinese editors responding? Bahr (1998) argues that labor is organizing in new ways and coping with the challenges of technological developments and institutional convergence worldwide. Converging technologies and converging companies have led media workers to come together across various knowledge industries, in order to seek improved collective bargaining opportunities and successful political interventions. Mosco and McKercher (2008, 11) also maintain that "organized labour has undertaken its own form of convergence, responding to technological and corporate convergence in the knowledge economy, by bringing together workers once divided by technological, craft, and industry barriers." In other words, worker organizations and trade unions are becoming important for knowledge workers because they can be effective in offering a highly mobile workforce with plausible benefits, and providing workers who are not eligible for employer-paid benefits with lifelong training, job placement, counseling, and health care plans.

Specifically for Chinese editors, either worker organizations or trade unions were once an integral part of the state socialist system, not as representatives of the working class in opposition to their employer—the state—but as the means of integrating workers into the state socialist system by performing state functions in the workplace and beyond (Luo 1995; Zhang 2001; Shen 2003; Wang 2003). This function, however, has greatly changed due to current social reform and the emergence of the global division of labor: at present, both worker organizations and trade unions have been transformed into organizations that aim to represent the interests of editors instead of the state, and take an active role in regulating the employment relationship. In this sense, Chinese editors are becoming less and less dependent on the party-state, and more reliant on higher worker organizations or trade unions, for example, the All-China Federation of Trade Unions (ACFTU), which offers legal and political channels to defend their political and economic rights and interests. The ACFTU possesses the expertise, resources, and connections to make sustainable efforts to extending the influences of either worker organizations or trade unions, as well as strengthening their roles in protecting the legitimate rights and interests of the working class, including editors.

Research Questions

To conclude, the primary research question that this book addresses is as follows: *how are knowledge workers in China's publishing industry, particularly editors, responding to the pressure brought about by media reform and social transformation, in the context of technological developments in the information age as well as China's increasing integration into the global political economy?* To be more specific, the book seeks to explore:

1. What are the major changes in the labor process for Chinese media workers, particularly editors today?
2. How are these changes connected to the combined pressure of media reform and social transformation? In detail, first, with the implementation of the marketization process in the Chinese publishing sector, how are editors coping with, on the one hand, the political restrictions and propaganda functions of the state, and on the other hand, the demanding need to generate profit for their companies? To paraphrase, how are they serving the political interests of the state, expanding democracy, and promoting political and social reforms at the same time? Second, are Chinese media workers, particularly editors, in a precarious condition, considering the steady rise of contingent employment, the significant decline of social welfare benefits, and intense work pressure? Third, when Chinese editors are examined from a political economic perspective, is there any inner division, in association with the dominant hierarchical structure, among editors themselves? How do such differences, for example, the differences between senior editors and junior editors, relate to social relations, particularly the power relations in China's media industry?
3. With technological developments as well as China's increasing integration into the global political economy, what are their impacts on editors? To what extent have technological developments changed the labor process of editors, and resulted in their deteriorating conditions? Also, are Chinese editors benefiting from the global division of labor in the publishing industry? What have they gained and lost when the copyright trade between domestic and foreign publishing houses has become frequent?
4. How are Chinese media workers, particularly editors, responding? Specifically, what types of organizations are they establishing (e.g., worker organizations and trade unions), and how effective are these organizations?

METHODS

For methodology, this book principally draws from several approaches that rest upon *qualitative* traditions to critically analyze the factors leading to the precarious condition of Chinese media workers, particularly editors, and more importantly, to examine their responses. Such approaches include archival studies, surveys, and semi-structured interviews.

Archival Studies

This book examines a large number of newspapers, magazines, pamphlets, government and business reports, and press releases, as the main sources of the data collection.

First, various Chinese government sources are collected and studied to trace the recent development in China's media industry. The most important sources are government reports, white papers, and policy documents, such as those of the Central Propaganda Department (CPD), the General Administration of Press and Publication of China (GAPP), and the State Council Information Office. For the official information on labor and employment relations, statistics from the Ministry of Labor and Social Security and the State Council are consulted.

Second, yearbooks are also useful sources. In China, they are considered the most comprehensive and professional sources, based on their quality, availability, and costs (Vallas, Finlay, and Wharton 2009). This book has used the annual *China Labor Statistical Yearbook*, *China Journalism Yearbook*, *China Publishers' Yearbook*, and *Yearbook of China Information Industry* as references. They provide a comprehensive description of the annual growth of China's media industry, as well as technological developments in China's industrial relations.

Third, it is essential to supplement official statistics with reports from nongovernmental organizations or reports written by university professors. As Hong (2008) argues, there is a possibility, even likelihood, that the official statistics have been manipulated or that they are mistaken because sometimes they also perform a propaganda function. Therefore, this book has paid specific attention to several important nongovernmental reports in the fields of China's media industry and labor relations. Such reports include: "The Report on the Chinese Publishing Industry" by Zhou Weihua (2005b), chief editor of China Renmin University Press; "The Annual Report on China's Media Development Index 2010" by the School of Journalism, China Renmin University; "The Report on the Development of China's Media Industry 2010" by the Chinese Academy of Social Sciences and Tsinghua University; "The Report on Chinese Labor Issues" by the Labor and Social Security Forum, Beijing; "The Report on Chinese Labor Relations" by Tong Xin, professor from the Department of Sociology, Peking University; and "The Report on Human Resources Development in Shanghai" by the Human Resources Research Center and the Population and Development Research Center, the Shanghai Academy of Social Sciences.

Surveys

In addition to the extensive archival studies, surveys have been conducted for a better understanding of editors' work and life, including not only their personal information, but also other important information, such as the changes in their working conditions and the decline of their social welfare benefits. In the survey, I sent out 150 questionnaires via e-mail to the editors in most of the large publishing houses in Shanghai.[2] The editors were selected randomly from a list that was provided by an official who works in the Publishers Association of Shanghai (PAS), and 128 completed questionnaires were returned.

The survey questions are divided into four sections: personal information, the changes in the working conditions, the changes in the social welfare benefits, and the comments on China's media reform. To be more concrete:

The first section, "Personal Information," attempts to gain basic information about the editors, such as their age, gender, marital status, and educational background.

There are fifteen questions in the second section, "The Changes in the Working Conditions," to examine the following five aspects of editors: the length of their services in the publishing house, their actual and expected monthly incomes, the number of overtime hours they work, their attitudes toward contingent employment, and how often they sign contracts. Also, several detailed questions are designed to specifically investigate whether editors are satisfied with their working conditions, such as "Have you ever changed your job?"; "What are the problems of the evaluation system in the publishing house?"; and "What is the major pressure as an editor?"

The third section, "The Changes in the Social Welfare Benefits," intends to figure out whether editors are receiving subsidies for housing, medical insurance, and unemployment benefits.

In the last section, "The Comments on China's Media Reform," editors are invited to comment on current Chinese media reform, specifically on both its positive and negative effects, and more importantly, on how worker organizations and trade unions are taking an effective role in protecting their legitimate rights and interests.[3]

Semi-Structured Interviews

This book looks into two cases—one is the Shanghai Science and Technology Publishing House, and the other is the Shanghai Education Publishing House. As Yin (2009) maintains, case studies allow for not only the examination of the particular complexities of a case, but also enable the researcher to gain incredible insight into larger systematic issues—an appropriate meth-

odology for the researcher who wants to look at an issue using both close-
and long-focus lenses.

What Makes the Two Publishing Houses Special?

The Shanghai Science and Technology Publishing House, established in
1956, is one of the largest and most comprehensive publishers in China. It
puts out nearly one thousand books every year, together with five different
journals and seven different magazines. Because of its wide variety of publications and the large scope of its readership, the Shanghai Science and Technology Publishing House enjoys an elevated reputation in China's publishing
industry. Also, it is one of the first Chinese publishers to begin cooperation
with international publishers. This serves as the main reason why I chose it as
the case study for my research. As of 2012, it had published more than two
hundred titles of co-publications, cooperating with many publishers all over
the world, including publishers from the United States, Germany, Britain,
Japan, and France. Therefore, the study of the Shanghai Science and Technology Publishing House has shed light on the understanding of editors'
work process, as well as how it has been changed with China's increasing
integration into the global political economy, and with the influences of the
global division of labor.

The Shanghai Education Publishing House is a professional publishing
house for the education sector, offering educational service and disseminat-
ing information about diverse cultures. Thus, each year, newspapers and
magazines are published specifically for students at all levels. About two
thousand different kinds of books, newspapers, and magazines have been
published since its foundation in 1958. Most importantly, as a publishing
house that mainly deals with educational materials, the Shanghai Education
Publishing House used to be a public institution, and was affiliated to the
Shanghai Education Bureau. However, with the implementation of media
reform and media marketization, it changed into a company. As a consequence, fundamental changes have occurred. First, the Shanghai Education
Publishing House now needs to support itself financially, while profit was
never a concern before the reform. Second, it used to receive many subsidies
from the municipal government; however, government subsidies are becoming less and less available. Third, the publishing house is now operating in a
more open market, accompanied by the fierce competition with other state-
owned publishing houses, private publishing houses, and even foreign publishing groups that also produce educational materials. For the above reasons,
the Shanghai Education Publishing House serves as an ideal case study to
scrutinize both the opportunities and challenges for editors brought about by
current media reform. To be more precise, how has their work process been
changed? Have their social welfare benefits been affected? To what extent

have their working conditions become precarious? These are the key questions in this case study.

Basic Interview Questions

For the interview, the participants—both editors and union officials—were selected from the pool that was recommended and authorized by the "leaders" (*lingdao* in Chinese) of the publishing houses, including editors and union officials of different ages, genders, and occupational ranks. Altogether, four editors and two union officials in each publishing house were interviewed.

The interviews combined both structured and open-ended questions, and each interview lasted for two to three hours. Most of them were conducted in the publishing houses where the editors work. The questions that were asked basically followed the interview outline. However, different questions for different groups were emphasized: the questions for editors mainly focused on their changing labor process as well as their declining social welfare benefits; for interviews with union officials, questions about the main functions of trade unions in publishing houses and the practical problems for better organizing editors were raised.[4]

Supplementary Interviews

I also supplemented two case studies with another five interviews of three editors and two union officials, who work in other major publishing houses in Shanghai.[5] Additionally, I conducted two interviews with the officials from the Shanghai Publication Bureau and the PAS. These interviews, when combined with the first-hand data collected from the case studies, helped to comprehensively understand the precarious condition in which editors, Chinese media workers in general, are situated.

In the research, the questions for the government official from the Shanghai Publication Bureau concentrated on how all levels of government in China (central, provincial, and local) are responding to the precarious condition that media workers are now faced with, particularly the decline of social welfare benefits. I was also interested in knowing more about the policies that have been implemented, and will be implemented, to expand the influences of both worker organizations and trade unions. The questions for the official from the PAS mainly explored the activities organized by the association to link together editors of different age, gender, job title, and educational background from different publishing houses, and more significantly, to investigate the institutional arrangements that can unite editors. Appendix D outlines all the interview participants and their basic background information.

To conclude, in both surveys and interviews, a mixed-methods approach, known as *triangulation* has been adopted, to conduct the research. Denzin and Lincoln (2008) argue that studies that rely on multiple sources of data are more likely to be accurate. *Triangulation*—examining the same research questions by using multiple sources (in this book: documents, observations, surveys, and interviews)—has offered a more accurate picture of what is being studied.

ORGANIZATION OF THE BOOK

This book seeks to provide a panoramic view of Chinese media workers, particularly editors, by developing a systematic examination of the three entry points of the political economy of communication—*commodification, structuration,* and *spatialization,* according to Mosco (2009), with its application to understanding the challenges confronting Chinese editors, brought about by recent social development and China's increasing integration into the global political economy. More importantly, the book also tries to understand how Chinese media workers, mainly editors, are effectively responding to both national and international changes aforementioned. The book is organized as follows.

Chapter 1 takes on the question of how this research is empowered by political economic theories of communication and development. Within the overall framework of the political economy of communication, two central concepts are addressed: Chinese media reform and knowledge workers. First, to better understand China's media reform, chapter 1 offers a thorough analysis of the relationships between current media reform and the Party principle, media commodification, and media democracy. As for the examination of knowledge workers, it is critical to explore their connections to industrial workers as well as to the party-state, the influences of globalization, particularly neoliberalism and the global division of labor, and the functions of trade unions when they are responding to the challenges brought about by current social reform.

The following three chapters develop a substantive map of the political economic analysis of Chinese media workers, particularly editors. To specify, chapter 2 concentrates on the *commodification* process of the political economy of communication by focusing on Chinese media reform, especially the publishing conglomeration process since 2002, as an indication of social development. It is undeniable that the intense competition for the media market has resulted in more diverse and autonomous media, which has significantly promoted media democracy. However, at the same time, with regard to media reform, and social development in a broader sense, editors are increasingly confronted with the problem of contingent employment, declining social welfare benefits, and intense work pressure, all of which largely contribute to their precarious working and living conditions.

Addressing the *structuration* process of the political economy of communication, chapter 3 reveals that in addition to the problems brought about by Chinese media reform, editors are faced with the following five critical problems, as a result of a series of fundamental social changes, including technological, political, and economic ones, and most importantly, the changes in class relations and power dynamics. Therefore, editors' positions have become even more precarious. The five problems are: problems related to technological changes, the problems on how to follow the Party principle in the media marketization process, those on the marketization process in the social welfare system, the problems brought about by the smashing of the work-unit system, and the conflicts resulting from the inner division within the working class. Special attention is drawn to the inner division among editors because there is a growing tension between senior and junior editors in publishing houses, manifested in struggles for power in the publishing industry hierarchy.

As both chapters 2 and 3 have situated editors, and Chinese media workers in a larger sense, in domestic social economic and political development, chapter 4 attempts to broaden the theoretical horizon into a global perspective with China's increasing integration into the world economy, concentrating on the *spatialization* process of the political economy of communication. It is essential to examine how editors have encountered globalization, embodied in the widespread influences of neoliberalism, as well as the unbalanced global division of labor. On the one hand, this chapter explores how neoliberal ideas have influenced editors to "dance with chains" (Zhao 1998, 161), under the construction of a particular kind of market economy that increasingly incorporates neoliberal elements along with authoritarian centralized control (Harvey 2005). On the other hand, it examines how editors have financially profited from the copyright trade between domestic and foreign publishing houses that has developed in an extremely unbalanced manner, and how they get exploited when connected to the global networks of wealth, power, and symbols.

In chapter 5, I aim to seek a plausible solution for Chinese media workers, and editors in particular, to overcoming the above problems. I will address the benefits of labor convergence, the basic functions and major limitations of worker organizations and trade unions, and how they can, for example the ACFTU, further help Chinese media workers better deal with the challenges associated with current Chinese media reform.

It is important to emphasize that in China, while capitalist interests are becoming more integrated at a global level, together with the decentralizing power of social networks, divided bargaining does not help Chinese media workers, particularly editors, because it leads to the development of a status hierarchy within the group that benefits some workers at the expense of others. At the same time, it also creates opportunities for bargaining that plays one unit of labor against another, thereby fomenting conflicts within and between different groups of workers (Mosco and McKercher 2008). Centralized bargaining and convergence in the forms of worker organizations and trade unions, however, have become effective weapons for Chinese media workers to enhance their collective identity, and attain values of long-term stability and labor harmony. Specifically in the Chinese publishing industry, as the surveys and interviews reveal, both worker organizations and trade unions are effective in promoting regulatory protections that limit work hours and set a minimum wage, carrying out workplace health and safety standards, and establishing centralized and standardized union structures for editors.

Under the umbrella of transcultural political economy (Chakravarrty and Zhao 2008), the concluding chapter summarizes the findings of this research. It becomes significantly important to examine Chinese media workers, particularly editors, by inquiring into the possibilities of reconstituting the party-state, restructuring the Chinese publishing industry, as well as reshaping the state's ideological, cultural, and normative underpinnings, with the emphasis on the *commodification, structuration,* and *spatialization* processes of the political economy of communication.

To conclude, by scrutinizing the trajectories of the labor process transformation of editors; their changing social, economic, and political roles; and their dilemma, challenges, and opportunities in relation to current social reform and China's growing integration into the global political economy, I aim to help Chinese editors, and generally knowledge workers in the Chinese media industry, better understand their work, the difficulties associated with it, and how it compares with the work of knowledge workers worldwide. I also intend to benefit the research community by applying the processes of *commodification, structuration,* and *spatialization* of the political economy of communication to the analysis of the challenges that are confronting Chinese media workers, particularly editors, due to social transformation, as well as China's increasing integration into the global political economy. In other words, this book aims to advance theory and research on knowledge workers in China, especially through a political economy approach. Most importantly, I attempt to benefit the sociology of knowledge, technology, and culture, especially the political economy of communication in contemporary China, by providing suggestions about how to improve the working conditions of knowledge workers who play a pivotal and ever-growing role in the information era.

NOTES

1. All Chinese names in the text are listed by family name followed by given name, as is customary in China. The references section alphabetizes entries by family name.

2. The publishing houses where the editors in my surveys are working include: the Shanghai People's Publishing House, the Children's Publishing House, the Shanghai Science and Technology Publishing House, the Shanghai Education Publishing House, the Shanghai Translation Publishing House, the Shanghai Lexicographical Publishing House, the Shanghai Ancient Books Publishing House, the Shanghai Century Publishing Group Distribution Center, the Shanghai Literature and Art Publishing House, the Shanghai Culture Publishing House, and the Shanghai Music Publishing House.

3. See appendix A for the original survey questions.

4. See appendix B for "Interview Outline," and see appendix C for "Interview Questions for Editors and Union Officials."

5. The three editors come from the Shanghai Art and Literature Publishing House, the Shanghai Lexicographical Publishing House, and Fudan University Press. Meanwhile, one union official works at the Shanghai Art and Literature Publishing House, and the other works at Fudan University Press.

Chapter One

Political Economy, Media Reform, and Knowledge Workers

What is political economy? What are the characteristics of political economy? This chapter starts by answering these two questions with the purpose of offering a brief overview of political economy, which lays the theoretical foundation of this book. Then, this chapter continues with the examination of two central concepts that are closely related to editors in the Chinese publishing industry: media reform and knowledge workers. Interestingly, Chinese editors are trapped in a dilemma: they face the dual challenge of dealing with the state elite as described by the propaganda model, as well as dealing with the commodification process led by the economic elite who have profited from it. A detailed analysis of such a dilemma involves exploring three major components of China's media reform: the Party principle and the propaganda model, media commodification, and media democracy. Furthermore, it is important to explore the relationships of knowledge workers to industrial workers as well as to the party-state, the influences of globalization, particularly neoliberalism and the global division of labor, and the responses of knowledge workers in China's media industry, particularly those in the publishing industry, to the challenges brought about by current social reform. Therefore, class analysis, globalization, and trade unions have become the three key aspects that I would like to address in the analysis of knowledge workers in the Chinese publishing industry.

POLITICAL ECONOMY

What Is Political Economy?

My research on knowledge workers in the Chinese publishing industry primarily draws on the theoretical trajectory of political economy. Political economy can be described as *"the study of social relations, particularly the power relations, that mutually constitute the production, distribution, and consumption of resources, including communication resources"* (Mosco 2009, 2). According to this definition, political economists are not merely interested in analyzing the meaning of media messages, but more profoundly, they intend to explore the social process through which these messages are constructed and interpreted, and the contexts which shape and constrain these constructions.

From a broader sense, political economy deals with a wide range of issues, relating to both *control* and *survival* in social life. In order to study the *control* in social life, political economy specifically looks at how a society organizes itself, with the analysis of how the internal organization of social group members adapts to or fails to adapt to the inevitable changes that all societies are faced with. For the study of *survival*, political economy examines how people produce what they need to reproduce themselves and to keep their society going. That is to say, it is important for political economists to examine not only the *political* aspect of social life, by concentrating on the *control* process (encompassing the social organization of relationships within a community), but also the *economic* aspect (focusing on the *survival* process which involves production and reproduction) (Mosco 2009).

Essentially, political economy addresses the operation of power, which, by contrast, contemporary economic theory largely ignores in its examination of the marketplace (Rothschild 2002). To specify, the analysis of power relations links political economy with communication because both of them discuss critical issues related to capitalism and democracy, directly deal with commercial and material issues, and are concerned with issues of social justice and political self-government. Therefore, the following issues are generally listed on the agenda of the political economists of communication: market structure, advertising support, labor relations, profit motive, technologies, and government policies that are shaping media industry, journalistic practices, occupational sociology, and the nature and content of the news and entertainment (Mansell 2004).

Furthermore, the political economy of communication also aims to understand how power is structured and differentiated, where it comes from, and how it is renewed (Garnham 2000). This notion suggests an examination of communication to show how the structuring of global networks, and the flows and consumption of digital information are informed by both predominant and alternative principles, values, and power relations. According to William Melody (1994), political economists of communication have drawn increasing attention to the circumstances that give rise to any given distribution of power and of the consequences for consumers and citizens.

To summarize, the political economy of communication focuses on the nature of the relationship between media and communications systems, in a larger sense, the social structure of society. It attempts to examine how media and communications systems and content reinforce, challenge, or influence existing class and social relations, and it particularly seeks to explore how economic factors influence politics and social relations. In addition, as Robert McChesney (2000, 2007) argues, the political economy of communication specifically looks at how ownership, support mechanisms, and government policies, in association with power relations, influence media behavior and content. It concentrates on the structural factors and the labor process in the production, distribution, and consumption of communication.

Central Qualities of Political Economy

According to Mosco (2009), there are a set of central qualities that characterize the political economy of communication, which have broadened its meaning beyond what is typically provided in definitions. The political economy of communication is characterized by addressing *social change and historical transformation, the totality of social relations, moral philosophy,* and *social praxis.*

First, political economists of communication have consistently concentrated on understanding *social change and historical transformation.* The founding figures, such as Adam Smith, David Ricardo, and John Stuart Mill, primarily explored the capitalist revolution, and the social transformation that had led to the emergence of an industrial society in their times. Karl Marx critically examined the dynamic forces within capitalism and the relationship between capitalism and other forms of political-economic organizations, in order to comprehensively understand the process of social changes that would result in socialism (Mosco 2009). Contemporary political economists of communication attempt to take on the central questions of our time, trying to figure out the fundamental rearrangement of social structure and process, particularly with the examination of the following four historical processes: the growth of the media, the extension of corporate reach, commodification, and the changing role of state and government intervention (Golding and Murdock 2005).

Second, political economy is holistic in the sense that it concentrates on examining *the totality of social relations* that involve the economic, political, social, and cultural aspects of social life. This argument indicates that compared with mainstream economics, which predominantly sees the economy as a separate and specialized domain, political economy focuses on the interplay between economic organizations and political, social, and cultural life (Golding and Murdock 2005). To elaborate, a commitment to the social totality not only means understanding the connection between the political and the economic, but also means linking society's political economy with the wider social and cultural field. Therefore, most political economists try to understand how power and wealth are related, and how they are in turn connected to social and cultural life. Political economists of communication in particular are keen to understand the relationships of power and wealth to mass media, information, and entertainment.

Third, Mosco (2009, 4) implies that "political economy is also noted for its commitment to *moral philosophy*, which means that it cares about the values that help to create social behavior and about those moral principles that ought to guide efforts to change it." In other words, political economy goes beyond technical issues of efficiency and effectiveness to engage with such basic moral questions as social justice, social inequality, and the public good. The moral dimension of political economy remains strong because it provides a powerful defense of democracy, equality, and the public sphere in the face of dominant private interests (Artz, Macek, and Cloud 2006).

In detail, political economists pay close attention to the distortions and inequalities of the market system. Peter Golding and Graham Murdock (2005) argue that the concept of the "public good" is the basis for the analysis of the balance between the public and private sector, as well as the analysis of constructing a public cultural space, which is open, diverse, and accessible. According to Jurgen Habermas (1991), communication has become a central component of democracy, and therefore, the central problem of the political economy of communication has been the matter of determining a more democratic media system than that provided by the market. The political economy of communication addresses the key issues surrounding the relationships among communication, democracy, and capitalism, thereby promoting a deeper understanding of democracy.

Fourth, political economy is concerned with *social praxis*, or the unity of thinking and doing. Against traditional academic positions, which separate research from social intervention and the researcher from the activist, political economists have consistently viewed intellectual life as a means of bringing about social change and social intervention as means of advancing knowledge. Political economists of communication have conducted many field studies, and been fully engaged with the participants of their researches. For example, by leading a field study in an Indian village called Ramanagara, Manjunath Pendakur (1993) highlights the postcolonial condition of the Indian economy, where its integration into the world capitalism is well on its way. He also highlights the changes in the way that people think about locale, identity, and culture. More importantly, he addresses the uneven development process, due to the distribution of power in association with class, caste, and gender. In "Women and Knowledge Work in the Asia-Pacific: Complicating Technological Empowerment," McLaughlin and Johnson (2007) closely examine female knowledge workers in Singapore and Malaysia, and find that discrimination, based on both structural and social elements, is reproduced in women's use of technologies. As such, they critically urge a change of hierarchical and patriarchal authority, including the changes in social attitudes, cultural ideologies, and gender stereotypes.

In fact, many political economists of communication have turned out to be social activists in social movements in pursuit of moral philosophy that is deeply rooted in the tradition of the discipline. They are promoting women's rights and opposing domestic violence, defending the rights of gays and lesbians, promoting the rights of migrant workers, and becoming leaders of environmental movements (Ogden 2004). Specifically, in alliance with feminists, political economists have pushed government officials to implement social policies that facilitate women's agency and protect their interests in the name of social justice, more than just offering women more education and job opportunities solely for the purpose of national economic development (Riordan 2002). Working together with union officials, political economists have also succeeded in advancing numerous trade union movements in the information age by incorporating the new tools of information technology and telecommunications. Most ambitiously, they are still striving to fabricate a complex web of communication networks and information sources, which could possibly link national unions, workplaces, nongovernmental organizations, and other popular organizations (Sussman and Lent 1998).

In short, political economy concentrates on the issues that are intimately associated with audience commodities, corporate power, the social totality, the propaganda model, and the public sphere. In other words, rather than scrutinizing texts, discourses, or symbolic meanings, political economists aim to understand the production of meaning as the exercise of power, the construction process of public discourses by promoting certain cultural forms over others with the economic dynamics of production, and the barriers that limit the freedom of consumption, for example, time, space, and cultural competence.

MEDIA REFORM

From the time China's economic reform began in 1978, many political commentators have tried to characterize China's transition from a planned economy to a market economy under various formulations: post-socialism, state capitalism, even social capitalism (Dirlik 1989). The regime has settled on "the socialist commodity economy," along with the one-size-fits-all epithet, "socialism with Chinese characteristics." In such a context, media reform was implemented, with three key concepts associated with it, namely, the Party principle and the propaganda model, media commodification, and media democratization.

The Party Principle and the Propaganda Model

The Party principle is a good starting point for understanding that Chinese media workers, including editors, are still obliged to serve the political interests of the authoritarian state. In *A Teaching Program for Journalism Theory*, Tong and Cheng (1993) mention that with the legacy of Party journalism, at the present time, the media structure is dominated by the Party committee at each hierarchical level. As a consequence, the Party principle is unconditionally and strictly obeyed in the media sector, and it comprises three basic components: "that the news media must accept the Party's guiding ideology as their own, that they must propagate the Party's programs, policies, and directives, and that they must accept the Party's leadership and adhere to the Party's organizational principles and press policies" (Tong and Cheng 1993, 148).

In *Media, Market and Democracy in China between the Party Line and the Bottom Line*, Zhao (1998) furthers Tong and Cheng's arguments by indicating that in responding to the Party principle, Chinese media workers (also applicable to editors) are therefore required to fulfill two interrelated tasks. On the one hand, from a *bottom-up* approach, Chinese media workers ought to report people's opinions, concerns, and aspirations to the cadres who are working directly with the people in the Party committee, so that a strong connection between the Party and the masses can be achieved. On the other hand, from a *top-down* approach, Chinese media workers are assumed to "bring the Party program, the Party line, and the Party's general and specific policies to the people in the quickest and most extensive ways" (Mao 1991, 241). Specifically in the publishing industry, according to Gan Xifen (1994), Chinese editors should take the responsibilities to educate the people to be more united and to make improvements in socialism. They must not do the opposite by publishing materials (mainly books, journals and magazines, and newspapers) to create political division or ideological backwardness among the people. This is the lofty sense of responsibility of the socialist journalistic enterprise.[1]

One consequence of the unconditional obedience to the Party principle is that the mass media in China have performed a propaganda role. According to the propaganda model, as proposed by Edward Herman and Noam Chomsky (1988), the mass media are carefully selecting contexts, promises, and the general agenda in order to serve the interests of the elite. It is critical to consider the propaganda model as a key element to understanding the role that Chinese media workers, particularly editors, are actively playing because it deals with the inequality of wealth, and most importantly, it involves power analysis at its core. Herman (1998, 2000) also argues that in accordance with the principles of the propaganda model, the mass media are highly functional for the established power and responsive to the needs of the government, the social elite, the leaders of the corporate community, and the top media owners and executives. Therefore, the analysis of the propaganda model is a useful tool within the overall political-economic model.

Specifically, in China where the levers of power are in the hands of the state bureaucracy, the monopolistic control over the publishing industry, often supplemented by official censorship, makes it clear that the Chinese publishing industry serves the ends of the dominant political and economic elites. In this regard, Chinese editors are expected to commit to their social responsibilities, not the responsibilities to enable the public to assert meaningful control over the political process, but the responsibilities to inculcate and defend the economic, social, and political agenda of the privileged groups. In practice, this can be achieved in various ways, for example, through the careful selection of topics, selective distribution of concerns, framing of issues in favorable language, filtering of information according to the interests of the Party, and keeping economic, social, political, and cultural debates within the bounds of acceptable promises.

Media Commodification

Following the Party principle, Chinese editors are supposed to serve the propaganda function of the mass media. However, it is equally important to pinpoint that they are also currently faced with the challenges of media commodification and democratization, both of which are brought about by current social reform.

Mosco (2009) defines commodification as *a process of transforming things valued for their use into marketable products that are valued for what they can bring in exchange*. In other words, "Commodification is the process of transforming *use values* into *exchange values*" (Mosco 2009, 129). The public's growing demand for more media service, as well as fewer economic subsidies by all levels of government, has motivated the Chinese media industry to seek other sources of financing by promoting media commodification. According to Dallas Smythe (1977), the mass media are constituted out of a process which sees media companies producing audiences and delivering them to advertisers. This process is also known as commercialization, a process concentrating on the use of media advertising to perfect commodification in the entire economy (Garnham 2000; Mosco 2009).

To elaborate on this point in the Chinese context, advertising has become China's fastest growing industry since the early 1980s with favorable government policies and a rapidly expanding market economy. When the mass media are increasingly linked with business through advertising and sponsorship, they no longer simply perform a propaganda role, especially with the emergence of business conglomerates in the media sector. Susan Shirk (2011) compares the role that the mass media play before and after current media reform in her latest edited book *Changing Media, Changing China*. She argues that in the pre-reform era, the Chinese public received all of its highly homogenous information from a small number of officially controlled sources. The media were called the "throat and tongue" of the Party, and their sole purpose was to mobilize public support by acting as loudspeakers for the policies of the Communist Party of China (CPC). However, beginning in the early 1980s, the structure of China's mass media changed because newspapers, magazines, and television stations were driven to enter the market and to earn revenue. With the audience becoming eager for information and manufacturers constantly advertising their products, the increase of profit in the media sector has been steady. In addition, when examining the influences of media commercialization, professionalism, and the Internet on China's emerging public sphere in an era of transition, Gang and Bandurski (2011) emphasize that media commodification has accelerated since 2000, especially after the media conglomeration process that started in 2002, as the central government sought to strengthen Chinese media organizations in order to compete with foreign media companies.

Both Zhao (1998, 2008) and Shirk (2011) have drawn specific attention to the practical impacts of media commodification in their works. According to *The General Report on the Development of China's Media Industry 2010*, the financial impacts of media commodification are rather obvious given that the total outcome of China's media industry reached 126 million *yuan* in 1998, and by 2010, that figure had nearly quadrupled to around 490 million *yuan* (Cui 2010). However, the social impacts of media commodification, especially the commodification process in the Chinese publishing industry, are more profound according to these two scholars.

First, the CPC has eliminated mandatory subscriptions to official newspapers and ended subsidies to most papers. Even nationally circulated, official papers like *The People's Daily*, *The Guangming Daily*, and *The Economics Daily* are now sold at retail stalls and are competing for audiences.

Second, about a dozen commercial newspapers with national circulations of over one million readers are printed in multiple locations throughout the country. It is also worth highlighting that although most of the commercial publications are part of publishing groups led by the Party, they appear to be very different. In contrast to the stilted and formulaic language of official publications, the language of the commercial press is lively and colloquial. Because of this difference in style, people are more apt to believe that the content of commercial media is true.[2]

Third, regarding the power shift brought about by the growth of media commodification, unsurprisingly, the number of reports on issues at national and provincial levels has remarkably decreased, based on the fact that these issues are more likely to be involved with propagating the policies of the Party. By contrast, Chinese media workers, particularly editors, have shown their growing interests in metropolitan issues, which are more relevant to the affairs closer to the daily lives of the urban population. These issues are normally less political, and more consumer-oriented.

To conclude, it is apparent that in China, with the implementation of the media commodification process, the levels of bureaucratic control in the media sector have been reduced. This trend in turn makes the entire media sector less political. In China's publishing industry, with editors gaining increasing autonomy, they have accumulated a sense of job satisfaction derived from the relevance of their work to the daily lives of the audience. Thus, they have managed to produce new publications that are mostly devoted to business information and infotainment.

Media Democratization

As mentioned above, in order to follow the Party principle and meet the challenges of media commodification at the same time, Chinese editors are assumed to act as the defenders of the Party, but equally significant, they are supposed to pursue business interests. How would they respond if these two missions conflict? The question falls back on media democratization, another key aspect in the examination of knowledge workers in China's publishing industry (Hackett and Carroll 2006).

According to Crawford Macpherson (1977), media democratization comprises efforts to change media messages, practices, institutions, and contexts *inside* the media system, including changing state communication policies, in a direction which enhances participation and equality, and helps to build a social order which nurtures the autonomy of individuals and their developmental power. More importantly, media democratization also involves efforts *outside* the media system, for example, the democratization of the economy and the state, and the equalization of communicative and material resources available to citizens. Both of them have played a pivotal role in the process of media democratization from a much broader political and cultural perspective.

In "Political Communication Systems and Democratic Values," Gurevitch and Blumler (1990) specifically concentrate on the functions and services that media perform and provide in pursuit of democracy. The functions and services include:

1. Surveillance of the sociopolitical environment, reporting developments likely to impinge, positively or negatively, on the welfare of citizens.
2. Meaningful agenda-setting, identifying the key issues of the day, including the forces that have formed and may resolve them.
3. Platforms for an intelligible and illuminating advocacy by politicians and spokespersons of other causes and interest groups.
4. Dialogue across a diverse range of views, as well as between power holders (actual and prospective) and mass publics.
5. Mechanisms for holding officials to account for how they have exercised power.
6. Incentives for citizens to learn, choose, and become involved, rather than merely to follow and kibitz over the political process.
7. A principled resistance to the efforts of forces outside the media to subvert their independence, integrity, and ability to serve the audience.
8. A sense of respect for the audience member, as potentially concerned and able to make sense of his or her political environment. (Gurevitch and Blumler 1990, 25–26)

Then, how is China's media democratization progressing, which focuses on the values of inclusivity, mutuality, and justice? According to Zhao (1998), journalism practices in the popular commercial sector have made some important contributions toward democratization, with an appreciation of the importance of media professionals who speak on behalf of the people, and public participation which dethrones the self-important, self-appointed media. Zhao reflected, "It is rather obvious that the emergence of a commercialized sector, in favor of ordinary people, has been addressing their concerns, speaking their languages, and treating them as protagonists" (1998, 156).

However, numerous scholars have argued that such changes are not fundamental, even though the public's need for entertainment, social, and business information, and more generally, its participation in economic and cultural life through the media are acknowledged and partially fulfilled (Lee 1994a; Sun 1994; Hackett and Zhao 1997). To be more specific, Pei (1994) contends that *inside* the media system, the accessibility to political information, the meaningful participation in political life, and the significant role in making key economic decisions of the mass media are not encouraged by the Party, and sometimes they are opposed. *Outside* the media system, it is also taken for granted that the Party principle must not be directly challenged under any circumstance. As a result, Chinese media workers, particularly editors, survive by merely softening the tones of political propaganda—moving beyond its narrow concentration, and broadening its content to include social and personal issues. Therefore, in reference to media democratization, it is more accurate to maintain that China's mass media (including the publishing industry) serve as a supplementary rather than an oppositional institution to the more conventional Party organs. Thus, Chinese media workers have to gain the ability to put on a good show while "dancing with chains" (Zhao 1998, 161).

"Globalization and the Chinese Media: Technologies, Content, Commerce and the Prospects for the Public Sphere" explores the relationship of Chinese media democratization to globalization. According to McCormick and Liu (2003), the flow of media technologies, content, and business models across China's boundaries has increased, and globalization has also significantly transformed the public sphere.

First, in terms of linking media technologies to globalization, each of the media technologies, including gramophones, radios, videos, and televisions, has had an impact on the social distribution of ideas and information. More critically, each of them has exerted an enormous impact on the changing configuration of institutions—successive new media technologies have enjoyed progressively less centralized, less politicized, and more commercially oriented institutional frameworks.

Second, to associate media content with globalization, it is worth mentioning that while China's political authorities retain a heavy hand, globalization has increased the volume and diversity of images and information available to the Chinese audience. Globalization also offers Chinese citizens new resources that have the potential to establish a more open and reasonable public sphere. According to Daya Kishan Thussu, "mobility of the media is a key characteristic of the increasingly digitised global communication ecology" (2007, 1). In a digitally connected globe, flows of all kinds of information—political discourse, scientific research, corporate data, personal communication, and media entertainment—circulate around the world at a speed unimaginable even a decade ago.

Third, connecting business models to globalization, McCormick and Liu (2003) argue that due to the widespread expansion of media commodification, influenced by the Western concept of consumerism, the Chinese audience is less exposed to official public discourses, and more exposed to such topics as fashion, education, community, and professional training. As Davis echoes:

> [R]apid commercialization . . . broke the monopolies that had previously cast urban consumers in the role of supplicants to the state. . . . [R]eformers became increasingly indifferent to how citizens used their new commercial freedoms. And in this more lightly censored terrain, urban residents initiated networks of trust, reciprocity, and attachment that differed from the vertical relationship of obedience between subject-citizens and Party or government officials . . . the greater affluence and new consumerism of the 1990s have weakened the hege-

monic sureties that defined urban life throughout the 1960s and 1970s. (Davis 2000, 2–3)

To conclude, according to Donald, Keane and Hong (2002), media reform in China concentrates on the gradual decentralization of management, deregulation for media industry, and diversification of publications, with the emergence of a new middle class that controls economic and social capital. However, the central government has never lost the control of media industry. With regard to the Chinese publishing industry, it is owned and operated either by the Central Committee of the CPC or by municipal/provincial Party organs at various levels. Also, by serving as an instrument of the Party and the state for political propaganda and political conformity, the Chinese publishing industry (mass media in a broader sense) still remains a prerequisite for both the Party and state leaders to maintain their balance of power and domination.

KNOWLEDGE WORKERS

In the introduction of *The Critical Communications Review: Labor, the Working Class, and the Media*, Vincent Mosco and Janet Wasko maintain that in order to challenge the individualistic, pluralistic, and developmentalist paradigm of established research, scholars should focus on the "social relations of communication" and "wider institutional power structure of society" that shape media and communications (Mosco and Wasko 1983, ix). Therefore, my analysis of knowledge workers in China's publishing industry is intimately associated with class analysis, globalization, particularly the widespread reach of neoliberalism with the emergence of the global division of labor, and trade unions—how Chinese editors are organized to respond to both the domestic and international challenges aforementioned.

Labor and Class Analysis

As Mosco points out in "The Laboring of Communication," despite a number of outstanding exceptions, "media labour and class formation is a blind spot in communication studies" (2006, 493). However, the growth of employment in the communication industry, and the technological and institutional changes unleashed by corporate concentration and informationalized capitalism, have alerted communication scholars to the changing nature of work and of worker organizations. In doing so, communication scholars attempt to advance the understanding of the broader transformative historical processes that both shape and are carried out through media and communications (Mosco 2008, 121). In this sense, when analyzed from the perspective of class relations and class struggles, the control and deployment of media and communications becomes a key to understanding the broader transformative historical process. As such, my examination of knowledge workers in the Chinese publishing industry gives special attention to class analysis, which serves as the defining feature of social relations and power structure in China. More importantly, class analysis offers a comprehensive and compelling theoretical framework within which to understand the possibilities for and the obstacles to emancipatory social changes (Adams and Welsh 2008).

First, it is important to acknowledge that knowledge workers, playing a critically important role in the current social transformation, are important compositions of the working class in China (Zhu and Dai 2009). To specify, according to Marx, who defines class at the point of production, the working class is a definite social group, whose common identity is rooted in the non-ownership of the means of production, selling labor power for wages, and holding the status as an employee (Braverman 1974). Following Marx's definition, in the Chinese context, the working class is comprised of "people who, by their physical strength and skills, directly or indirectly operate the tools of production to produce physical products, provide labor service or assistance to such production or service, and are supervised by managers" (Lu 2002, 127). To be more concrete, in China, the working class is considered to manufacture *material* commodities, such as clothes, gas, chemicals, and machines, as well as to offer *nonmaterial* commodities, which include knowledge, information, management, and service.

In the transition to a market economy, the Chinese working class is also in the process of changing and restructuring (Jin 1998). Before the economic reform, the common conception of the Chinese working class was that it was a social group comprising urban laborers who did not possess any means of independent production and reproduction of their livelihoods, living primarily from wages based on employment. Thus, the main bodies of the working class were industrial workers. Nevertheless, China's economic reform has broadened such a concept and led to a new understanding of "the working class," which includes four social divisions: workers who provide their physical labor (blue-collar workers); workers who provide their mental labor (white-collar workers); intellectuals conducting educational or scientific work; and civil servants and managerial cadres in public sectors (Liu 2001). That is to say, the working class in China has expanded and now includes: workers in state-owned, collective, and private enterprises; the peasantry; intellectuals; cadres; cadres and intellectuals in the countryside; private entrepreneurs working on their own; private entrepreneurs with enterprises of their own; soldiers; college students; and the underclass composed of migrant laborers, beggars, and prostitutes.

In a nutshell, mental labor, like manual labor, is also considered to be work that contributes to China's socialist construction, and therefore, knowledge workers engaged in education, science and technology, and medical service, including knowledge workers in the publishing industry, are an indispensable part of the working class (Zhu 1994; Chang 1998). From this viewpoint, the idea of a single, unified class of workers began to emerge in China.

Second, Zhang and Peng (2001b) maintain that according to the Party, knowledge workers are not regarded as a separate class. They are part of the working class, and their class interests are intrinsically linked to other members of the working class to which they attach themselves through their work. Accordingly, it becomes essential to examine the identities, consciousness, and behavior of knowledge workers in association with industrial workers, not only because the labor of knowledge workers needs to be treated as a form of work to be combined with manual labor in the production of a commodity, but also due to the common problems that confront the working class as a collectivity. According to Lee Ching-Kwan (2007a), gone are the days when Chinese workers are given the institutional guarantee of social welfare benefits, lifelong employment, and pension security. Contradictorily, for both industrial and knowledge workers, labor discontent and workplace tensions have been reported, for example, layoffs, bankruptcies, insecurity of jobs and rewards, the failure of enterprises to pay wages over months and even years, the nonpayment of benefits accumulated over a lifetime of labor, and the unsettled nature of legal and organizational frameworks regulating work relations and workers' rights.

The class analysis of knowledge workers is specifically concerned with the relationships of knowledge workers and industrial workers to the party-state. On the one hand, the party-state still possesses the power to control the working class. In *Class in China: Stratification in a Classless Society*, Wortzel (1987) implies that neither knowledge workers nor industrial workers are fully able to articulate their material interests and translate these interests into political programs or changes in the allocative process in China because important economic decisions, with regard to the direction of the national economy or of an enterprise, may not be undertaken without the approval of the CPC. Therefore, both knowledge workers and industrial workers are relegated to the same conditions regarding their subordination to the central authority of the Party, which essentially possesses the ownership of social resources.

On the other hand, in *Working in China: Ethnographies of Labor and Workplace Transformation*, Lee (2007a) asserts that labor policy reform has reshaped the legal context of work and employment, and as a result, the state's political control over workers and workplaces has declined. The gradual dismantling of the "iron rice bowl" system (*tiefanwan* in Chinese, also known as the permanent employment system for state employees) began with the introduction of labor contracts in the early 1980s and became universally mandatory in 1995, when China's first Labor Law was implemented (amended in 2008). Since then, employment relations are regulated by the Labor Law, instead of managerial or Party policies, and accordingly, labor conflicts are resolved according to the "Regulations on the Treatment of Enterprise Labor Disputes." Effective in 1993, it involves a three-stage procedure of *mediation, arbitration,* and *litigation* (Ho 2003). The procedure implies that the mechanisms of labor markets have replaced labor administrations in the allocation of labor. The increasing importance of both the law and the markets partially frees workers from their past economic and political dependence on the party-state, but enhances their dependence on market forces.

Third, the power of the working class keeps declining. Knowledge workers, from technicians to researchers, and from media workers to consultants, have increasingly opened up more space for their personal choices and career development than ever before. They have gained more financial and intellectual autonomy, as marketization proceeded in China. However, as Taylor, Kai, and Qi (2003) reveal, the transformation of the economy has essentially resulted in the status of the working class, including both industrial workers and knowledge workers, changing from being a component of the leading class to a lower stratum in the social structure in China. From Ng and Warner's (1998) viewpoint, the Chinese working class has been transformed from a rhetorical leading class into a group of wage laborers, who have become the producers of private profit, rather than of social wealth. Moreover, Qin (1999) maintains that owing to the ever-present possibility of a reduction in income or dismissal, the Chinese working class has been rendered vulnerable to employers' intensification of productivity pressure. In fact, the working class is increasingly frustrated with the deepening social inequality and economic exploitation, layoffs, unpaid wages, cadre corruption and abuse, unequal distribution of resources, high taxes, and so forth (Hao 2003). These are the same problems facing knowledge workers in the Chinese publishing industry as well as in other media sectors.

Labor and Globalization

Mass-mediated communication processes, institutions, and technologies have both contributed to, and been affected by the broader wave of globalization. With the predominance of transnational media firms and markets, China has witnessed privatization, commercialization, trade liberalization, and overall, the deregulation in the national media systems in the past three decades (Zhao and Hackett 2005). *The neoliberal revolution* and *the emergence of the global division of labor* are regarded as the two most far-reaching impacts of globalization on Chinese media workers, particularly editors.

Neoliberalism is an important facet that needs to be closely examined in the analysis of Chinese editors. Neoliberalism is understood in contemporary social theory as "a concept of a larger social and political agenda for revolutionary change," which is "aimed at nothing less than extending the values and relations of markets into a model for the broader organization of politics and society" (Robison 2006, 4). Neoliberalism has forged a market state in the global political economy since the late 1970s, and the rise of neoliberalism in China has addressed the state's attempt to incorporate neoliberal elements in conformity with authoritarian centralized control. The defining characteristic of neoliberal governmentality, namely, the infiltration of market-driven calculations into the domain of politics, has in many ways featured China's post-1978 accelerated social transition from a planned economy to a market economy.

In *Neoliberalism as Exception: Mutations in Citizenship and Sovereignty*, Aihwa Ong aims to analyze Chinese media workers within the framework of "the twin modalities of the neoliberal governmentality" (2006, 3). To specify, on the one hand, certain populations, places, and socioeconomic domains in China are subject to neoliberal calculations to maximize entrepreneurial dynamism and facilitate interactions within the global market. This modality is known as "*neoliberalism as exception*" to the authoritarian centralized control. On the other hand, it is also known as *exceptions to neoliberalism*, when political decisions are still invoked to exclude populations and places from neoliberal calculations and choices in order to maintain social equality. The two modalities indicate that for Chinese media workers, the party-state has tentatively stimulated market-oriented development in the media sector, while the control over the system is still tight. In brief, for Chinese editors, as a part of media workers, they are working in such a context that the state, forged in a communist revolution, still claims to build socialism, even though essentially it has been turning socialism into "a cover for policies of development inspired by capitalism" (Dirlik 2005, 157).[3]

Recently, Yu (2011) specifically explores the inherent tensions and pitfalls of Chinese neoliberal developmentalism. She argues that the party-state, capital, and popular aspirations are mingling together in the restructuring of the Chinese publishing industry and of other mass media and communications industries as well. Interestingly, in such interplay, neoliberal strategies are wrapped in socialist legacies, traditional values, and post-socialist dilemmas. Indeed, Chinese media workers (including editors) must deal with both market power and the Party logic: while market power is unleashed and harnessed to stimulate domestic media and communications industry (particularly publishing industry), the Party logic dominates how media are managed and who controls the backbone of China's media and communications infrastructures (including publishing infrastructures).

The *global division of labor*, with its relation to the changing labor process of Chinese editors, also sheds light on the challenges that they encounter. According to Burawoy (1979, 30), the essential characteristic of the labor process in the capitalist mode of production is defined as "the simultaneous obscuring and securing of surplus value." Although the separation of *conception* and *execution* of work posited by Braverman (1974) is a fundamental method of obscuring surplus value, Burawoy (1979) argues that the most crucial and effective means of securing surplus value, still the most important for capitalists, is through the worker's free compliance rather than the capitalist's coercion. For him, the *political* aspects (production of social relations) and *ideological* aspects (production of an experience of those relations) in the analysis of the labor process are tantamount to the *economic* dimension (production of things). Thus, labor process theory has been shifted from a focus on the point of production to a more satisfactory political economy of the labor process.

In recent years, Chinese editors have experienced dramatic changes in their work process as well as working conditions. The rapid development of information and communication technologies has reshaped the structure of the workplace, transformed the required skills and tasks for most editors, and changed their labor-employer relations (Liu 2006). As a result, as Im (1997) argues, many editors have been transformed from the role of social critic, interpreter, and contemporary historian to a species of technical worker. After the reconstruction of the production process by new technologies, many jobs in the Chinese publishing industry have been trivialized into merely physical activities; thus demanding only unskilled or semi-skilled workers. Therefore, editors have lost their control over the goals and values of their products, and become less skillful due to their specific roles in the production process. Apparently, deskilling, or in Braverman's words, "the degradation of work" still exists, and is becoming even more severe in the Chinese publishing sector (1974, 425).

Critically, when companies are making use of communication and information technologies to find the most efficient means of production, globalization brings about massive changes in the global division of labor. With the uneven geographical development and strong competitive pressure between various political-economic powers, deep inequalities persist among different nations, leading to an unbalanced global division of labor. Accompanying the global division of labor, a unity of the work process throughout the complex global network of interaction has emerged, when the life of global capital depends less and less on specific labor, but more and more on accumulated, generic labor (Castells 1996). At the same time, the differentiation of work, segmentation of workers, and the disaggregation of labor on a global scale become so distinct and forceful that labor is significantly specialized and impersonalized, which creates a tight tension between the bare logic of capital flows and the cultural values of human experiences, especially when the outsourcing process is involved.

It is well accepted that China has become a manufacturing colossus, dominating global production of textiles, footwear, and toys. "Made in China" signifies cheap goods for consumers, and simultaneously a flood of jobs from the developed economies. In "From Made in China to Created in China," Keane supplements this statement by arguing that in the information age, China not only excels in labor-intensive industries, which cost "less energy, capital, and resources," but also in creative industries, particularly evident in the animation industry (2006, 291).[4] In China's media industry, within the context of "socialism" and "marketization" broadcasting policies, both private studios and the practice of outsourcing began to emerge in the Chinese market in the wake of less restrictive policies of the 1990s. As a result, over 1,500 private television production companies have been set up since the first private TV production company was established in China in 1994 (The State Administration of Radio, Film, and Television 2006). For editors in the publishing industry, major foreign publishing companies have established many branches in China, specializing in copyright trade, business cooperation, as well as market research and development. In addition they have also been involved in the production of audiovisual and electronic publications in the form of joint ventures in most of the large cities in China.

To conclude, the impacts of globalization on Chinese media workers, particularly editors, are twofold. On the one side, *neoliberalism*, understood as a type of economic policy, a cultural structure, a set of particular attitudes toward individual responsibility, entrepreneurship, and self-improvement, and a form of governmentality, has pushed Chinese editors into the dilemma brought about by current media reform. On the other side, the rapid development of information and communication technologies has reshaped the work process and working conditions of Chinese editors. With the prevalence of *the global division of labor*, outsourcing is becoming common in China's publishing industry. As a consequence, government policies have gradually been less restrictive, and international cooperation between the domestic and foreign publishing houses has increased to a large extent, which has resulted in a growing copyright trade, productive market research and development, and strategic co-production of audiovisual and electronic publications.

Labor and Unions

How are Chinese media workers, particularly editors, working together to defend their rights to communicate in the face of the accelerated commodification process of information and education initiated by the government? With combined effects of technological changes, increasing corporate power, the rise of neoliberal government, and problems internal to trade unions as well as to labor movements, organized labor is facing daunting challenges and difficulties. However, in the Chinese media sector, worker organizations and trade unions are still being formed, based on the assumption that converging technologies and companies have led media workers to come together across various knowledge industries, in order to seek improved collective bargaining opportunities and successful political interventions (Bahr 1998; McKercher 2002). Mosco and McKercher (2006) also maintain that the position of labor, as a source of resistance to the erosion of public service, can be strengthened by a series of approaches, such as mergers between previously separate trade unions, attempts to use bases in one trade union to organize bases in others, and efforts to consolidate bargaining units in companies where multiple unions exist as well as to build bridges to connect organized workers with unorganized ones, both at home and abroad.

Specifically, in China's publishing industry, editors are taking the initiative in fighting for their rights with management because, as a result of the economic reform, the party-state management of the publishing sector was replaced by a management-responsibility system. In "China's Developing Civil Society: Interest Groups, Trade Unions and Associational Pluralism," Ogden (2000) concludes that new leaders are now under contract with the state that pressures them to increase productivity and profit even at the expense of the workers' interests. Therefore, in the Chinese publishing industry, faced with the end of the "iron rice bowl" system as well as the possibility of unemployment and the elimination of pensions, Chinese editors began to demand greater organizational autonomy vis-à-vis their new managers (Warner and Zhu 2000; Chan 2000a; Ng and Warner 2000). In order to avoid thousands of editors, and Chinese media workers as a collectivity, taking to the streets to protest about working conditions, the party-state has turned to the trade unions to resolve the conflicts media workers (particularly editors) have with management.

It is important to note that trade unions have been gradually transformed into organizations which can represent their members, and participate in the regulation of the employment relationship with their increasing independence from the party-state. Regarding the tension between trade unions and the party-state, Lee's analysis is rather illuminating. In "Pathways of Labor Activism," he argues that "the emergence of autonomous trade unions and their alliances with intellectual and human rights dissidents are most politically unsettling to a regime which still proclaims itself the embodiment of the dictatorship of the proletariat" (2007b, 73). In the Chinese publishing industry, the reform era has marked a period of unprecedented ferment in organized labor dissent in the history of post-1949 China, and therefore, the interests of the party-state and editors are no longer identical. Thus, the days are gone when Chinese editors do not need autonomous organizations to represent their interests. For this reason, only can improved working conditions and social welfare benefits be successfully negotiated when Chinese editors are organized.

Interestingly, Hong and Ip (2007) observe that trade unions in the Chinese publishing industry are increasingly dependent on higher trade unions, such as the All-China Federation of Trade Unions (ACFTU), which offer legal and political channels to defend the rights and interests of their members. The ACFTU has set up a nationwide network of service centers to offer advice to the jobless, and it has been very active in exploring new avenues of employment opportunities in the labor market, in collaboration with Chinese trade unions at all levels. Specifically in an attempt to protect the interests of laid-off workers, the ACFTU endeavors to:

1. Integrate the re-employment of laid-off workers into the overall plan for national economic and social development.
2. Improve the working body for re-employment and promote re-employment work.
3. Boost the reform of the social security system, thus guaranteeing the basic needs of laid-off workers.
4. Intensify the supervision and combat the infringement of the workers' right to work. (Hong and Ip 2007, 68)

As a consequence, in some districts, the re-employment rate has been significantly raised. In some cases, guidance becomes instrumental in encouraging the setting up of small businesses run by laid-off workers. Some union officials even offer assistance to start businesses that would hire newly trained laid-off workers.

Last but not least, Johnston's article "Organize for What? The Resurgence of Labor as a Citizenship Movement" opens up a new window for political economists to rethink labor and unions, by introducing the idea of labor citizenship. He emphasizes that labor citizenship has been an extremely popular concept among labor scholars. To reframe the labor movement as a citizenship movement, one of the most effective approaches of labor unionism is to "defend, exercise, and extend the boundaries of citizenship" (Johnston 2001, 35). In detail, it involves envisioning claims and orienting strategies to the status and fate of communities, not just to the benefits of a specific bargaining unit. In a much broader sense, the construction of labor citizenship implies that "labour power should be based on heterogeneous coalitions growing out of a common vision of the future, or a common potential political agenda, and that these visions should not be dependent on market forces" (Mosco and McKercher 2008, 52). Basically, by forming such heterogeneous coalitions, knowledge workers, in China's publishing industry in particular, can perhaps unite globally.

CONCLUSION

In this chapter, I have argued that Chinese media workers, particularly editors, are trapped in a two-track system in media and communications—a state-controlled news and current affairs sector in combination with a market-oriented entertainment business. In detail, on the one hand, Chinese editors are unconditionally obedient to the Party principle; thus, the Chinese publishing industry performs a propaganda role, serving the interests of the dominant political and economic elites. On the other hand, as a result of the implementation of the media commodification process, Chinese editors are increasingly devoted to business information and infotainment. The increasing importance of the law and the markets partially frees workers from their past economic and political dependence on the party-state, but enhances their dependence on market forces. The next chapter will specifically examine the commodification process of the political economy of communication, by analyzing Chinese media reform, particularly the reform in China's publishing industry, and its substantial consequences for Chinese media workers, mainly for editors—the problem of contingent employment, declining social welfare benefits, and intense work pressure.

NOTES

1. Under the guidelines of the "Four Cardinal Principles," which serve as the foundation of socialism, Chinese media workers, particularly editors, are supposed to uphold the socialist road, the dictatorship of the proletariat, the leadership of the CPC, and Marxism-Leninism-Mao Zedong Thought, in order to stabilize the political and ideological fields for post-Mao transformation.

2. This statement is echoed by Daniela Stockmann. She (2011) maintains that consumers seek out commercial publications because they consider them more credible than their counterparts from the official media. Surprisingly, even in Beijing, which has a particularly large proportion of government employees, only about 36 percent of residents read official papers, for example, *The People's Daily*, and the rest read only semi-official or commercial papers.

3. A plethora of scholars have been working on the application of the concept of neoliberalism to the analysis of what is currently happening in China. According to Robison, neoliberalism in China is not "just a reincarnation of laissez-faire sentiment or a simple neo-classical attachment to the idea of the inherent efficiency of markets" (2006, 4). Nor is it just the economic policies of market liberalization, deregulation, privatization, and fiscal austerity associated with the Washington Consensus, the shock therapy, and the structural adjustment programs applied to Russia and other transnational economies (Huang and Cui 2005). Together with the idea of the twin modalities of the neoliberal governmentality, it is concluded that, within the Chinese context, neoliberalism is specifically understood as a system of justification and legitimation for whatever needed to be done to restore or to create the power of an economic elite. It is also understood as a means for the more general instrumental harnessing of the authoritarian state to serve the public or socialist interests.

4. According to some estimates, up to 90 percent of the world's animation is produced in Asia (Miller et al. 2001). It is also important to note that Japanese animation producers are using many low-cost Chinese animation factories in their animation production.

Chapter Two

The Commodification Process

Publishing Reform in China

This chapter and the following two chapters develop a substantive map of the political economic analysis of knowledge workers in the Chinese publishing industry, utilizing the three entry processes of the political economy of communication: *commodification, structuration,* and *spatialization.*

First, *commodification* is the process of transforming *use values* into *exchange values.* The key element of Chinese publishing reform is to introduce the commodification process into the Chinese publishing industry. As Mosco (2009) maintains, the political economy of communication has been notable for its emphasis on examining the significance of institutions, especially those businesses and government responsible for the production, distribution, and exchange of communication commodities, and for the regulation of the communication marketplace. Therefore, to investigate the media commodification process in China, it is very important to understand that the Communist Party of China (CPC) has promoted a market-oriented reform in China's economic base, while it still keeps a tight grip on the country's mass media system and political superstructure (Gordon 1997; Huang and Yu 1997). In such a context, as a result of the commodification process, in the publishing industry, Chinese editors are in a precarious condition, and they are increasingly faced with the problem of contingent employment, declining social welfare benefits, and intense work pressure.

Second, *structuration* is the process of constituting *structures* with *social agency.* The concentration on social structures, by incorporating the ideas of human agency, social process, and social practice, brings valuable insight into the understanding of class relations and power dynamics. In China, editors are confronted with five critical problems in relation to the structuration process: problems related to technological changes, the problems on how to follow the Party principle in the media marketization process, those on the marketization process in the social welfare system, the problems brought about by the smashing of the work-unit system, and the conflicts resulting from the inner division within the working class. In addition, it is crucial to examine the inner division and tension among editors, manifested quite clearly in struggles for power in the publishing industry hierarchy.

Third, *spatialization*, the transformation of space, or the process of institutional extension, is another process that I aim to address. Castells (1996) implies that business, aided by developments in communication and information technology, transforms space. The structural changes are the results of a shifting use of space and time, and such changes are fundamental. Moreover, spatialization encompasses the process of globalization—the worldwide restructuring of industries, companies, and other institutions. It is not only important to examine how editors, and generally Chinese media workers, are dealing with the challenges inside the "propaganda-commercial model of journalism" (Zhao 1998, 151), but also essential to investigate how they are responding to globalization, particularly the challenges that arise when China further integrates into the global political economy. Such challenges include the widespread expansion of neoliberal policies, and the emergence of the global division of labor.

In fact, the three processes are interconnected. To be more specific, with the widespread expansion of the *commodification* process, Chinese editors are more dependent on market forces. This dependence consequently leads to the dilemma that I highlight in the *structuration* process: on the one hand, Chinese editors need to serve the political and ideological interests of the state; on the other hand, they are pressured to pursue the economic interests. Also, the Chinese publishing reform, closely associated with the media *commodification* process, was influenced by the movement toward global neoliberalism in the late 1970s. Neoliberalism constitutes a major aspect of my analysis of the *spatialization* process, and in China, it mainly addresses the state's attempt to incorporate neoliberal elements in conformity with authoritarian centralized control. Furthermore, the *spatialization* process strengthens the tension within the "propaganda-commercial model of journalism" (Zhao 1998, 151) because Chinese editors are faced with the challenges of the global division of labor, which largely changes their work process and working conditions—a point addressed in the *structuration* process of the political economy of communication.

In terms of the basic structure of this chapter, I intend to systematically review commodification theory in the first section. Commodification theory is proposed and developed by numerous scholars, particularly political economists, such as Dan Schiller (2007), Vincent Mosco (2009), Dallas Smythe (1977), Eileen Meehan (2002), and Harry Braverman (1974). For these political economists, commodification is important in the analysis of the capitalist expansion process, including the global extension of the market as well as the privatization of public space. Also, to comprehensively understand the commodification process of communication, political economists attempt to scrutinize the commodification processes of media content, audiences, and labor.

Based on the theoretical framework of commodification, the second section of this chapter explores China's media reform, particularly the reform in the publishing industry. It becomes rather apparent that both the political and economic reforms in China since 1978 have accelerated the media commodification process, which has not only led to a profound development of the publishing industry, but also resulted in the following three dramatic changes: a change in the nature of publishing houses from public institutions to companies, the formation of publishing conglomerates, and the widespread expansion of private and foreign investment in the Chinese publishing industry. Most importantly, the advertising industry in China has grown to be one of the largest of its kind in the world today (Scotton and Hachten 2010).

The third section of this chapter seeks to understand the various impacts of current media reform on media workers, particularly editors in the publishing industry. According to the findings from the surveys that I conducted in China in 2010, editors have increasingly faced the problem of contingent employment, declining social welfare benefits, and intense work pressure with the changes in work hours, locations, main tasks, and monthly incomes. These impacts and changes are both real and profound.

THE COMMODIFICATION PROCESS

What is a commodity? According to Schiller (2007), a commodity is not merely a product or a resource, a thing of use to anyone, anytime, and anywhere. A commodity also can be defined as a product, which is produced for the market by wage labor. Thus, a commodity contains defining linkages to capitalist production and, secondarily, to *market exchange*.

Schiller further contends that it is helpful to focus not on the commodity itself, but rather on the commodification process. The commodification process, defined by Mosco, is a process of "turning *use values* into *exchange values*, of transforming products whose value is determined by their ability to meet individual and social needs into products whose value is set by their market price" (2009, 129). As Sreberny (2001) and Khiabany (2006) point out, the general, worldwide expansion of commodification in the 1980s, responding in part to global declines in economic growth, has led to the increased commercialization of media programming, as well as to the privatization of once public media and telecommunication markets, including in places where commodification had been limited.

Political economists argue that an uneven but ongoing process of commodification is foundational to capitalist development, and its historical generalization throughout the informational sphere constitutes a landmark of contemporary political economy (Schiller 2007). In other words, capitalism has been sustained by ceaseless enlargement of markets for commodities, and this trend continues today in information and culture. In this view, commodification is important in the analysis of capitalist expansion process, including the global extension of the market (Fursich and Roushanzamir 2004) and the privatization of public space (Gibson 2003).

To elaborate, in "Corporate Expansion, Textual Expansion," Fursich and Roushanzamir propose a commodification model of communication, to "reevaluate the importance of the economic foundation of mass communication as much as the communicative reach of the corporate structure" (2004, 376). Different from the former models of communication, which basically situate mass media and public communication within the political realm of nations, the commodification model of communication insists on linking corporate communications such as traditional advertising and public relations with marketing. More significantly, the commodification model of communication insists on the increasing privatization and commercialization processes of public spaces of discourse when public/democratic images are produced. As media messages and texts reach a global population, the new model is especially convincing in explaining how these messages and texts have expanded to accommodate corporate expansion, as well as how they have reworked earlier concepts of public goods and public service to equate those with corporate interests. Therefore, the new model highlights the corporate basis of its origins and regards audiences as consumers, while the old ones concentrate on their political origins and regard audiences as citizens (Fursich and Roushanzamir 2004).

Commodification is also important in the analysis of the privatization of public space. To examine this notion, Gibson introduces the concept of the "spectacular city" (2003, 83). According to his case study of Seattle, probusiness urban redevelopment strategies do not necessarily provide equitable distribution of public resources, such as truly accessible urban public spaces, affordable housing, and retail establishments for modest-income shoppers. On the contrary, those strategies motivated to promote the development of large, glittering office towers (yield to the demands of developers who bring remarkable profit to the city), provide subsidies for large-scale development, and invest public funds in upscale shopping districts and buildings that provide high-culture experiences. All these efforts have created, in Gibson's words, the "spectacular city" (2003, 83). It is important to understand that the growth of the "spectacular city" has been accomplished at the expense of the development which benefits a wider public. Likewise, the urban fabric created does not provide true public urban space, but rather space that is privately controlled by those corporations who own it. In this sense, the "spectacular city" is essentially a city of privatized commercial space.

In addition to acknowledging that commodification is important in the global extension of the market and the privatization of public space, Mosco (2009, 12) maintains that "when it has treated the commodity, political economy has tended to concentrate on media content, audiences, and the labour involved in media production."

To explain, first, the process of commodification in communication means transforming messages into marketable products. Indeed, the emphasis on media content is vitally important because of the increasing significance of global media companies and the growth in the value of media content. Different from the analysis of media content from a cultural studies perspective, which basically elaborates on symbols and images, the political economy of communication specifically associates the commodification process of media content with labor, consumers, and capital. These elements help to better understand the complex network of social relations that is connected to the commodification process, especially when exchange value in the content of communication is created (Mosco 2009).

Second, as Smythe (1977) advocates, the audience is the primary commodity of the mass media. This statement indicates that the mass media are constituted out of a process which sees media companies producing audiences and delivering them to advertisers. In this respect, the media commodification process has brought together a *triad* that links media companies, audiences, and advertisers in a set of reciprocal relationships—to put it briefly in Mosco's words, "media firms use their programming to construct audiences; advertisers pay media companies for access to these audiences; audiences are thereby delivered to advertisers" (2009, 136–37).

In more detail, in "Communications: Blindspot of Western Marxism," Smythe (1977) argues that the commodity form of mass-produced, advertiser-supported communications under monopoly capitalism comprises audiences and readerships. According to Smythe, the mass media intend to attract and keep the audience attending to the program, newspaper, or magazine, and at the same time, they aim to cultivate a mood conducive to favorable reaction to the explicit and implicit advertisers' messages. Therefore, the central purpose of the information, entertainment, and educational material transmitted to the audience is to ensure their attention to the products and service being advertised. The audience commodity plays a significant role in the marketing of the advertiser's product. The mass media and advertising are dominant through the process of consumption, as well as through the ideological teaching which permeates both the advertising and ostensibly nonadvertising materials with which they produce the audience commodity (Smythe 1977).

Moreover, Meehan's work has contributed to the critical understanding of the relationship between gender and audience commodity. In "Gendering the Commodity Audience: Critical Media Research, Feminism, and Political Economy," she attempts to challenge the ungendered markets and ungendered corporations that have been taken for granted in the previous studies (Meehan 2002). She echoes Smythe's statements by arguing that the main product manufactured by networks and sold to advertisers is the audience commodity. She also agrees that the political economic approach is very convincing in demonstrating the key role that capital is playing in manufacturing the audience commodity, which is predominately dependent on the changing power relations within the market. What is more critical, however, is her suggestion that in order to incorporate feminist analysis into a political economic understanding, it should be emphasized that the social divisions of labor based on gender, plus prejudicial assumptions about gender, are crucial in defining and differentiating the audience commodity (Meehan 2002).

To specify, Meehan (2002) finds that, as an audience commodity, the white male has a "higher quality" for which advertisers are willing to pay. In the commodification process of audiences, labels (such as "working women," "upscale," and "downscale") have been widely used to identify the social status attached to occupation and income. Not surprisingly, there is a widespread belief about what sort of people ought to be the audience, and such a belief follows familiar patterns of discrimination on the grounds of gender, race, social status, sexual orientation, and age. According to Meehan (2002), ideologies that are naturalizing the oppression of women have shaped corporate decisions. She concludes that restructuring markets to foster the liberation of women actually undermines the interests of individual capitalists and of capitalism because both have profited from disparities in income as well as from oppressive social relations. In this account, media serve as the instruments of oppression, and the commodification process of audiences internalizes, reflects, and strengthens such social oppression.

Third, in addition to examining the commodification processes of media content and audiences, it is equally important to emphasize the commodification process of media labor. According to Braverman (1974), in the process of commodification, capital acts to separate *conception* (the power to envision, imagine, and design work) from *execution* (the power to carry it out). It also addresses conceptual power in a managerial class that is either a part of capital or represents its interests. He maintains:

> Labor power has become a commodity. Its uses are no longer organized according to the needs and desires of those who sell it, but rather according to the needs of its purchasers, who are, primarily, employers seeking to expand the value of their capital. (Braverman 1974, 82)

Essentially, these purchasers have a special and permanent interest to cheapen the labor commodity. According to Braverman (1974), the most common mode of cheapening labor power is exemplified by the application of detailed and intrusive "scientific management" practices, pioneered by Frederick Taylor. The transformation of the labor process first emerged in large scale industries, and then extended to service, information, and commu nication sectors. For media workers worldwide, they are also being commod- ified as wage labor, and they are faced with the problem of the devaluation of knowledge that they have gained, the declining purchasing power of the money that they have earned, and the cut in the social welfare benefits that help to improve their living conditions. Accordingly, media workers have responded to these problems by bringing together people from different me- dia sectors into worker organizations and trade unions that represent large segments of the communication workforce (McKercher 2002; Mosco and McKercher 2008; Mosco 2009). Ursula Huws (2003) argues that in addition to Braverman, numerous scholars have concentrated on the commodification process of labor, and their interests include: addressing its contested nature, highlighting the active agency of workers, and examining how the transfor- mation of the labor process is experienced differently by industry, occupa- tion, class, gender, and race. Specifically for Chinese editors, the commodifi- cation process of labor brings them tremendous challenges, including the problem of contingent employment, declining social welfare benefits, and intense work pressure. I intend to discuss these challenges in more detail in the rest of this chapter, starting with a discussion of China's media reform.

CHINA'S MEDIA REFORM

During the last three decades, China has been engaged in a process of rapid social transition from a centrally planned economy to a market-based econo- my. The economic reform process, first initiated in 1978 by Deng Xiaoping in the aftermath of the Cultural Revolution, has since transformed China into one of the world's largest economies, poised for a complete integration into the international capitalist market. It has also brought about vast changes, particularly the extensive media commodification process, in China's public- ly owned mass media system. As a result, the problem of contingent employ- ment, the changing work process, and the precarious condition of Chinese media workers came to light and have become common topics of discussion.

Background of the Chinese Media Reform

The Party established the basic structure and functions of the mass media in the second half of the twentieth century. According to the Party principle, "The purpose of the mass media is to strengthen socialist education to promote proletarianism, and wipe out capitalism" (Ze 1995, 449). In 1983, the Central Committee of the CPC announced, "Our cause of the mass media is fundamentally different from those of capitalist countries in that it is a part of the socialist cause under the leadership of the Party and it must promote Marxism, Leninism, and the thoughts of Mao Zedong" (Ze 1996, 15). Therefore, ideologically, the CPC saw the mass media as tools in propagating socialist ideals and in executing Party policies.

However, China started to introduce the market mechanism when it shifted its social focal point from class struggle to economic development in 1978. Following the end of the Cultural Revolution in 1976, the new government of the 1977–1978 period wholeheartedly began to pursue the path of economic expansion and modernization with the support of the majority of the population. As Hua Guofeng (1980) remarked in the third session of the Eleventh Central Committee of the CPC, "Class struggle is no longer the principal contradiction in our society; in waging it, we must center around and serve the central task of socialist modernization." Accordingly, the main slogan of that period became the four modernizations of agriculture, science and technology, industry, and national defense. Numerous new economic policies were announced in 1979 at the second session of the Fifth National People's Congress, to readjust, restructure, consolidate, and improve the national economy.[1]

Among them, one of the most creative *economic* policies was to promote a rural reform process in China. Guided by the Party, Chinese farmers began to engage in business activities in cooperation with township and village enterprises (TVEs). The rapid growth in the number of TVEs, followed by the gradual emergence of private enterprises and foreign investment, created an irreversible momentum toward the expansion of market reform by the mid-1980s (Akhavav-Majid 2004). These developments resulted in the creation of a new social and political discourse, legitimizing market-oriented reform as an appropriate economic policy by the state (Wang 1995). In this context, the commodification process was introduced into the Chinese media industry. Together with nationwide economic reform, China's media reform has been designed to reduce governmental influences on the mass media, and expand market forces through the adoption of a market-based economy.

In association with the *economic* reform, a series of *political* reforms took place in China in 1978. According to O'Leary and Watson (1985, 7), during that period, "There has been . . . a significant reconceptualization of politics, substantially redefining the overall political agenda, redesigning much of the political framework, and changing the scope of political activities." The three most prominent *political* changes are the open-door policy, the decentralization policy, and the pluralism policy, all of which have largely affected China's media industry, specifically the publishing industry.

First, the open-door policy intends to bring China "out of its self-imposed isolation and toward a rapprochement with the industrialized countries in the West" (Wu 1985, 242–43), followed by a dramatic expansion of cultural and economic transactions between China and these industrialized countries. Because of this open-door policy, many news items about other countries have entered China's TV news programming, and much of the up-to-date technology for news broadcasting has also been widely adopted.

The second change is the decentralization policy. For several decades, local television stations have only repeated the central TV station's programming, and this restriction seriously limited the development of local TV stations. However, due to the decentralization policy, local TV stations have enjoyed more flexibility during the period of reform. Also, the decentralization policy has quickened the development pace of local TV stations, including an increase in news broadcasting hours, the formation of regional TV networks, and the launching of various local news services.

The third change is the pluralism policy. According to Barnett (1986), the CPC has allowed—within limits—increased diversity and pluralism, and has permitted a greater circulation of information and ideas. It has also stressed "social legality" and tried to broaden grassroots participation in political life. The state's penetration of society has been dramatically reduced and many areas of life have been depoliticized. In such a context, critical and popular programs have been able to appear on the screen. Such programs include "From Our Viewers" (revealing the audience's views on issues ranging from TV programs to social problems), "News Analysis" (discussing the current events related to Party policies), and "Life and Fashion" (introducing the latest global fashion and popular restaurants).

In sum, China initiated both *economic* and *political* reforms in 1978 and implemented various new policies that have affected the mass media to a degree unprecedented in China's media history. Different from previous reforms, the essence of current media reform is to bring the commodification process into China's media industry, and as a result, the state-owned media have become self-sustaining, making the economic reform to achieve more profit and meet the challenges of the international market (McGowan 2003). Therefore, the mass media started to serve the purpose of "informing, educating and entertaining people," and with constant efforts, they are more "reader-oriented" rather than "leader-oriented" (Greenberg and Lau 1990, 23).

China's Publishing Industry Reform

As Zhou Weihua (2005b) maintains, since the late 1970s, along with vigorous economic and political reforms, the Chinese mass media have undergone drastic changes and transformations in practice. To understand such changes and transformations, first and foremost, it is essential to clarify both the administrative management and laws in the Chinese publishing industry. In addition, a comparison of what media industry, particularly the publishing industry, looked like before and after current media reform fully demonstrates the rapid media development in China. Not only has the gross output value of the Chinese publishing industry significantly increased during the past thirty years, but most importantly, the Chinese advertising industry has enjoyed a substantial growth, and become an indispensable component of the media sector. Now, advertisements can be found in book publishing, on radio and television, in audiovisual production, and on the Internet.

Administrative Management of China's Publishing Industry

In China, national publications are dominated and regulated by the General Administration of Press and Publication of China (GAPP), and regional publications are regulated by the authorities of the relevant provinces, municipalities, and autonomous regions. To be more specific, the GAPP is the senior regulatory body for printing, publishing, and distribution, and it controls numerous Chinese publishing organizations, such as the Publishers Association, the Copyright Agency, and the National Copyright Administration. It has continued to censor materials that might be objectionable to the Chinese government or cultural standards. Also, it is responsible for managing the country's existing publication infrastructure, approving the establishment of new publishing houses, and promoting international trade between Chinese and foreign publishing houses. As an executive branch under the State Council, it possesses a status practically equivalent to that of a ministry (Xin 2005).[2]

The GAPP maintains a close liaison with the State Administration of Radio, Film, and Television (SARFT), an executive branch agency under the State Council. Different from the GAPP, which specifically monitors the publishing industry, the main task of the SARFT is the administration and supervision of state-owned enterprises engaged in the television, radio, and film industries. It also directly controls such enterprises at the national level, including China Central Television, China National Radio, China Radio International, as well as other movie and television studios and non-profit organizations.

Importantly, the Central Propaganda Department (CPD) is also responsible for the management of publications, and maintains large influences on the GAPP and the SARFT, as well as on all component units within the industry. The CPD is the CPC's counterpart to the GAPP and the SARFT. Whereas the GAPP and the SARFT exercise their censorship powers through their authority to license (and to rescind the license of) publishers, the CPD is the organization primarily responsible for monitoring content to ensure that publishers in China do not print anything that is inconsistent with the Party principle. According to *The Dictionary of the Organization of the CPC*, the main responsibilities of the CPD are described as:

> Screening all books and articles dealing with the Party's or the nation's leaders, significant political issues, and policies relating to foreign diplomacy, nationalities, or religion; issuing notices informing publishers and editors what stories can and cannot be covered, and telling them what ideological standpoint should be taken when discussing certain issues; and requiring editors and publishers to attend workshops where they are instructed on the proper ideological approach to use when reporting on politically sensitive topics. (The Central Organization Department of the CPC 2009, 48)[3]

In March 1998, at the first session of the Ninth National People's Congress, the Ministry of Post and Telecommunications, the Ministry of the Electronics Industry, and parts of the Ministry of Radio, Film, and Television merged to form the Ministry of Information Industry (MII). The MII is responsible for overseeing the management of Chinese information networks, and coordinating state policies on the construction and management of electronic media as voice, video, and data technologies converge (Redl and Simons 2002).

To conclude, the GAPP manages the Chinese publishing industry, and it also maintains a close liaison with the SARFT, CPD, and MII. At the same time, these are the same agencies responsible for censorship in China's publishing inudstry.

Publishing Industry Laws

The supreme legislative body in China (the National People's Congress) has not enacted laws specifically governing publishing. Currently, the most important publishing regulation is the "Regulations on Administration of Publications," which was promulgated by the central government (the State Council). In addition, the "Regulations on Administration of Audiovisual Products" and "Regulations on Administration of the Printing Enterprises" were effective in 1994 and 1997, respectively. The GAPP has issued some other related regulations and rules, which include the "Regulations on Administration of Periodical Publications," "Provisions on Administration of Electronic Publications," "Provisions on Administration of the Publications Market," and "Measures on the Recording of Important Topics of Books, Journals, Magazines, Audiovisual Productions, and Electronic Publications." For foreign investment, the GAPP and the Ministry of Commerce co-issued the "Measures on Administration of Foreign-funded Distribution Enterprises of Books, Newspapers, Journals, and Magazines."

On copyright protection, the National People's Congress issued the "Copyright Law of the People's Republic of China" in 1991. Also, in the same year, the State Council promulgated the "Regulations on the Implementation of the Copyright Law" and "Regulations on the Protection of Computer Software."

The above laws, regulations, and rules constitute the major legal documents that govern China's publishing industry. Table 2.1 summaries the laws, regulations, and rules relevant to publishing, with their effective and amendment dates.

Changes in China's Publishing Industry

Rapid media development can be fully demonstrated by a comparison of what the media industry looked like before and after current media reform. To take the publishing industry as an example, at the end of the 1970s (before current media reform), there were 158 organizations registered to publish books: about sixty in Beijing, fifteen in Shanghai, and eighty in the rest of the country. At the national level, there were ten specialized publishers directly under the GAPP. These ten specialized publishers are the People's Publishing House (specialized in works by Marx, Engels, Stalin, and Mao Zedong), the Sanlian Bookstore (specialized in works on social sciences), the Commercial Press (specialized in reference books and works on social sciences in different languages), the Zhonghua Publishing House (specialized in classical works), the People's Literature Publishing House (specialized in works on Chinese and foreign literature), the People's Fine Arts Publishing House (specialized in works on Chinese fine arts), the People's Music Publishing House (specialized in works on Chinese music), the Encyclopedia of China Publishing House (specialized in encyclopedias and dictionaries), the China Photographic Publishing House (specialized in works on Chinese photography), and the Beijing Braille Publishing House (specialized in Braille texts for the blind).

There were about fifty other specialized publishers, regulated, in varying ways, by the GAPP, the CPD, and the State Council and its ministries. Among them, major specialized publishers include the Science Press (specialized in science textbooks), the Foreign Language Press (specialized in foreign language books, journals, and magazines), the China Youth Publishing House (specialized in children's books), the People's Education Publishing House (specialized in textbooks), the Cartographic Publishing House (specialized in maps and charts), the People's Sports Publishing House (specialized in works on sports), and the Social Sciences Publishing House (affiliated to the Chinese Academy of Social Sciences).

At the regional level, there were about eighty publishers, regulated by the regional or local Propaganda Department of the CPC. In 1978, according to the GAPP, about 15,000 different kinds of books were published. The total printed copies of books and sheets were 3.86 billion and 13.54 billion, re-

Table 2.1.   Laws, Regulations, and Rules Governing China's Publishing Indus-try.

Law, Regulation, or Rule	Effective Date and Amendment Date	Issued by
Regulations on Administration of Publications	Effective Date: February 1, 1997 First Amendment Date: December 25, 2001 Second Amendment Date: March 16, 2011	The State Council
Regulations on Administration of Audiovisual Products	Effective Date: October 1, 1994 First Amendment Date: December 25, 2001 Second Amendment Date: March 16, 2011	The State Council
Regulations on Administration of the Printing Enterprises	Effective Date: May 1, 1997 First Amendment Date: August 2, 2001	The State Council
Regulations on Administration of Periodical Publications	Effective Date: December 1, 2005	The GAPP
Provisions on Administration of Electronic Publications	Effective Date: December 30, 1997 First Amendment Date: April 15, 2008	The GAPP
Provisions on Administration of the Publications Market	Effective Date: November 22, 1999 First Amendment Date: September 1, 2003 Second Amendment Date: March 17, 2011	The GAPP
Measures on the Recording of Important Topics of Books, Journals, Magazines, Audiovisual Productions, and Electronic Publications	Effective Date: October 10, 1997	The GAPP
Measures on Administration of Foreign-funded Distribution Enterprises of Books, Newspapers, Journals, and Magazines	Effective Date: May 1, 2003	The GAPP and the Ministry of Commerce
Copyright Law of the People's Republic of China	Effective Date: June 1, 1991 First Amendment Date: April 1, 2010	The National People's Congress
Regulations on the Implementation of Copyright Law	Effective Date: June 1, 1991 First Amendment Date: September 15, 2002	The State Council

| Regulations on the Protection of Computer Software | Effective Date: June 4, 1991 First Amendment Date: January 1, 2002 | The State Council |

spectively. At the same time, 168 different kinds of newspapers and 930 journals and magazines were published.

During the past thirty years, the acceleration of reform in China, especially that required for entry into the World Trade Organization (WTO), has been gradually increasing the overall capacity of the Chinese publishing industry. According to *The General Report on the Development of China's Media Industry 2010*, 275,668 titles were published in 2010, of which 125,680 were new. The total printed copies of books and sheets reached 6.936 billion and 56.073 billion, respectively, with the total revenue of 79.14 billion *yuan* (Cui 2010). Book printing consumed 1.32 million tons of paper. In addition, according to *China Statistics Yearbook 2008*, publishers produced 43,799 billion copies of 1,943 different kinds of newspapers, 3,041 billion copies of 9,549 journals and magazines, 258 million copies of 16,641 audiovisual products, and 135.84 million copies of 8,652 electronic publications (CD-ROMs, VCDs, DVDs, and e-books) in 2008 (China Statistical Yearbook Editorial Department 2008). There were also 579 publishing houses (220 directly belong to the central government, and the other 359 operate at the provincial level), 363 audiovisual publishing units, and 228 electronic publishers across the country (see table 2.2). In tandem with the rapid development in the publishing industry, the number of editors has grown incredibly in the past few years, and up until 2008, there were 60,906 full-time editors. In sum, the rapid growth that the Chinese publishing industry enjoyed thirty years after the implementation of China's media reform has been unparalleled and astonishing. The gross output value of the Chinese media industry in 2010 hit 490.796 billion *yuan*.

The publishing industry has long been one of the most heavily government-controlled industries in China. Before current media reform, all Chinese publishing houses were state-owned, nonprofit organizations. A step-by-step reform has been introduced and resulted in the steady withdrawal of the state from the industry, forcing state-owned publishing houses to become more market-oriented. Over the past decade, three significant changes have been observed in China's publishing industry.

First, the nature of publishing houses has changed from public institutions to companies. Apart from several publishing houses that still remain nonprofit, most publishing houses are required to change from nonprofit organizations to enterprises.[4] In other words, according to Guo Minggang (1994, 86), publishing houses were no longer budgeted by the central government, as in the days of the centrally planned economy, but "obtain programmatic

Table 2.2. Top 50 Chinese Publishers in 2002.

Rank	Publisher	Sales[a]
1	People's Education Press	1,159
2	Higher Education Press	621
3	Gansu People's Publishing House	376
4	Liaohai Publishing House	359
5	Foreign Language Teaching and Research Press	355
6	Jiangsu Education Publishing House	351
7	China Cartographic Publishing House	285
8	Science Press	284
9	Tsinghua University Press	280
10	Yunnan People's Publishing House	275
11	China Light Industry Press	252
12	Chongqing Publishing House	247
13	People's Medical Publishing House	245
14	Zhejiang Education Publishing House	239
15	Shanghai Foreign Language Education Press	232
16	Beijing Normal University Press	231
17	China Machine Press	211
18	Guangdong Education Publishing Press	206
19	Shanxi People's Publishing Press	203
20	Shandong Education Publishing Press	202
21	Beijing Publishing House	199
22	Shanghai Education Publishing House	191
23	Commercial Press	184
24	Anhui Education Publishing House	179
25	World Publishing Corporation	175
26	China Financial and Economic Publishing House	166
27	Planet Cartographic Publishing House	164
28	Hubei Education Press	162
29	Publishing House of Electronics Industry	157
30	China Renmin University Press	157
31	Central Radio and TV University Press	154
32	Hebei Education Press	152
33	Shanghai Literature and Art Publishing House	148

34	Guangxi Normal University Press	148
35	Peking University Press	148
36	Inner Mongolia Education Press	146
37	Shanghai People's Fine Arts Publishing House	140
38	Shaanxi People's Publishing House	139
39	Xinjiang Education Publishing House	138
40	China Architecture and Building Press	132
41	Hu'nan Education Publishing House	132
42	Hainan Publishing House	130
43	Shanghai Science and Technology Publishing House	123
44	Future Publishing House	122
45	China Labor and Social Security Publishing House	121
46	China Financial Publishing House	120
47	Elephant Publishing House	119
48	Educational Science Publishing House	116
49	Shaanxi Normal University Press	116
50	Fujian Education Press	116

Source: Xin (2005).

[a] Millions of *yuan*.

and directive significance in developing the cultural industry to fit into the market system."

Along with the transformation process, it is worth mentioning that as a result of market competition, many leading publishers with absolute advantages in some professional fields have been formed. Examples in the field of education are the Higher Education Press, the People's Education Press, Peking University Press, and the Foreign Language Teaching and Research Press. In professional publishing, examples are the China Cartographic Publishing House, the China Machine Press, and Tsinghua University Press. Currently, these publishing powers have become the leading forces in the fields of education and professional publishing, and they also turn out to be the key productive forces for the further development of China's publishing industry. Based on the survey of 2,800 readers in six big cities in China (Beijing, Shanghai, Guangzhou, Chengdu, Wuhan, and Shenyang), a report published by the Open-Book Book Market Research Center lists the three most popular publishing houses in Education, English, Literature, Computer Science, and Finance in 2004, respectively (see table 2.3).

Second, publishing houses are increasingly merging into publishing conglomerates. Large publishing groups have appeared within many provinces,

Table 2.3.   The Most Popular Chinese Publishing Houses in Education, English, Literature, Computer Science, and Finance in 2004.

Category	Rank in Popularity	Publisher
Education	1	Higher Education Press
	2	People's Education Press
	3	Peking University Press
English	1	Foreign Language Teaching and Research Press
	2	Foreign Language Press
	3	Shanghai Foreign Language Education Press
Literature	1	People's Literature Publishing House
	2	People's Publishing House
	3	Chinese Writers Publishing House
Computer Science	1	Tsinghua University Press
	2	People's Posts and Telecom Press
	3	Publishing House of Electronics Industry
Finance	1	China Financial Publishing House
	2	CITIC Publishing House
	3	Tsinghua University Press

Source: Shi, Wang, and Dong (2008).

municipalities, and autonomous regions. At first, these publishing groups were pure products of top-down policies—a way for the central government to strengthen the domestic publishing industry. In fact, the media conglomeration process started in 2002, as the central government sought to enhance the competence of China's publishing industry in order to compete with foreign media companies. As a consequence, a number of powerful publishing groups emerged, such as the Shanghai Century Publishing Group (Shanghai), the Beijing Publishing Group (Beijing), the Guangdong Publishing Group (Guangzhou, Guangdong province), and the Liaoning Publishing Group (Shenyang, Liaoning province). Table 2.4 provides a summary of China's publishing groups in 2006.

Table 2.4. China's Publishing Groups in 2006.

Publishing Group	Date of Establishment	Headquarter	Total Number of Publishers	Total Printed Titles	Total Printed Copies[a]	Total Printed Sheets[a]	Total Revenue from Books[b]
Shanghai Century Publishing Group	February 24, 1999	Shanghai	12	7,253	137.04	1,008.03	1,418.13
Beijing Publishing Group	July 7, 1999	Beijing	7	2,870	41.94	329.988	525.11
Guangdong Publishing Group	December 22, 1999	Guangzhou	6	2,565	68.45	386.750	565.86
Liaoning Publishing Group	March 29, 2000	Shenyang	9	3,020	93.12	572.951	735.93
China Science Publishing Group	June 25, 2000	Beijing	2	5,393	74.60	770.335	1,061.43
Hu'nan Publishing Group	September 1, 2000	Changsha	7	845	137.04	1,991.27	1,293.26
Shandong Publishing House	December 12, 2000	Ji'nan	9	3,648	177.45	1,103.15	1,155.26
Zhejiang Publishing Group	December 21, 2000	Hangzhou	8	4,498	142.59	781.851	1,021.95
Jiangsu Publishing Group	September 28, 2001	Nanjing	8	4,579	225.83	1,394.54	1,697.44
China Publishing Group	April 9, 2002	Beijing	20	5,705	94.80	1,101.63	1,753.38
Jilin Publishing Group	December 12, 2003	Changchun	8	966	11.55	100.197	167.44
Chinese Writers Publishing Group	December 22, 2003	Beijing	1	361	7.91	110.186	175.89

Group							
He'nan Publishing Group	March 28, 2004	Zhengzhou	9	2,671	90.00	448.093	549.88
Hebei Publishing Group	April 15, 2004	Shijiazhuang	6	1,770	111.05	523.743	581.19
Hubei Changjiang Publishing Group	October 12, 2004	Wuhan	7	3,024	121.59	626.314	768.35
Shanghai Literature and Art Publishing Group	June 22, 2004	Shanghai	7	213	142.59	62.578	200.36
Jiangxi Publishing Group	December 21, 2004	Nanchang	6	1,806	74.60	322.471	467.76
Yunnan Publishing Group	January 25, 2005	Kunming	5	1,990	148.34	821.555	786.68
Chongqing Publishing Group	April 28, 2005	Chongqing	1	783	74.52	423.734	456.51
Guizhou Publishing Group	September 30, 2005	Guiyang	4	869	68.45	486.107	352.96
Anhui Publishing Group	November 28, 2005	Hefei	7	2,814	41.94	516.041	549.86
Gansu Readers Publishing Group	January 17, 2006	Lanzhou	7	788	177.45	319.404	299.88
Shanxi Publishing Group	December 21, 2006	Taiyuan	8	1,951	93.12	744.931	969.21

Source: Shi, Wang, and Dong (2008).

[a] Million.

[b] Millions of *yuan*.

There were twenty-four registered publishing groups in China until 2004. These publishing groups were highly important industrial organizations and were integral to the development of China's publishing industry. They accounted for 31.3 percent of all published titles (65,129 different kinds of books), 37.8 percent of all copies of printed books (2,422.88 million), 31.4 percent of all copies of printed sheets (14,618.489 million), and 30.2 percent of all the revenue from books (17, 932.47 million *yuan*).[5]

Third, it is very important to recognize that both private and foreign investment boomed in China's publishing industry. There are around 10,000 private publishers in China, among which two hundred to three hundred are of considerable size. Prior to 2006, they mostly found themselves working in a kind of "underground economy" (Chen 2008; Yin 2008). Since they were not permitted to apply for publishing licenses, these companies were often registered as cultural companies. They had to find a way to purchase ISBNs (International Standard Book Number), and thus ISBNs became marketable goods between state-owned and privately owned publishers. Nevertheless, the private sector has played a powerful role in the Chinese book market: they purchase 12 percent of the total copyrights from international counterparts every year; they successfully conduct publishing operations at a high level of professionalism and market-orientation; and 50 percent of the bestseller titles come from private publishing companies (Ge 2010). According to the Open-Book Book Market Research Center, net sales in the Chinese book market in 2008 were about 65 billion *yuan*. Among them, 52 billion *yuan* was created by state-owned channels, and the remaining 13 billion *yuan* was earned through private channels.[6]

A significant change took place in April 2009 when chief minister of the GAPP, Liu Binjie, confirmed that private publishers are officially and legally permitted in the publishing industry. At present, approximately 110,000 private organizations control 78 percent of publication and distribution networks. In addition, twelve of the fifty-seven integrated publication complexes are run by private investors. There are twenty-five national chain-bookstore complexes registered with the GAPP—eight of them (32 percent) are private organizations (Yi 2011). In this account, the powerful influence of private investors in the development of China's publishing industry cannot be disregarded. Many small- to medium-sized publishing houses are inseparably tied to private funds, which are more sensitive to consumer requirements. Private investment is structured as a helpful supplement to state-owned publishers, and therefore, in order to achieve maximum market profit in the publishing industry, it is necessary to find a balance between state-owned assets and private investment.

Furthermore, the new policy in China encourages the investment of capital into the publishing industry from international corporations. In 1997, the German company, Bertelsmann AG, launched its first book club in Shanghai.

Around the same time, many foreign publishers began to set up offices in China. In December 2003, Bertelsmann AG obtained partial ownership of the 21st Century Chain. This new joint venture is the first foreign-owned national chain-bookstore complex. Anther example is that in February 2002, Sony Music Entertainment Inc. established the Shanghai Epic Music Entertainment Co., Ltd. with Chinese partners (the Shanghai Media Group and the Shanghai Jinwen Investment Co., Ltd.). It became the first cooperative joint venture to gain national distribution rights for audiovisual products.

There are two publishing joint ventures of note: the Commercial Press International (CPI) and the Children's Fun Publishing House (Xin 2005). The CPI consists of five companies from China (including Taiwan and Hong Kong), Singapore, and Malaysia. Over the past ten years, it has been devoted to the publications of language learning materials and reference books, with an annual output value of around 20 million *yuan*. The Children's Fun Publishing House is primarily invested by Egmont (Demark) and the People's Posts and Telecom Press (China). Its main product is a simplified Chinese bi-weekly edition of "Mickey Mouse Magazine," and each issue sells 350,000 copies. In 2002, the Children's Fun Publishing House published 424 new titles and achieved an annual output value of 84 million *yuan*. It had become one of the top five children's book publishers by 2002.[7]

It is also worth mentioning that three publishing groups, from Liaoning, Sichuan, and Guangdong provinces, have registered themselves on the stock market. Specifically, the Sichuan Publishing Group was formally listed on the Stock Exchange of Hong Kong Ltd. on May 3, 2007. The China Sunshine Media, indirectly controlled by the Guangzhou Publishing Group, was formally listed on the Shenzhen Stock Exchange on November 16, 2007. The Liaoning Publishing Group was formally listed on the Shanghai Stock Exchange on December 21, 2007.

To conclude, during the past thirty years, the Chinese publishing industry has experienced a profound growth and transformation with an increase of total titles, total printed copies of books and sheets, total revenue from books, and gross output value. This development is also in tandem with an incredible growth in the number of publishing houses and full-time editors. Most importantly, a step-by-step reform has been introduced to accelerate the state's withdrawal from the publishing industry and to promote market competition. As a consequence, three fundamental changes occurred: a change in the nature of publishing houses from public institutions to companies with the emergence of many leading publishers in different professions, the formation of publishing conglomerates to enhance the competence of the Chinese publishing industry, and the widespread expansion of private and foreign investment in the publishing industry of China. In the last part of this section, I intend to specifically concentrate on the growth of the advertising industry, the most direct and significant result of the ongoing Chinese media reform.

The Advertising Industry in China

One of the most obvious and, for many people, the most startling, aspects of China's media reform is the boom in advertising. Since it became legal again in China in 1979, the advertising industry has grown to be one of the largest of its kind in the world today (Scotton and Hachten 2010).[8] To be more specific, in 1979, advertising revenue accounted for 0.002 percent of China's gross domestic product (GDP), and in 2003, the figure went up to 0.92 percent—the highest so far in terms of advertising's share of China's GDP. Also, in 1979, advertising revenue in China was approximately 10 million *yuan*, and fewer than 1,000 people were employed in the industry. By 2007, advertising had grown into a 40,463.5 million *yuan* industry with more than 1.1 million employees. Over the past thirty years, the Chinese advertising industry has expanded at an average annual growth rate of 35 percent, one of the fastest growth rates among all industries in the country (Datamonitor 2010).

Abplanalp (2009) mentions that in China, domestic and international corporations have invested heavily in advertising their products to meet and stimulate consumer demands across numerous product categories, ranging from daily products to luxury goods. Therefore, advertisements are ubiquitous in China today—on taxis and buses, billboards, radio, television, the Internet, and mobile phones, in airports, subways, shopping malls, sports venues, and above all, magazines and newspapers. The rapid and sustained growth of the Chinese advertising industry has been fueled by two major forces.

The first force comes from China's robust economic development since Deng Xiaoping initiated free market reform in the late 1970s; China has since become one of the world's fastest-growing economies. From 1979 to 2007, China's GDP grew at an average annual rate of 9.8 percent. In fact, the dynamic growth of China's advertising market has directly reflected the massive scale of investment in China's economy in recent years. Also, advertising is important in building brand quality and driving consumer sales. The large middle class, estimated at 197 million in 2008, has turned China into a "king maker" market that neither foreign nor local marketers can underestimate (Adler 2008). The second force shaping the Chinese advertising industry comes from the intense inter-firm competition as the country continues to deregulate its markets, especially since 2001 when China became an official member of the World Trade Organization (WTO). Advertising has become vital, not only for international corporations, but also for local firms that attempt to largely challenge the competitive positions of international corporations (Hung, Gu, and Tse 2005). Nowadays, the leading advertising companies in China include the Beijing Dentsu Advertising, Dahe Media, and Saatchi and Saatchi China (Wang 2008a).

In essence, China's explosive economic development has transformed the country into one of the largest economies in the world and has given rise to roughly 350 million urban consumers. Particularly in the Chinese media industry, this consumerism has in turn created one of the largest and most dynamic global advertising markets in just over a decade. Until now, advertising has provided at least 80 percent of the revenue for the Chinese mass media. This high percentage has given strong impetus to China's media industry, and more fundamentally, it has reduced the media's dependence on government funds and has promised more opportunities for creativity and variety in media products.

It is also important to address the sustained growth of professional advertising companies in the Chinese media industry. There are two reasons for such a growth. First, with the development of new media, advertising content is delivered in many formats through diverse channels, ranging from sponsorship of sports events and teams to Internet advertising campaigns. This simply means that reaching the audience now is complicated and often costly. For example, in the past, an advertisement during a prime-time TV show would have certainly reached a large audience. But nowadays, with a plethora of entertainment media available, such as TV, DVDs, and the Internet, the audience is less concentrated in one medium, and therefore, advertising through all media formats needs to be considered. In such a context, professional advertising companies have emerged due to their specific knowledge of the market and audience. Second, the advertising industry is supposed to quickly adjust to meet the challenges of the audience, media segmentation, and the rapid development of technology. As the audience is increasingly fragmented due to technological advances and different consumer habits, players in the advertising market need to constantly innovate and improve their practices to ensure that clients' needs are thoroughly met. Thus, much more attention has been paid to the clients' needs when manufacturers and consumers have interacted through various advertising channels. Not surprisingly, businesses are seeking advice from external advertising/marketing agencies, particularly professional advertising companies, in order to reduce expenditures.

However, most fundamentally, the advertising industry still needs to follow the Party principle despite its incredible expansion accelerated by market forces. It is suggested that the purpose of China's media reform is to strengthen the Party's leadership and supervision, not to discard them (Chu 1994). Thus, the mass media are supposed to deliver political and commercial messages without apparent contradiction, combining intense commercial pressure and highly charged political responsibilities. In other words, the mass media are obliged to persist in unconditionally guiding the people forward with correct public opinions when they are also required to advocate healthy, lofty ideology and culture in order to give a moral support to contemporary socialist construction. Therefore, both domestic and international advertisers are working closely with the government to jointly improve production quality through practical and politically safe initiatives. This further reinforces the notion that as a result of the widespread expansion of China's media reform, Chinese media workers are trapped in a two-track system, namely a state-controlled media sector in combination with a market-oriented entertainment business. What does this mean for Chinese editors, as a main component of Chinese media workers? The following section attempts to specifically examine the actual impacts of the media commodification process on Chinese media workers, particularly on editors in the publishing industry.

PRECARIOUS CHINESE EDITORS

Basic Information of the Surveys

In this section, I intend to examine the precarious condition of Chinese editors using the findings from my surveys carried out in China. I sent out 150 questionnaires via email to the editors in most of the big publishing houses in Shanghai. These editors were selected randomly from a list that was provided by the official who works in the Publishers Association of Shanghai (PAS). Among 150 questionnaires, 128 were completed and have been received. The ages of the editors participating in the surveys are as follows: 23 percent, between twenty and twenty-nine years old, 47 percent, thirty to thirty-nine years old, and 30 percent, forty to forty-nine years old. The average age of the participants is around thirty-six years old. In addition, 85 percent of the editors are female, while 15 percent are male; males are more likely to be the leaders of publishing houses. In terms of marital status, 74 percent of the editors are married, and 26 percent remain single or divorced. It is also important to note that 25 percent of the editors hold master's degrees or above; the rest of them have obtained bachelor's degrees. Among them, 24 percent have graduated from prestigious universities in China, for example, Fudan University, Shanghai Jiaotong University, and the East China Normal University. Their majors include linguistics (22.5 percent), literature and art (12.5 percent), philosophy (2.5 percent), foreign languages (15 percent), economics (5 percent), publishing and editing (15 percent), accounting (2.5 percent), science and technology (22.5 percent), designing (2.5 percent), and education (2.5 percent).

As knowledge workers, editors are considered to obtain high levels of education, various personal skills, and strong social responsibilities. Thus, an editor is supposed to possess a high social status with a decent income. However, as mentioned in the previous two sections, due to the media commodification process in the publishing industry, Chinese editors are trapped in a two-track system: a state-controlled media sector in combination with a market-oriented entertainment business. In such a context, they have constantly faced the problem of contingent employment in association with the changing mode of management, the isolation from any protective framework of social insurance, and intense work pressure with the changes in work hours, locations, main tasks, and monthly incomes.

Contingent Employment

The changing mode of management basically manifests in signing a contract that is based on a fixed time period. Thus, the employment pattern in the Chinese publishing industry has changed from lifetime employment to contingent employment. According to the surveys, 42 percent of the editors sign their contracts annually, 8 percent sign contracts once every two years, and 30 percent sign contracts once every three years. Also, 20 percent of the editors in the surveys sign their contracts in different ways; for example, some editors sign contracts once every five years, and some senior editors sign contracts that guarantee their lifetime employment.

Junior editors usually sign contracts once every year in the first three years. From their fourth year, only those "excellent" (well-behaved) editors are allowed to sign contracts once every three years. Maybe a few years later, they can sign contracts once every five years, depending on their performances (namely, the profit that they have generated for the publishing house). In contrast, senior editors first signed three-year contracts when the Labor Law was implemented in 1995, and afterward they signed contracts that guaranteed their lifetime employment. Nonetheless, before media reform, no contract was required in the publishing industry (Gao 2000).

The Decline of Social Welfare Benefits

In the publishing industry, with the processes of marketization, privatization, and deregulation, social welfare benefits have been cut dramatically. The third section of the survey primarily focuses on this decline. I asked the following questions:

1. Do you have a child? If yes, have you ever taken a maternity leave?
2. Have you received any subsidy for your housing? Do you have to pay a mortgage every month? If yes, how much do you have to pay?
3. Do you receive medical insurance and unemployment benefits?

For the first question, 38 percent of the editors have a child, while 62 percent do not. The decline of maternity leave strongly implies that social welfare benefits have been radically cut in the publishing industry. Maternity leave used to be one year, but now it has changed to four months for a natural delivery, and four and a half months for a Caesarean birth. However, in practice, these expectant mothers have to work as ordinary editors, and sometimes they even work twelve hours a day. The only privilege that they might enjoy is to work at home. In addition, after giving birth to their children, female editors try to go back to work as soon as possible due to their intense concerns about losing their jobs. What is even worse is that most publishing houses are reluctant to recruit female editors because according to the Labor Law, female editors should be fully paid during their maternity leaves (Bie 2007).

In terms of the answers to the second question, 81.8 percent of the editors do not receive any subsidy for housing. In contrast to 63.8 percent of the editors who have bought their own houses, 36.2 percent of them still cannot afford one. The surveys also indicate that 53.5 percent of the editors have to pay monthly mortgages, which range from 2,000 to 5,000 *yuan*. To specify, 41.2 percent of them pay less than 2,000 *yuan* for their monthly mortgages, 29.4 percent between 2,000 to 3,000 *yuan*, and 29.4 percent between 3,000 to 5,000 *yuan*. Considering their monthly incomes, editors are enormously pressured to meet their mortgage payments.

To supplement this analysis, it is rather illuminating to analyze the concrete regulations on housing subsidies in the Shanghai Education Publishing House, combined with the findings from the interviews with the editors who work there. The Shanghai Education Publishing House offers senior editors 140,000 to 180,000 *yuan* (depending on their administrative roles in the publishing house) in total as a subsidy to purchase a house. In practice, editors receive 300 *yuan* per month before their retirement, and get the rest of money when they are retired. Meanwhile, it offers junior editors around 120,000 *yuan* as a subsidy for house purchasing, with 100 *yuan* distributed to them per month. Interestingly, in order to be eligible for such a subsidy, editors, both senior and junior, are required to sign contracts which stipulate that they should work in the publishing house for the next five consecutive years after the contract is signed.

Generally, in association with the enormous pressure to pay off the mortgage, one of the most effective means for the government to maintain its control over society is by successfully tying people to the pressure of purchasing their accomodations. This tremendous economic pressure has motivated editors to work hard, and caused them to feel excessively insecure given that they can easily lose their jobs, and by no means can they afford such a loss. This point is further strengthened by the answers to question 14 in the questionnaire, which specifically looks into the frequency that editors change their jobs. According to the surveys, 62.5 percent of the editors have never changed their jobs, 25 percent have changed once, 7.5 percent have changed twice, and only 5 percent have changed three times or more. In fact, editors are fearful of losing their jobs if they complain too much about their work, work less intensely than their colleagues, or fail to achieve the profit required by the leaders. Likewise, it is not only important to understand that editors cannot afford to lose their jobs due to the high living costs, but more critically, specific attention should be drawn to the surplus of labor in China. Every year, a large number of local students, graduated from universities and colleges, who major in journalism, history, political science, and finance, plunge into the job market. With very limited job opportunities, most of them remain unemployed. There is no doubt that they constitute constant threats to those editors who are working in the publishing industry.[9]

As a result, editors have become docile, indifferent to politics, and exclusively concerned about their personal affairs instead of being interested in the common problems facing editors as a collectivity (Li 1997a; Ma 1998). This, to some extent, explains why social resistance on the part of editors has not been widespread in China, even though the decline of social welfare benefits has been significant.

In response to the third question, 95.7 percent of the editors receive medical insurance and unemployment benefits, while 4.3 percent of them do not. According to the regulations issued by the Shanghai Municipal Human Resources and Social Security Bureau, employers and employees are paying contributions to pensions, medical insurance, unemployment benefits, and housing funds together. The exact amount is listed in table 2.5.

Basically, the more employees pay to the government, the more employers will pay for them to the government. However, for those 4.3 percent of the editors who are not paying anything, with employers paying nothing for them either, they will end up receiving neither financial assistance nor social welfare benefits from the government after their retirement (Li and Zhang

Table 2.5. Percentage Employers and Employees Paid for Social Welfare Benefits.

Item	Employees' Part	Employers' Part
Pensions	8%	22%
Medical Insurance	2%	12%
Unemployment Benefits	1%	2%
Housing Funds	7%	7%
Total	18%	43%

Percentages are based on the percentage of the employee's monthly income. *Source*: The Shanghai Municipal Human Resources and Social Security Bureau (2011).

2008). Furthermore, some publishing houses used to buy extra commercial health insurance for editors on behalf of unions. Also, they used to offer extra housing funds for editors as social welfare benefits, which could be used to buy, rent, or decorate houses. But now, fewer and fewer publishing houses carry out these two policies, and the amount spent on either commercial health insurance or housing funds has been shrinking substantially. [10]

To conclude, according to the surveys, in the Chinese publishing industry, along with the media commodification process, government no longer provides free education, housing, and medical service. At the same time, publishing houses are trying to minimize their expenditures on social welfare benefits, by providing neither sufficient medical insurance nor unemployment benefits. Even though some forms of social welfare benefits have not been removed completely, for example, maternity leave, food and transportation subsidies, and travel grants, they have been reduced to a large extent. Most importantly, several insignificant forms of social welfare benefits, for example, distributing gift cards and transportation tokens, have slightly increased at the expense of the dramatic decline of the basic social welfare benefits that editors badly need, including medical insurance, housing funds, and unemployment benefits.

Intense Work Pressure

Work pressure has become intense due to the changes in work hours, locations, main tasks, and monthly incomes.

Changes in Work Hours

Questions 10 and 11 in the questionnaire specifically deal with the changing work hours of editors in the publishing industry. Even though the regular work hours before and after current media reform remain the same, eight hours a day and five days a week, it is apparent that after current media reform, editors usually work overtime in order to finish their monthly workload, as their incomes are largely determined by the profit that has been generated. As the surveys demonstrate, 94.9 percent of the editors work overtime, and among them, 19.4 percent work an extra one to five hours per week, 41.9 percent work an extra six to ten hours per week, 19.4 percent work an extra eleven to twenty hours, and 19.4 percent work an extra twenty-one hours or above per week. Interestingly, although editors are confronted with the enormous economic pressure aforementioned, 98 percent of them do not take any part-time job. This phenomenon partially reflects the heavy workload of editors in a very implicit way because as their incomes are predominately determined by the profit that they can generate, editors have to work outside of their regular work hours frequently. Therefore, the line between work and leisure is blurred. So is the boundary between office and home (Wang 1994).

Changes in Locations

Before media reform, editors exclusively worked in their offices. But now, within their regular work hours, editors mainly work both in the offices and at home, while outside of their regular work hours, the places where they work include: home (86.3 percent of them prefer working at home), offices (22.7 percent), restaurants (31.8 percent), hotels (9 percent), and other miscellaneous places (18.1 percent). In general, editors' workplaces have become very flexible.

Nevertheless, according to the surveys, 97.7 percent of the editors have admitted that everyday attendance is still strictly recorded in the publishing house. Actually, in most publishing houses, the physical attendance of editors is precisely recorded by a machine that is installed at the entrance of the publishing house. Only with the leaders' permission can editors leave the publishing house during regular work hours. In most cases, editors are allowed to chat with the author of a forthcoming book outside of the publishing house, and they are also allowed by the leaders to attend conferences organized by the PAS. Besides, sick leave will not be approved until an official note from a doctor is provided.

Changes in Main Tasks

Editing no longer remains the only important task for editors. Once, editors were mainly responsible for editing and word processing. However, as a result of media commodification, editors need to be good at, or at least familiar with, editing, wording processing, marketing, book planning, sales, and publishing. The boundaries between different tasks are blurred, and as a consequence, it becomes imperative for editors to frequently renew their knowledge. According to the surveys, 37.5 percent of the editors are mainly responsible for *editing* (word processing), 22.5 percent take care of *book planning* (marketing, sales, and publishing), and 40 percent need to fulfill both tasks.

In fact, after current media reform, editors' responsibilities for *book planning*, particularly marketing and book sales, turn out to be more substantial. As such, the working conditions of editors have largely changed because most of them are now increasingly concentrating on the promotion of books instead of *editing* them. Not surprisingly, editors have spent a great amount of time traveling to different provinces to promote books instead of merely working in their offices.

It becomes rather enlightening to investigate the main problems regarding both *editing* and *book planning* for editors. For the problems in *editing*, 29.2

percent of the editors have realized that the leaders have excessively emphasized the economic interests of publication, which leads to a fast pace of
work and tremendous work pressure. Other major *editing* problems include:
the lack of systematic training in the publishing house (mentioned by 12.5
percent of my survey participants), the decline of editors' social responsibilities as a result of the widespread expansion of utilitarianism as a guiding
social principle (8.3 percent), the deteriorating quality of books with less
effort made to polish and proofread (1.4 percent), and the challenge of mas-
tering new skills required by modern word processing techniques (8.3 percent). The problems in *book planning* include intense competition among
different publishing houses (50 percent), the need to develop personal social
networks to effectively promote books (24.1 percent), the rigid hierarchical
system in publishing houses as an impediment to generating profit (16.75
percent), the comparatively low incomes for authors that lead to poor quality
books (7.4 percent), and the lack of institutionalized and routinized training
(8.3 percent). Thus, it has become clear that *editing* and *book planning* share
many common problems.

Changes in Monthly Incomes

The current distribution system is guided by "market-based and profit-orien-
tated" principles. The monthly incomes of editors thus consist of both basic
wages and bonuses (Sun 2006). In general, basic wages of editors are determined by their job titles and the length of their services, while bonuses are
calculated considering their monthly workload, profit that has been generated, and the administrative roles that editors are playing in the publishing
house. Comparatively, before media reform, the monthly incomes of editors
largely equalled their basic wages with the job titles and the length of services being the two dominant indices. Questions 7 and 8 in the questionnaire
specifically look into the changing monthly incomes of editors.

To be more specific, question 7 attempts to understand both the monthly
and annual incomes of editors. The surveys show that 55.5 percent of the
editors earn below 5,000 *yuan* per month, 18.8 percent earn between 5,000 to
6,000 *yuan*, 7.3 percent earn between 6,000 to 7,000 *yuan*, 9.1 percent earn
between 7,000 to 10,000 *yuan*, and 9.3 percent earn more than 10,000 *yuan*.
To calculate, in 2009, the average annual incomes of editors are roughly
around 60,000 *yuan*, which is less than that of most knowledge workers in
other professions, including finance, telecommunications, and scientific research. It is even less than that of some industrial workers, including min-
ers.[11]

As shown above, editors are not well paid in general. Therefore, question
8 further seeks to learn how much they expect to earn, with regard to increasing living costs in Shanghai. It is interesting to find that 10 percent of the

editors expect their monthly incomes to be up to 6,000 *yuan*, 6 percent expect incomes from 6,000 to 7,000 *yuan*, 32 percent expect incomes between 7,000 to 10,000 *yuan*, and 26 percent anticipate their monthly incomes to be more than 10,000 *yuan*. In order to better understand the actual living costs as well as the actual purchasing power of *yuan*, table 2.6 lists several major expenses for editors in their daily lives in Shanghai.

In conclusion, Chinese media workers, particularly editors, are in a precarious situation with the advance of China's social reform. Table 2.7 summarizes the changes in the mode of management, social welfare benefits, work hours, locations, main tasks, and monthly incomes that editors have been experiencing. Also, it is important to acknowledge that these changes are interconnected. When the impacts of contingent employment are examined, editors believe that contingent employment not only manifests in signing a contract based on fixed time periods (85 percent of them mentioned this point in the surveys), but more critically, it leads to a series of other crucial problems, including taking part-time jobs (58 percent), the decline of social welfare benefits (90 percent), working overtime (45 percent, and among them 32 percent maintain that they have to work at home frequently), receiv-

Table 2.6.   Major Expenses for Editors in Their Daily Lives in Shanghai.

Expense	Estimated Cost
kindergarten	3,000 *yuan* / per month
tuition fee for public elementary school	3,000 *yuan* / per term
tuition fee for private elementary school	8,000 *yuan* / per term
tuition fee for public secondary school	5,000 *yuan* / per term
tuition fee for private secondary school	12,000 *yuan* / per term
meat	40–70 *yuan* / per kilogram
vegetables	10–25 *yuan* / per kilogram
seafood	60-90 *yuan* / per kilogram
gas	7.60 *yuan* / per liter
housing to buy[a]	25,000–40,000 *yuan* / per square meter
housing to rent	1,600–5,000 *yuan* / per month, one unit
transportation	400–800 *yuan* / per month

Source: The Shanghai Municipal Statistics Bureau (2009c).

[a] To highlight, accommodation has become extremely expensive in Shanghai. In order to buy a house, according to their average incomes, editors need to work for nearly fifty years. The economic pressure has successfully motivated editors to work hard so as not to lose their jobs.

ing less payment (88 percent), and getting fewer chances to get promoted (38 percent).

None of the editors are satisfied with their current jobs. In association with the answers to questions 19 and 20 in the questionnaire, editors are suffering from enormous pressure owing to other factors that I have not elucidated above. Such factors include intense living pressure (mentioned by 86 percent of the survey participants) and ineffective reward system (71.7 percent). Table 2.8 illustrates the major factors that have also led to the precarious condition of editors in the publishing industry.

Question 24 concentrates on editors' comments to the media commodification process. For editors, the negative impacts of publishing reform are rather obvious, which makes the reform itself problematic. First, according to 46.1 percent of the editors, it is impossible, or at least too demanding, for them to acquire the abilities of editing, word processing, marketing, sales, and publishing at the same time, not to mention the fact that training is not easily accessible to every individual in the publishing house. Second, there are 20.5 percent of the editors pointing out that most of the leaders are not editors themselves, and thus their guidance is not professional, and sometimes can be very misleading. Third, rigid bureaucratic structure is an important factor that contributes to the poor efficiency in the publishing house (mentioned by 10.2 percent of the editors in the surveys). Finally but most importantly, administrative power is still essential in regulating the publishing industry through very tight censorship and effective control over social resources, and accordingly, editors have to dance with much more powerful

Table 2.7.   Differences between the Two Employment Patterns before and after China's Publishing Reform.

	Before Publishing Reform	After Publishing Reform
Employment Pattern	lifetime employment	contingent employment
Mode of Management	no contract is required	signing a contract based on a fixed time period
Social Welfare Benefits	all-inclusive	shift from government to publishing houses and individuals
Work Hours	regular work hours	regular and extra work hours
Work Places	office and home	multiple locations, including home, offices, restaurants, and hotels
Main Tasks	editing and word processing	multitasks, including editing, word processing, marketing, book planning, sales, and publishing
Monthly Incomes	basic wages	basic wages with bonuses

Table 2.8.   Major Factors Leading to Enormous Pressure on Editors.

Factor	Percentage
intensive living pressure	86%
ineffective reward system	71.7%
various pressure to raise a child	32.3%
too much involvement in housework	27%
the limitation of time and strength	12.7%
disadvantage of age	9.2%
deteriorating personal health condition	7.7%
unfair promotion	7.7%
unpredictable future career	7.7%
complicated relationships with colleagues	4.6%
decline in work ability	4.6%
subjectivity of the leaders	4.6%
gender discrimination	4.6%
weak personality	2.3%
lack of work experience	2.3%
inadequate educational background	2.3%

"chains." In this regard, it is not difficult to find that the Chinese government has not completely withdrawn from the publishing industry. In addition to implementing tight censorship and controlling social resources, government also needs to be largely responsible for improving the working conditions as well as increasing the social welfare benefits of editors.

CONCLUSION

The development of the mass media, the most political and commercial aspect of modern industries, provides unique insight into the reality of "socialism with Chinese characteristics" and the challenges facing China as it emerges as a major world economy and cultural force. In no other sectors are the powerful forces of politics and economics so graphically and publicly joined together as a single product. Therefore, Chinese media workers, particularly editors, are constantly faced with tremendous challenges brought about by both the ongoing political and economic reforms. It has become more apparent when China's media reform started in the late 1970s, with the widespread expansion of the media commodification process.

This chapter specifically examined China's media reform, particularly the reform in the publishing industry. In essence, a step-by-step reform has been introduced to accelerate the state's withdrawal from the publishing industry and to promote market competition. The widespread expansion of the media commodification process has resulted in a series of fundamental changes. Meanwhile, in this chapter, I have also described how media commodification has led to a two-track system for editors—a state-controlled media sector in combination with a market-oriented entertainment business. Therefore, editors are in a precarious situation. More critically, according to the findings from my surveys, junior editors are confronted with more challenges than senior editors, for example, they sign contracts based on shorter time periods, receive fewer housing subsidies, and get a heavier monthly workload. Thus, it becomes crucial to examine the inner division even among editors because the tension is manifested quite clearly in their struggles for power in the publishing industry hierarchy. This leads to my discussion of the structuration process of the political economy of communication in the Chinese publishing industry, which concentrates on the five critical problems facing Chinese editors in relation to the fundamental social changes, including technological, political, and economic ones, and most importantly, the changes in class relations and power dynamics.

NOTES

1. In China, each congress lasts for five years and holds one session in each of those five years.

2. To note, the State Council is largely synonymous with the central government of China. It is the chief administrative authority.

3. For an example of how the GAPP and the CPD work together to ensure that in China people are not able to print criticisms of their own leaders, see the "Regulations on Strengthening the Administration of Publications Describing Major Party and National Leaders" (effective on May 5, 1990, promulgated by the GAPP and the CPD).

When relevant publishing houses are arranging for the publication of topics for these types of books, local publishing houses shall provide a draft to their local Press and Publication Office, which shall read and evaluate the manuscript and offer their opinions. After receiving approval from the Propaganda Department, local publishing houses shall provide the manuscript to the General Administration of Press and Publication for examination and approval. Central level publishing houses shall provide a draft to their responsible department. After the responsible department has reviewed the manuscript and provided opinions, central level publishing houses shall provide the manuscript to the General Administration of Press and Publication for examination and approval. Manuscripts written about major Party and national leaders who are currently living must ask for the opinions of that person prior to submission to the General Administration of Press and Publication. (article 4)

4. There are still several nonprofit publishing houses existing in China, which are directly affiliated to, and are largely subsidized by, the Central Committee of the CPC, for example, the Party Building Books Publishing House.

5. This book specifically looks into two publishing houses: one is the Shanghai Science and Technology Publishing House, and the other is the Shanghai Education Publishing House. The Shanghai Science and Technology Publishing House ranked 43 among 568 publishing houses in China in 2002, in terms of the gross output value, and the Shanghai Education Publishing House ranked 22. Both of them have become important publishing houses of the Shanghai Century Publishing Group, the first Chinese publishing group that was established in 1999.

6. The Open-Book Book Market Research Center is a private organization, and it is the only organization that provides continuous sales monitoring service for books in China. Retrieved May 1, 2011 (www.openbook.com.cn/EN/).

7. According to the market share in 2002 (The Book Publishing Management Department of the GAPP 2008), the five largest children's book publishers are: the Zhejiang Children's Publishing House (6.2 percent of the market share), the Children's Fun Publishing House (5.21 percent of the market share), the 21st Century Publishing House (4.6 percent of the market share), the Shanghai People's Fine Arts Publishing House (3.46 percent of the market share), and the Jilin Fine Arts Publishing House (3.34 percent of the market share).

8. The word "again" is used purposefully. In fact, China's first advertising agency, the Shanghai Advertising and Packaging Corporation, was set up in 1962. It kept busy promoting national products and advertising on the packaging of products for exports. However, the Cultural Revolution was thoroughly opposed to advertising activities, and the corporation ceased to function until 1978 when it rose again as the Shanghai Advertising Corporation. Since then, advertising agencies have been widely established in Guangzhou (Guangdong province), Qingdao (Shandong province), Nanjing (Jiangsu province), Dalian (Liaoning province), and Tianjin.

9. According to the survey, 75 percent of the editors choose being editors as their lifetime careers. In fact, many editors are reluctant to change their jobs not just because of the external factors as I have argued previously, such as the surplus of labor, the increasing living costs, and the widespread expansion of contingent employment. Internal factors, including the love and enthusiasm that editors have toward their jobs, the aspiration and respect for knowledge as intellectuals, and the high social status associated with editors, need to be considered as well. According to the findings from my surveys, 60.7 percent of the editors refuse to work outside of the publishing industry.

10. The Shanghai Education Publishing House still offers very sick editors a living allowance. To specify, those editors who are suffering from any cancer, kidney disease, or mental disease can receive 300 *yuan* per month. In addition, 300 to 500 *yuan* is given to the editors who need operations. However, no more than 1,000 *yuan* is granted to each editor within one year.

11. According to the report of the Shanghai Municipal Statistics Bureau (2009a, 2009b), the average annual income in Shanghai was around 40,000 *yuan* in 2009. The average annual incomes of knowledge workers in finance, telecommunications, and scientific research were 117,463, 98,548, and 74,611 *yuan*, respectively. The average annual income of industrial workers in mining was 61,533 *yuan*.

Chapter Three

The Structuration Process

The Five Critical Problems

The current Chinese economic reform has brought about remarkable social changes. The emergence of contingent employment and the deteriorating working conditions of the working class are among the most evident of labor relation changes. As mentioned earlier, in the Chinese publishing industry, such changes have resulted in the decline of social welfare benefits and intense work pressure on editors, with the acceleration of the media *commodification* process. In this chapter, I intend to examine the *structuration* process of the Chinese publishing industry by analyzing the findings from my interviews in China. Specifically, I intend to concentrate on the five critical problems confronting Chinese editors that came about as a result of various ongoing social changes. These changes include technological, political, and economic ones, and most importantly, the changes in class relations and power dynamics.[1]

THE FIVE CRITICAL PROBLEMS

According to Mosco (2009, 185), *"Structuration describes a process by which structures are constituted out of human agency, even as they provide the very 'medium' of that constitution."* In other words, social life is comprised of the mutual constitution of *structure* and *agency*. *Structure*, as Anthony Giddens argues, is regarded as rules and resources recursively implicated in social reproduction. Structure is out of time and space, and marked by an "absence of subject" (1984, 25). However, social systems, in which structure is recursively implicated, also comprise the situated activities of *human agents* that are reproduced across time and space. Therefore, analyzing the structuration of social systems means incorporating the ideas of agency, social relations, and social practice into the political economic analysis of social structures. In this regard, the theory of structuration, defined by both Mosco and Giddens, attempts to bridge a gap between theoretical perspectives that foreground *structure* and those that emphasize *action* and *agency*. Thus, *structures* and *agents* are not two independently given sets of phenomena. Instead, they are interconnected in the ongoing patterning of social life (Mosco 2009). From this viewpoint, I aim to address an interconnection between *structures* (the dominant Chinese political, economic, and social structures) and *agents* (Chinese editors) when analyzing the structuration process of the Chinese publishing industry.

Furthermore, both Mosco and Giddens acknowledge that one of the most important characteristics of structuration theory is the prominence it gives to *social change*—a process that is described as the way structures are produced and reproduced by human agents who act through the medium of the structure. According to Hobsbawn (1973), the theory of structuration can never be fully understood without comprehending the stabilizing and disruptive elements that either lead to the maintenance of a system or to the inevitability of social change. As such, in this chapter, it is essential to connect the problems facing Chinese editors to the broader ongoing social changes in China. In more detail, they are challenged by five critical problems brought about by the rapid technological changes, following the Party principle in the media marketization process, changes in both the pension and health care systems, the smashing of the work-unit system, and the internal differences with the working class.

TECHNOLOGICAL CHANGES IN CHINA

Since the 1990s, with the purpose of integrating China into the global political economy, the nationwide economic reform has shifted its concentration to the promotion of information technology, particularly the widespread expansion of the Internet. The past thirty years has witnessed an extensive application of information technology by professionals, managers, and media workers in China. The consequences are twofold in the Chinese publishing industry. On the one hand, it is much easier for Chinese editors to use databases, manipulate text and quantitative data, generate tables and graphic displays, and utilize analytical software. In light of the rapid technological developments in telecommunications, Chinese editors are able to communicate with one another through a computer network, renew their knowledge and upgrade their professional skills at a relatively low cost, and gain quick access to external databases and communication networks that can be either used independently or in conjunction with internal databases (Zhang 2004). As a result, both organizational and national boundaries have been blurred. On the other hand, in recent years, as technological developments advance, Chinese editors are experiencing numerous problems resulting from the dramatic changes in both their work process and working conditions.

First, it is evident that editors' jobs have been simplified in company with the deskilling effects of new technology. In the interview with Li, who started working in the Shanghai Science and Technology Publishing House in 2009, he maintained that:[2]

> I am completely unsatisfied with my work in the publishing house. I graduated from one of the leading universities in China, and my major was editing and publishing. When I first entered the publishing house, I thought I would be very successful due to my educational background and professional training. I was wrong. I have never been allowed to choose which book to publish or to edit. Even highly profitable books cannot be published without the leader's agreement. I only work on the books assigned by the leader. I check for typos, and most importantly, I read drafts to make sure nothing will be published that criticizes the Party's leadership. I am very good at advertising and promoting new books. I can design very attractive posters, and I know a lot about marketing. It is frustrating, however, that these skills are becoming less and less important due to the use of professional software in the publishing house. I am not the only person who has this problem. To be honest, a lot of junior editors feel the same way. (Li 2010)

According to Aronowitz and DiFazio (1994), the application of information technology has moved the deskilling trend up the occupational ladder. Deskilling is not just a feature of industrial workers but of knowledge workers as well. For most editors, the introduction of new technology has largely removed them from the *conception* stage of production. In most Chinese publishing houses, editors are mainly responsible for checking the typos on the screen, and reading drafts to ensure their political correctness of the material. There is a growing awareness among editors that new technology has devalued much of their professional knowledge and abilities upon which they had once prided themselves (Liu 2006). Such professional knowledge and abilities for editors include the solid background of grammar and sentence rules, the accurate understanding of the logic of language, and the abilities to connect book contents to readers' interests.

Second, in association with the deskilling effects of new technology, job opportunities for most of the editors have greatly decreased. McKercher (2002) argues that the introduction of computers in the workplace creates new opportunities for a small number of people, mostly technicians. Yet, for the immense majority, job opportunities have decreased. It is not difficult to understand that as the technical skills appear to be more crucial, most leaders in publishing houses are more inclined to hire a less qualified but technically adept editor instead of an experienced editor with fewer technical skills (Zhao 2001). By placing more value on editors' technical skills than on their professional experience and knowledge, leaders have successfully degraded editing work, and the uniqueness of each experienced editor has been eliminated. As a consequence, positions for experienced editors are threatened because leaders have realized that in order to minimize wage costs, it is advantageous to employ young editors with adequate technical skills instead of the experienced ones who are normally highly paid.

Third, editors are increasingly challenged by intense work pressure. Leaders in most Chinese publishing houses have put enormous pressure on editors with a heavier workload because they assume that the Internet enables editors to finish their work much faster than before. According to the findings from my interviews, it is fairly common for editors to work outside of their regular work hours due to their heavy workload. The growing pressure of working overtime has blurred the boundary between editors' work and leisure time, as well as the boundary between office and home (Wang 1994; The International Labor Organization 2000). Additionally, editors who spend most of their time working on computers are vulnerable to repetitive strain injuries, asthenopia, backaches, and other health problems.

Fourth, while a large amount of information from the Internet provides editors with a new source of knowledge, it has also resulted in information overload (Garrison 2000; Keane and Donald 2002). Given the speed of technological change, editors need to expand and update their professional knowledge as often as possible, and the value of their old knowledge decreases at an incredibly fast speed. In other words, due to information overload, most editors find that their traditional professional skills of editing are not enough, and they are obliged to acquire additional technical skills. For example, in most publishing houses, editors feel it necessary to learn how to use several different software systems to process either text or pictures. They are also responsible for taking on more administration and research work formerly done by more advanced technical workers. It is clear that as the required skills in the workplace are changing constantly, the abilities of editors to learn new skills and to gain up-to-date information have become essential; however, they do not necessarily receive any higher income or job title (Halford and Savage 1995).

Fifth, the introduction of new technology has enhanced management control over the work process of editors. Editors are facing greater surveillance, and are increasingly subject to the "electronic panopticon" (Adams and Welsh 2008, 221). As a senior editor who has worked in the Shanghai Education Publishing House for more than twenty years, Gao stated in the interview that:

The leader of our publishing house uses his mobile phone to micromanage the book editing process. I frequently receive work-related text messages from him, sometimes even when I am having dinner with my family. I feel extremely depressed because I no longer enjoy the independence and autonomy that I once had. The leader can reach me, whenever he chooses. What is worse, I am expected to keep my mobile phone on even when I am off-duty or on vacation, so that he can assign me new jobs at anytime. (Gao 2010)

It is suggested that the shift to an electronic infrastructure for office work allows leaders in publishing houses to adopt additional control mechanisms that are embedded within the computer systems themselves. In both the Shanghai Science and Technology Publishing House and the Shanghai Education Publishing House, surveillance cameras have become quite common in the workplace to monitor what editors are doing in their regular work hours. Moreover, the editors' phone calls and emails with authors of publications are censored by leaders after the introduction of specific software. The enhanced surveillance has added to editors' stress and discomfort.

With the widespread expansion of new technologies, the Chinese publishing industry has become more competitive, and it requires more skilled employees with better professional expertise and abilities. Therefore, editors are pushed to take various measures to respond to the challenges brought about by technological changes. In detail, according to the findings from my interviews in the Shanghai Science and Technology Publishing House, editors often attend different lectures to upgrade their knowledge structures when the technological changes in the publishing industry turn out to be rapid and wide. The lectures are primarily sponsored by the publishing house, and in most cases, they are given by professional technicians either inside or outside the publishing industry. As a nongovernmental organization, the Publishers Association of Shanghai (PAS) also plays an active role in organizing large lectures, aiming to link editors with different ages, genders, job titles, and educational backgrounds from different publishing houses to better accommodate themselves, particularly junior editors, to current media reform. In addition, as Xin Guangwei (2005) observes, some professional organizations, such as the China Book Business Report and the Open-Book Book Market Research Center organize various kinds of lectures at irregular intervals, focusing on book market research, book advertising and promotions, book distribution, publishing management and strategies, and other topics that seem to be especially relevant in relation to many changes that are taking place in the market.

Editors also take short-term training classes, which has become one of the most efficient ways to help them gain specific skills in a short time period (Tian 2010). The topics of the training classes are diverse, but basically they concentrate on the practical skills that good editors need to acquire in the information age. Such topics include the techniques to produce an attractive poster by using the latest software systems (Photoshop and CorelDRAW), the skills to search useful information on the Internet, the shortcuts to effective computer typesetting, and the online management of word processing (Deng and Huang 2001). Also, participating in numerous nationwide conferences, seminars, and forums every year, editors are clearly aware of the challenges of media reform, the guiding principles of the Chinese publishing industry, and the fierce competition among publishing houses accompanied by media digitalization (Sun and Yang 2002).

It is important to note that most publishing houses have strongly encouraged editors to participate in either lectures or short-term training classes, as part of their training programs in the industry. For more than twenty years, publishing houses have been paying constant attention to job training. Numerous formal training centers have been established in Beijing, Shanghai, and other large cities in China, to offer short-term job training projects that aim to extend professional knowledge to new employees in the publishing industry (Xin 2005). It is estimated that more than 41,600 employees have received job training in a total of 795 sessions since 1995 (Baensch 2003).

Last, but most importantly, with more and more Chinese universities adding a major specifically dealing with editing and publishing, a great number of editors, both senior and junior, feel that they need to receive further education for either degrees or certificates to improve their professional abilities, skills, and insights (Wang and Wang 1999). The following briefly offers an overview of universities that provide a major in editing and publishing in China.

Major in Editing

Anhui University (*undergraduate degrees*)
Beijing Normal University (*undergraduate and graduate degrees*)
Beijing Printing College (*undergraduate and graduate degrees*)
Fudan University (*undergraduate and graduate degrees*)
He'nan University (*undergraduate and graduate degrees*)
Nanjing University (*undergraduate degrees and two-year graduate programs*)
Nankai University (*undergraduate degrees*)
Peking University (*undergraduate degrees*)
Shanghai Professional University (*two-year training programs*)
Shanghai University (*undergraduate degrees*)
Sichuan Academy of Social Sciences (*graduate degrees*)
Sichuan University (*undergraduate degrees*)
Tsinghua University (*undergraduate degrees and a second bachelor's program*)
Wuhan University (*undergraduate and graduate degrees*)
Xi'an Highway University (*graduate degrees*)

Xi'an Jiaotong University (*graduate degrees*)

Major in Management of Publishing and Distribution

Beijing Institute of Technology (*two-year training programs*)
Beijing Printing College (*undergraduate and graduate degrees*)
Beijing Professional University (*two year training programs*)
Nanjing University (*undergraduate and graduate degrees*)
Shanghai Publishing and Printing College (*two-year training programs*)
Tsinghua University (*certificate programs*)
Wuhan University (*undergraduate and graduate degrees*)

Major in Book Design, Production, and Binding

Beijing Hongqi University (*certificate programs*)
Beijing Printing College (*undergraduate degrees*)
Shanghai Publishing and Printing College (*two-year training programs*)
Tsinghua University (*undergraduate degrees*)

Major in Printing

Beijing Printing College (*undergraduate degrees*)
Shanghai Publishing and Printing College (*two-year training programs*)
Wuhan Technology University (*two-year training programs*)
Wuxi University of Light Industry (*undergraduate degrees*)
Xi'an University of Technology (*two-year training programs, undergraduate and graduate degrees*)
Zhuzhou Institute of Technology (*undergraduate degrees*)

In the Shanghai Science and Technology Publishing House, it is common for junior editors, who have been working in the publishing house for a couple of years, to take graduate courses as part-time students in large local universities. The core courses included in the editing and publishing major are closely related to their professions, as indicated below.

Courses for Management Major

Management of Press
International Trade of Books
Economics of Book Industry
Fundamental Laws for the Book Industry

Courses for Editing Major

Editing

Courses for Printing and Distribution Major

Introduction to Printing

Courses for Publishing Major

Introduction to Book Distribution
Management of Book Distributing Corporation
Introduction to Publishing
History of Publishing
Comparative Publishing
Electronic Publication
Modern Technology of Publishing
Book Marketing

Other Courses

Professional English
Internship in the Publishing Industry

According to *The China Book Publishing Industry Report 2005–2006* (The Book Publishing Management Department of the GAPP 2008), in 2006, 16.4 percent of the editors possess master's degrees or above in the publishing industry in Shanghai, with the average of 18.83 percent in China, and 28.36 percent (Chongqing Municipality) as the highest (see table 3.1).

FOLLOWING THE PARTY PRINCIPLE IN THE MEDIA MARKETIZATION PROCESS

Mass media command a sensitive location in the Chinese Communist system because they are regarded as an important part of the ideological apparatus that is indispensable for legitimatizing the party-state, indoctrinating the public, and coordinating campaigns (Chan 2003). Thus, as Zhao (1998) maintains, the propaganda model has long been the dominant framework for analyzing the Chinese media industry, and accordingly, the publishing industry has become a tightly controlled instrument of political indoctrination and mass mobilization. Considered as the party-state's mouthpiece, the Chinese publishing industry has been broadly used to propagate the goals of the Communist Party of China (CPC) and promote changes in the attitudes and behavior of the Chinese people, leading to intentional political propaganda and indoctrination.

However, in the past thirty years, as a part of the massive state-directed transformation of the Chinese political economy, a media marketization process has widely expanded. In China, the marketization process contains substantive political implications. In Pei's (1994, 150) words, such implications can be summarized as "In a politically repressive environment, market forces

Table 3.1.   Percentage of Editors with Master's Degrees or above in 2006.

Rank	Region	Number of Editors with Master's Degrees or Above	Percentage (%)
1	Chongqing Municipality	194	28.36
2	Jiangsu Province	378	27.31
3	Beijing Municipality	258	26.43
4	Hubei Province	259	20.14
5	Shanghai Municipality	739	18.83
6	Shandong Province	192	16.62
7	Anhui Province	110	15.49
8	Zhejiang Province	120	15.38
9	Ningxia Hui Autonomous Region	27	14.36
10	Gansu Province	32	13.39
11	Hu'nan Province	116	13.20
12	He'nan Province	113	13.15
13	Liaoning Province	174	12.99
14	Guangdong Province	183	11.57
15	Guangxi Zhuang Autonomous Region	124	11.01

Source: The Book Publishing Management Department of the GAPP (2008).

became the principal means for societal actors to gradually and subtly influence the political process and alter the balance between the state and society."

Therefore, the Chinese publishing industry is defined as "both a state ideological apparatus and an integral part of the profit-oriented service industry" (Tong 2003, 18). To specify, the marketization process has brought about significant changes in the Chinese publishing industry. These changes include the rise of market competition, even stricter Party control, and the growing tension within the propaganda-commercial model. At the core, Chinese editors are bound to serve the political and ideological interests of the state. At the same time, they are required to meet the need to generate profit like business entities for their companies in the media marketization process.

The Rise of Market Competition

As one of its most profound influences, marketization has reduced institutional dependency of the media on the state, mainly through the commercialization process of the interests, behavior, and finally, the structural change of the mass media (White 1990; Lee 2000; Gang and Bandurski 2011). It is apparent that marketization has made the Chinese mass media essentially rely on market competition for their survival and prosperity, rather than as before, on their hierarchical locations within the media system and their connections with the state. Responding to the media marketization process, in China's publishing industry, editors endeavor to reorient themselves to the needs of the market in order to increase their financial resources by all legitimate means, and therefore, profitmaking turns out to be an important aim in their activities.

To be more specific, when advertising becomes an essential regulative power of a market-oriented media structure, an increasing number of editors start to concentrate on the informational and entertainment needs of affluent urban consumers—advertisers' most wanted audience. As an editor who has worked as chief editor in the Shanghai Education Publishing House for over thirty-five years, Qian mentioned in the interview:

> As an editor, I am fully aware of the tremendous impacts of the marketization process on the Chinese publishing industry. Most importantly, our publishing house no longer receives direct subsidies from the state, but it must earn revenue in the marketplace. Advertising has become a major revenue source. Our most popular journal is *Learning Chinese*, a journal that is designed to improve the reading and writing skills of middle-school students and foreigners learning Chinese as a second language. The journal makes substantial profit by selling advertisements to language training institutions. It also advertizes some private optometry clinics that offer special treatments for myopia. (Qian 2010)

In other words, when facing the increasing market competition, editors are more responsive to readers. With the deepening of media marketization, editors intend to provide information appealing to the audience, such as economic news, news on science and technology, sports news, social news, and useful daily information. Apparently, editors are also paying increasing attention to the interaction with the audience through feedback and audience participation (Zhao 2008).

In conclusion, the media marketization process has led to the diversification of information with the emphasis on the interests of the business and professional strata, as well as the construction of a consumerist paradise for the well-off urban population (Wu 2000; Zhao 2003). Therefore, despite the Party's continuing control over the publishing sector, the propaganda model is gradually challenged by the marketization process in the publishing industry because economic principles and the market logic maintain great importance in management decisions when the Chinese publishing industry first initiated the commercialization process.

Strict Party Control

Although both the roles and functions of the mass media have undergone a series of changes as a result of various substantial ongoing political and social changes associated with the marketization process, the fundamental guideline regarding the mass media never seems to change. That is, in principle, the Chinese mass media remain an instrument of both the Party and the government for political propaganda and the ideological indoctrination of the Chinese citizenry (He and Chen 1998).

The ideological control of the publishing sector still prevails. According to Shirk (2011, 7), "being highly conscious of public opinion, the CPC has devoted numerous resources to managing popular views of all issues." In other words, the Chinese publishing industry is assigned to mobilize the population for social development, disseminate information to promote mass mobilization, and support political power struggles in China's socialist construction. It becomes clear that acting as the "throat and tongue" of the Party, the Chinese publishing industry not only serves as an instrument for political struggles, but also as a public forum where propaganda and mobilization of the masses are conducted by the Party. Accordingly, the primary task for Chinese editors, in Zhao's (2000) view, is not to inform the masses, but rather to stimulate their action as well as to change their values, beliefs, and behavior.

Therefore, as they are strictly controlled by the Party, Chinese editors are supposed to follow the Party principle under all conditions. Instead of demanding more political autonomy from the state, many Chinese editors have been co-opted by the political and economic elite, and now they are acting as their supporters. In response to the increasingly blunt state censorship in association with the Party's coercive power and institutional control, editors in China's publishing industry have become quite self-disciplined (Pan 2000; Pan and Lu 2003). To specify, they carefully pick up the "right" vocabulary in their work. Also, among various tactics to appropriately express their ideas, they often take whatever official rhetoric can offer to selectively justify what they wish to achieve. For example, they attempt to frame business events by using Party rhetoric, and incorporate propaganda analysis into the market logic. This statement is echoed by my interview with Zhu. In the interview, she maintained:

> Years of restrictive regulations and coerced compliance have caused most editors to feel alienated from official Communist ideology. In order to function under such heavy state censorship, editors must possess "professional intuition," a sense of the ideological boundaries of editorial work. Such "professional intuition" helps the editor determine what topics and vocabulary are off limits. In my experience, successful editors employ several strategies to ensure good relations with the state: they use quotations from top leaders, they ana-

lyze social events from a dialectical materialist perspective, and they avoid either absolutism or extremism. Nowadays, finely-tuned "professional intuition" is not only a critical measure of "professional maturity," but more importantly, it saves a lot of trouble. (Zhu 2010)

To summarize, most of the recent studies on the commercial success of the publishing sector, and of the mass media collectively, have provided valuable insight into current media system, which is undergoing a dramatic transformation accelerated by the marketization process. However, at the same time, the strict Party control, indispensable to upholding the Communist ideology in the Chinese publishing industry, needs to be re-examined, because the coercive power of the CPC still dominates the publishing industry and regulates Chinese editors to a large extent.

The Growing Tension within the Propaganda-Commercial Model

It has been argued that in the process of media marketization, the party-state plays an important role in directing the development of the mass media through administrative means, such as policies, directives, and individual discretion. Meanwhile, the market creates the need for innovations that exert pressure on the party-state to carry out corresponding policy changes in the media industry. Therefore, each major Chinese media reform is the result of the interaction between the party-state and market.

There is, however, a structural contradiction between the CPC-dominated media system and the ongoing media marketization process in contemporary China, which is manifested in the discursive negotiation between partisanship and professionalism for Chinese media workers. This contradiction is also apparent in the Chinese publishing industry. Dong and Shi (2007) maintain that such a contradiction has led to numerous changes for Chinese editors, including changes in their identities, the nature of their work, their roles in society, and the principles and criteria for evaluating and rewarding their work. Among them, the most fundamental one is that Chinese editors are faced with the pressure to generate profit for their companies, as well as the pressure to expand democracy and to promote political and social reforms, to the extent allowed by the political interests of the authoritarian state. This remains the core of what Zhao (1998, 151) has defined as the "propaganda-commercial model," and it characterizes the context in which Chinese editors are situated.

Ke (2010) argues that most Chinese editors have fully realized that such a tension does not exist in abstract terms, but in their daily encounters and choices. As Luo indicated in the interview:

The publishing industry has become a special industry with a dual function. On the one hand, like most companies, publishing houses must generate profit, mainly through advertising. On the other hand, they are part of the nation's propaganda mechanism. As a result, our publishing house is regarded as a company, but it is not under the supervision of industrial and commercial authorities. Instead, it is under the direct control of the government's propaganda departments, which issue a lot of "DOs" and "DON'Ts" to regulate the publishing industry.

Due to the industry's dual function, we are "dancing with chains"—in pursuit of economic interests within a heavily restrictive ideological and political framework. Nevertheless, it is interesting to observe that the Chinese publishing industry has witnessed a gradual but clear shift from publishing political materials, such as pamphlets of leaders' speeches, to publishing nonpolitical materials, such as books on entertainment and public service. Books on fashion, gardening, travelling, and cooking have become very popular. Regardless of what material we publish, however, we exercise great creativity to maintain "political correctness." Most importantly, most editors and leaders in the publishing houses, as well as government officials, must exercise considerable "political wisdom" in order to creatively break through political taboos without overtly violating the official "ideological framework." (Luo 2010)

In response to the current framework of the paradoxical propaganda-commercial model, in general, Chinese media workers attempt to cultivate a new form of public/civic media. According to Sun (2003), public/civic media are mainly characterized by their concentrations on social conflicts and the problems of contemporary Chinese society when they adhere to a politically correct standpoint in the observation, interview, analysis, and programming of such conflicts and problems. One good example is the growth and substantial success achieved by "The Focused Interview."

"The Focused Interview" is a fifteen-minute in-depth news program, aired by the China Central Television (CCTV). The program started on April 1, 1994, and it focuses on current social affairs, investigative reports, and watchdog journalism. Since its beginning, the program has gained generous official endorsement from the topmost leadership, achieved high ratings from the general audience, and earned considerable revenue from advertisers. As one of its features, "The Focus Interview" predominantly relies on the public/civic sources as the basis of its news framing and production. Its editorial department receives over 2,300 news sources every day from all around China through various channels of correspondence, such as phone calls, e-mails, and mobile phone text messages (Chen 2004). Also, the program has been awarded several prestigious accolades from the CPC, and it has received praise from three former premiers. More importantly, "The Focused Interview" was granted a quota of 50 percent of muckraking reporting in its annual programming with the principle of following the Party's leadership.

However, the ratio by April 2004 had already exceeded 50 percent—perhaps a positive sign for further media reform (Li 2004; Sun 2009b). It is undeniable that the growth of public/civic media further drives the Chinese media industry and the government itself to become more transparent. In order to preserve its credibility, the government must release more information than it ever did before. In this sense, the growth of public/civic media improves the responsiveness and transparency of governance. However, what remains to be seen is how far public/civic media can go within the propaganda-commercial model, especially with their rising impacts on the Chinese publishing industry.

THE MARKETIZATION PROCESS IN
THE SOCIAL WELFARE SYSTEM

Changes in the Pension System

The economic reform beginning in the late 1970s triggered a widespread expansion of the marketization process in almost every facet of society. The market principle has also been largely applied to the Chinese social welfare system, leading to dramatic changes in both the pension and health care systems. First, in terms of the changes in the pension system, a multilayered system involving funds contributed by the state, companies, and individuals has been established (West 1999). The new pension system puts a heavy burden on individuals because the shared contributions of both the state and companies have significantly decreased. Second, as for the changes in the health care system, the previously freely provided medicines and medical service have been replaced by user-pay policies with the accelerated marketization process in China's health care sector. In such a context, Chinese editors are facing numerous new challenges and problems.

In China, the reform of the social security system also started in the late 1970s, together with the economic reform. As Ge (1998) argues, in the previous work-unit system, workers routinely enjoyed social security as part of their employment. Basically, for Chinese editors, their work units, including publishing houses and newspaper agencies, were responsible for their social security, primarily through offering them pensions when they retired. Since China moved toward a market economy, however, it becomes essential for the state to move the entire social security system out of the work units' control and shift it to a national social security program administered by government agencies.

It is difficult to carry out such a national security program due to the following three reasons. First, most workers are accustomed to pension systems managed by their work units instead of government agencies. Naughton (2007) claims that distributing pensions by their work units offers workers a sense of entitlement as well as a sense of belonging because most workers have been employed in their work units for decades. Second, it is not easy for some older companies, enormously burdened with a large number of retired workers, to cover the health care bills of their employees and retirees by strictly following the standards stipulated by the national social security program. As such, different companies might carry out the program very differently, and therefore, the final outcome of the program could strongly violate the purpose of establishing a unified social security system as a key to eliminating social inequality and disparity. Third, state-owned enterprises, as the financial base of the traditional social security system, have been shrinking, and at the same time, numerous joint ventures, foreign companies, and private companies have emerged. In this sense, the state has trouble setting a fixed standard for the national social security program, which is suitable for the vastly different nature of companies (Lin 2001).

After several years of experiments in various regions and companies, the State Council in March 1995 issued the "Directives on Further Reform of the Enterprise Pension System," which introduced a series of significant reforms in China's social security system. West (1999) maintains that the core of the new social security system is to establish a multilayered pension system involving funds contributed by the state, companies, and individuals.

In detail, in the publishing industry, editors receive their basic pensions in the form of individual accounts. Contributions to editors' individual accounts, approximately 16 percent of their total wages, consist of the following three parts: an individual contribution of 3 percent of the total wage, a company contribution of 8 percent of each editor's total wage, and a company contribution of 5 percent of the average local wage. The intention of further reform in the social security system is to increase the individual contribution over time and to decrease the company contribution (by 1 percent every two years for ten years) until individuals contribute half the total to their individual accounts. In its goal to substantially increase the individual contribution in the pension system, in July 1997, the State Council further issued the "Decisions on Establishing a Uniform Basic Old-Age Insurance System for Enterprise Employees," and stipulated that each company, including publishing houses, must contribute no more than 20 percent of the workers' total wages as social pension funds. Therefore, for individual editors, according to the Chinese Academy of Social Sciences (1998), the percentage of their wages paid into their individual accounts increased from 3 percent to 11 percent.

Furthermore, for most Chinese editors, more and more publishing houses and newspaper agencies are not willing to pay the contribution required by the new pension system because some of them do not have enough funds, and others prefer to save money for investment purposes. Rocca (2003) posits that especially for those editors working in the remote areas of China, the contributions of both the state and companies are transferred at an extremely slow pace into the editors' individual accounts, resulting in delays in the payments of pensions. Moreover, as funds are badly managed, it is not rare to find that a large amount of money has disappeared or has lined the pockets of corrupted high officials and local authorities (Zhu 1998). Also, there is a sense of growing anxiety among Chinese editors because taking into account the increasing living costs, the purchasing power of pensions keeps declining. The changes in the social security system, particularly in the pension system, have made most Chinese media workers, particularly editors, less protected by either the state or their companies, and therefore, they feel more insecure about their future lives.

Changes in the Health Care System

In the Chinese publishing industry, editors are facing increasing pressure to pay for their medicines and medical service due to the critical changes in the health care system accompanied by the marketization process. According to the "labor-protection medical care system" introduced in 1951, all editors' medical expenses and subsidies during their sick leaves should be financially handled by their work units. The units should also reimburse 50 percent of the medical expenses if any family member of editors suffers from a disease (Duckett 2004). However, in the new health care system, the central government has established individual medical care accounts to which a certain amount of money is allocated, and editors need to pay their own medical expenses first from their individual accounts. The deposits in their individual accounts can only be used for medicines and medical service. If the allocation for the current year is not used completely, the remaining amount can be transferred to and used in the following year (Lin 2001). However, when all the allocation in their individual accounts is used up, editors have to pay for their own medical expenses until a stipulated limit mutually agreed by them and their companies. A unified social insurance fund partially pays for the medical expenses exceeding that stipulated limit. The massive implementation of the health care reform did not begin until 2000, but 90 million Chinese workers, both industrial and knowledge ones, had been enrolled in the new system by 2004 (China Statistical Yearbook Editorial Department 2005).

As Naughton (2007) elaborates, the new health care system is adverse to the interests of individuals. First, the government has substantially withdrawn from offering free medicines and medical service throughout the country, and individuals have taken more responsibilities for their medical expenses since user-pay policies were implemented in the new health care system. In 1995, according to the World Health Organization, China spent 3.9 percent of its GDP on health care, rising to 5.3 percent in 2000 (The

World Health Organization 2002). However, the problem is that with the deepening of the marketization process, the proportion of the medical expenses paid by individuals has kept growing—53.3 percent in 1995 and 63.4 percent in 2000 (The World Health Organization 2002). Moreover, the government no longer struggles to bridge the gap in health care standards between rural and urban areas, and as a result, the differences in both health care provision and delivery between cities and the countryside have been substantial.

Second, the new health care system has been largely commercialized. It does not come as a surprise that many doctors write prescriptions with the purpose of generating profit rather than curing their patients. The costs of medicines and medical service increased by 14 percent annually between 1993 and 2003, and one of the major reasons was the practice by doctors of unnecessarily prescribing expensive medicines in order to increase hospital revenue (Markus 2004). Compared with the old health care system wherein inadequately trained medical practitioners were allowed to serve patients at a relatively low cost, there is a growing number of well-trained doctors providing better medical service for patients in the new health care system; however, medical expenses have continued to increase, and have become less affordable for most of the working class, with editors included.

Last, according to Murphy (2003), in the new health care system, there is more emphasis on new technology than there used to be. Undoubtedly, the increase of foreign medical equipment largely raises the costs of health care provision.

Therefore, most Chinese editors are overwhelmingly worried about their current and future medical expenses. Most of them are afraid of becoming sick. As Ma mentioned in the interview:

> Since the implementation of recent health care reform, fewer medical expenses have been covered by the publishing house. In the old health care system, I received full reimbursement for my medical expenses. The changes have been rapid and dramatic. Nowadays, not only am I responsible for a large portion of my own medical expenses, but there is less coverage available for many critical illnesses, such as cancer, heart disease, leukemia, and paralysis. Last year, I suffered a heart attack, and stayed in hospital for one week. The total cost was 30,000 *yuan*, around half of my annual income. I think the implication of recent health care reform is clear: excellent health care, good hospitals, and foreign equipment are for the rich, not for the average person. Consequentially, I have become depressed due to overtly concern about my health problems. (Ma 2010)

Indeed, Ma's concern is well founded, regarding the numerous problems faced by Chinese editors in the current health care system.

First, in most cities, the amount of money allocated by the government is insufficient, especially taking the increasing medical expenses into consideration. In Ma's case, he receives 800 *yuan* in his individual medical care account every year from the government. Even though the remaining amount of the allocation for the current year in the medical care account can be transferred to and used in the following year, Ma maintained that this never happens, as his medical expenses exceed far more than 800 *yuan* every year.

Second, the amount that individuals contribute to their accounts is always twice or three times as much as the amount allocated by the government. In fact, Ma has to pay 1,600 *yuan* annually into his account, and therefore, individuals, instead of the government, shoulder the major responsibility for the medical expenses.

Third, although a unified social insurance fund is raised to pay for the medical expenses exceeding the stipulated limit paid by individuals, the regulations involved are complicated and extremely adverse to the interests of the individual. To be more specific, in the publishing house where Ma works, the unified social insurance fund, mostly contributed by the publishing house, only covers the diseases specified on a list that is agreed by both editors and the publishing house—mainly critical diseases. Moreover, even if editors suffer from such a disease, their medical expenses are reimbursed at a stipulated percent. It is 60 percent in Ma's case. In other words, Ma needs to pay 40 percent of the medical expenses exceeding the stipulated limit when he suffers from diseases specified on the list. When editors suffer from diseases other than those specified, they would have to cover the full medical expenses themselves.

As a response to the dramatic decrease in social security and health care benefits, in China's publishing industry, editors are pressured to save a large portion of their incomes, and according to Chen (2008), more than 40 percent of their disposable earnings are deposited in case of an emergency. At the same time, most editors are buying various forms of private medical insurance, and consequently, the private medical insurance industry has experienced a substantial growth in China, and its annual growth rate reached 27 percent between 2000 and 2009. Nowadays, there are twenty-seven insurance companies providing private medical insurance, with eight domestic ones owning 96.31 percent of the market share and nineteen foreign ones owning the rest (Pressly 2011). In the Shanghai Science and Technology Publishing House, both senior and junior editors have purchased private medical insurance from the China Life Insurance Company. The insurance covers 90 percent of the editors' total expenditure of medicines and medical service, with the maximum annual reimbursement of 20,000 *yuan*. Since the costs of medicines and medical service keep rising, the reimbursement relieves the economic pressure when editors are sick; however, it is expensive to purchase private medical insurance, and it brings additional economic pressure to editors. Therefore, it is not surprising when Ma concluded at the end of the interview that, in recent years, with the widespread expansion of marketization in the social welfare system, the dramatic decrease in social security and health care benefits that Chinese media workers have been experiencing has led to a very precarious situation in which they are marginalized and worried about their future lives. This is compounded by the fact that there is no sign of improvement.

SMASHING OF THE WORK-UNIT SYSTEM

The marketization process of the social welfare system is closely associated with the smashing of the work-unit system. Prior to the economic reform introduced by Deng Xiaoping, work units provided a living for their workers in terms of fair wages and good working conditions; offered extensive social welfare benefits, including pensions, housing, paid sick leaves, meal service, recreational facilities, health care, daycare and school; and most importantly, promoted the Communist ideology to strengthen the Party's leadership (Bian 1994; Naughton 2007). Once workers entered the work-unit system, they expected to remain in work units for their entire lives.

Accordingly, in the work-unit system, like other forms of work units, Chinese publishing houses were not only economic organizations, but also served three non-economic functions, namely: as administrative units, as political vehicles, and as social welfare organizations. As a result, editors felt secure in the work-unit system.

First, publishing houses in the work-unit system played an important role in carrying out administrative initiatives and representing individuals. As soon as administrative orders, regulations, and policies of the central and local governments were sent to publishing houses, both editors and leaders were organized to study government documents. Also, within the party-state, editors were tightly connected to the state and society through publishing houses as their work units, which served as mediators between the state and individuals (Lu and Perry 1997). For example, editors who needed their birth certificates notarized by public notary agencies were required to obtain the approval from the publishing houses. Also, editors studying abroad who wished their spouse, children, or parents to visit them needed to get approval letters from the publishing houses where they were formerly affiliated.

Second, publishing houses acted as political vehicles. In China, editors' political lives were bound to publishing houses in the work-unit system. According to the provisions of the Constitution effective in 1954, it was stipulated that government leaders should be elected by people's representatives, and representatives should be chosen through primary elections in the work units. Therefore, in the work-unit system, editors elected their representatives in the publishing houses, and these representatives elected government leaders. At the same time, the CPC, the Chinese Communist Youth League (CCYL), and other democratic parties all had their representative bodies in every work unit.[3] Most editors intended to join either the CPC or the CCYL, as Party membership was a valuable political asset for their careers. Furthermore, every editor was obliged to attend political study meetings, and in doing so, the political control and management of editors by their work units was achieved. In every Chinese publishing house, editors were organized to study the Party's documents; topmost leaders' speeches; and government administrative orders, regulations, and policies (Warner 2000). In the political study meetings, editors were not only expected to express their attitudes toward the Party's new guidelines, but also were asked to examine the deviations of their behavior from the Party's guidelines and to make self-criticisms. It is important to note that for editors, both their participation and performance in the political study meetings were considered vital elements in the evaluation process for their job promotion, their salary and bonus raises, and their applications for Party membership (Zhu 1995).

Third, as social welfare organizations, publishing houses offered a wide array of benefits and services. Such benefits and services included labor insurance, housing, and collective welfare programs and facilities, for example, hospitals and clinics, dining halls, nurseries, recreational facilities, and libraries. Also, some educational institutions were sponsored by work units, such as elementary schools, high schools, technical schools, and even colleges. Apparently, in the work-unit system, editors were largely dependent on publishing houses, and they felt relatively secure in their work units.

However, interestingly, Stepanek (1992) maintains that in the work-unit system, most editors did not develop a very strong commitment to the publishing houses, indicated by their low levels of work effort and productivity. Additionally, they were disciplined neither by managerial rules nor procedures. For example, in their workplaces, the absenteeism rate was high, and editors frequently ran personal errands during their work hours. As such, creating a new system of management that would alter such unproductive attitudes and behavior has distinctively been one of the most important imperatives for China's social reform.

In such a context, under the banner of "creating a modern enterprise system," the work-unit system was smashed with a complete reshaping of the socialist employment structure. In 1986, the State Council started reconstituting labor relations with the introduction of the labor contract, which encouraged each individual company to hire and fire people according to its financial profitability. In other words, as Whyte (2010) concludes, in the publishing industry, publishing houses have been given growing power and autonomy to make decisions on personnel and wages, instead of following the previous pattern in which they simply accepted every worker assigned to them by the local labor bureau.

As a consequence, the working class is facing new hazards of being marginalized in the new enterprise system, because workers' incomes have been dramatically reduced, and they can be either fired or laid off by their companies with less and less protection from the state. In some specific cases, when companies are faced with bankruptcy, the jobs and livelihoods of their entire workforce have been severely threatened. Also, the work unit welfare system was replaced by a state welfare system, in which the changes in the distribution of bonuses, subsidies, and benefits for the working class are critical (Wong and MacPherson 1995). Benefit cuts have also been widely enacted. For example, as mentioned, in the work-unit system, the medical expenses of workers were fully covered, and half of the medical expenses of their family dependants were reimbursed as well. In the new system, however, even workers themselves receive very limited health care benefits.

In the publishing industry, the purpose of abandoning the work-unit system was to alleviate the social and political burdens of publishing houses and improve their financial situations in the marketplace. For work units, the financial burden of providing bonuses, subsidies, and benefits to both employees and retirees was a major contributing element to the fact that numerous publishing houses continued to report financial losses. By the mid-1990s, it was estimated that the value of bonuses, subsidies, and benefits received by editors in publishing houses had been equal to the salaries that they received (Goldman and Macfarquhar 1999). Responding to the tremendous financial burden, many publishing houses have attempted to reduce the benefits that workers were once entitled to; require partial and increasing payments for some benefits by editors themselves, such as continuing education and training, medical service, and housing; and make the distribution of bonuses, subsidies, and benefits performance-based rather than based on egalitarianism.

For Chinese editors, the implications of such changes are fundamental. As the reform advances, job security has weakened, and social welfare benefits have significantly decreased. In this regard, according to Rocca (2003), the privileged existence of workers (including editors) as the "master" of the Communist society has been transformed in many ways. Instead of maintaining lifetime employment, most Chinese editors need to sign fixed-term employment contracts, and almost all of their work is rewarded based on performance. The influence of the marketization process in the social welfare system is so profound that now even leaders in the workplaces have seen their roles and conditions become more dependent on market forces, not to mention ordinary editors in the publishing industry.

Therefore, it is not difficult to understand why most of the university and college graduates do not choose editing as their ideal jobs, although the social status of editors still remains high in contemporary China. According to "The Annual Report of Chinese University and College Graduates' Employment 2009," even graduates majoring in linguistics, literature and art, and editing and publishing prefer to become government officials, administrative assistants in state-owned enterprises, and interpreters and translators in international corporations (MyCOS 2009). Moreover, as mentioned before, my surveys of editors in most of the large publishing houses in China indicated that despite the tremendous economic pressure of losing jobs, 37.5 percent of the participants in my surveys acknowledged that they had changed their jobs at least once. The result is echoed by "The Ranking of University and College Graduates' Employment Ability 2010," implying that there are five majors whose graduates change their jobs most frequently in the first year of their work: editing and publishing, art design, advertising, wood science and management, and environment design (MyCOS 2010). Among them, the rate of graduates majoring in editing and publishing leaving their jobs reached 51 percent, as the highest. In response to the decrease in job security and social welfare benefits, a large number of editors intend to work in private or foreign companies in the publishing industry, because compared with state-owned publishing houses, most of them are able to offer editors higher salaries, even though their work pressure is more intense. As Cui Baoguo (2010) argues, with more and more graduates crowding into private or foreign companies in China's publishing industry, both the private and foreign publishing houses have enjoyed a drastic growth in the past thirty years, and their market share of book publishing has added up to approximately 50 percent of the total books published annually in China (Cui 2010).

To conclude, the smashing of the work-unit system has made editors much more vulnerable. The highly politicized work units were despotic because editors were caught in a web of intense organized dependence that forced them to rely on their work units to meet almost their every need. In the reform era, with the introduction of market forces, the retreat of politics from everyday economic life of editors has loosened the control that the workplaces once held over their editors. However, at the same time, the reform has also brought about equally despotic working conditions for editors because they are intricately caught in another web of intense organized dependence that forces them to rely on market forces. According to Lee (1999), in both state-owned and private enterprises, workers are now disciplined by piece-rate pay scales, strict controls over the work process, and other manifestations of managerial power. Specifically in the publishing industry, the monthly incomes of editors are primarily determined by the profit that they can generate for their publishing houses, and bonuses constitute a large portion of their incomes.

It is also equally important to note that in the publishing industry, leaders have gradually gained the power of distributing bonuses and making crucial decisions on personnel that most editors should follow. This has become the major managerial characteristic of most publishing houses since the work-unit system was smashed (Gallagher 2004). In this regard, the inner division of the working class is clear, reflected in the wide and unbridgeable gap between the leaders and editors in the publishing industry.

THE INNER DIVISION OF THE WORKING CLASS

As aforementioned, Chinese editors are experiencing serious loss of the privileges they once enjoyed as the "master" of the country in the work-unit system. Due to the imbalance between labor supply and demand, their bargaining power has also significantly declined. They have to work long hours for relatively low wages, and they are always reminded that many people are waiting to take their jobs. On the contrary, the leaders in the workplaces have enjoyed growing decision-making power over the distribution of bonuses for editors, the allocation of their social welfare benefits, and the management of human resources.

In addition to the differences between media workers and leaders, there is also a sharp rift among editors themselves. For example, based on my interviews conducted in both the Shanghai Science and Technology Publishing House and in the Shanghai Education Publishing House, there is a growing tension between senior and junior editors. Compared with senior editors, junior editors are confronted with more challenges, including signing a contract based on shorter time periods, taking more challenging work with intense work pressure, and obtaining fewer chances to get promoted, but receiving more severe financial punishment if they fail to meet their monthly workload or generate the amount of profit specified in their contracts. Therefore, the internal differences within the Chinese working class, embodied in the division between editors and leaders, as well as the inner division of editors themselves, have increased and become obvious.

Divisions between Editors and Leaders

The composition and characteristics of the Chinese working class greatly changed when dramatic transformation was taking place in the economic system. The study of social stratification has been a popular topic of sociological research in China (ACFTU 1997; Ip 1995; Warner 1995; Li 1999). According to Zhang's (1997) research, since the economic reform, the Chinese working class has been divided into several strata, based on their differences in access to power, income, occupational popularity, and social status. He also concludes that workers have been separated from the employers who own the means of production, and from the managers who control them. In his research entitled "Studying Report on the Stratum in Contemporary China," which was undertaken with the help of the Chinese Academy of Social Sciences, Lu Xueyi (2002) indicates that the Chinese working class has developed into ten strata that separately belong to five rankings within the existing social structure.

Upper Ranking

leading cadres
managers in larger companies
senior professional personnel
owners of larger-sized privately owned enterprises

Upper-middle Ranking

middle-level and lower-level leading cadres
managerial staff at the medium level in large-sized companies
managers in medium-sized and small companies
professional personnel at the medium level
owners of medium-sized privately owned enterprises

Middle-middle Ranking

junior professional personnel
owners of small-sized privately owned enterprises
office workers

Middle-lower Ranking

self-employed workers
original employees of commercial sectors
workers and peasants

Lower Ranking

workers and peasants in poverty and without job security
unemployed
semi-unemployed vagrant

From the top to the bottom in social hierarchy, the ten strata of the Chinese working class are: managerial staff, managers, owners of privately owned enterprises, professional personnel, office workers, self-employed workers, employees of commercial and service sectors, industrial workers, agriculture laborers, and unemployed and semi-employed workers in urban and rural areas.

For editors in particular, it comes as no surprise that they consider leaders to be "bosses," and that these leaders are no longer part of the working class. In addition, they deeply resent their leaders' corruption and misconduct as well as the unfair treatment that they have received. Therefore, as Bonnin (2000) advocates, Chinese editors are more class-conscious than before, especially with the decline of their management participation. As Zhuang indicated in the interview:

> In our publishing house, about thirty years ago, we were all encouraged to participate in management, planning, and the resolution of problems under the centrally planned economy. Since the implementation of current media reform, however, we are blatantly excluded from management decisions, and we have to passively accept the guidance and obey the instructions of the leaders. (Zhuang 2010)

Critically, in the publishing industry, leaders have formed an independent social stratum. From a micro level of analysis, leaders in the workplaces have become different from ordinary editors in their social status and rights defined by laws, ideological consciousness, and values based on their social experience (Chang 1995). From a macro level of analysis, both privatization and the modern corporate system encourage leaders to gain power and dominate ordinary editors. As such, Sargeson (1999) maintains that the direction of public opinion has become seriously biased, excessively propagandizing leaders' positions and roles. The terms "excellent leaders" and "star leaders" have come into use, but the positions of the broad masses of editors and their roles in publishing reform have neither been fully evaluated nor appropriately affirmed.

There are two profound influences brought about by the division between editors and leaders. First, most Chinese editors' enthusiasm for production, once encouraged by management participation, is now genuinely prompted by productivity-related wage payments and the threat of dismissal. As a response, when losing many of their privileges relative to other social groups, most Chinese editors are paying growing attention to their personal interests and incomes. To be more specific, Qi and Xu (1995) argue that as long as they no longer rely on their work units because the work-unit system in the centrally planned economy was smashed, editors in the Chinese publishing industry are inspired to pursue personal economic interests and address their rights to earn money in the marketplace. Such concepts as cost, price, and profit have become substantial for both editors and leaders when minimum labor costs are sought.

Second, with the enlarged gap between editors and leaders in power, the social connections of editors with leaders, also known as *guanxi* in Chinese, are playing a significantly important role in the media industry (King 1991). This means that for Chinese editors, the access to both material resources and opportunities is largely regulated by their relative positions in the highly complex and entangled networks of personal connections. Thus, editors are pressured to establish extensive and intimate personal connections with leaders.

Specifically, in the recruitment process, even though leaders often announce their preferences, conduct merit examinations, and select the best-qualified candidates, specific attention is paid to the applicants recommended by the person who establishes a good *guanxi* with the leaders. Chu and Ju (1993) claim that in the Chinese context, the general rule is: the more key officials and leaders in either governments or companies a person's network covers, the more social influence he or she has at his or her disposal, and the more easily he or she can get things done. Thus, in the Chinese publishing industry, individuals gain advantages by frequently using their networks of social connections instead of faithfully following the established rules and procedures.

For Chinese editors, *guanxi* also helps them apply for Party membership in their workplaces. In principle, the CPC uses membership as a way to select loyalists who will safeguard the Party's ideologies, interests, and political power. Party membership becomes a political status or privilege, as well as an effective path to get promoted (Bian 1994). Since Party membership is a prerequisite for high-ranking positions, editors, particularly junior editors recruited into low-ranking positions, are encouraged to apply for Party membership in the Party branches in their workplaces. They try to establish a strong *guanxi* with the Party branch secretaries who control the recruitment process as many editors desire to join the Party. In other words, editors in the Chinese publishing industry need to show their commitment to the Party's goals as well as the dedication of their lives to the Party; at the same time, they are obliged to prove their loyalty to the Party branch secretaries (Hu 2000).

Inner Divisions of Editors

According to Wortzel (1987), in the work-unit system, editors in different workplaces might have had competing and contradictory interests because of the unequal allocation of resources in the socialist state. Nevertheless, due to the fact that all editors were the owners of the state-owned enterprises, their competing and contradictory interests were non-antagonistic. According to my interviews in both the Shanghai Science and Technology Publishing House and the Shanghai Education Publishing House, however, the non-antagonistic relations among editors have been largely challenged by China's media reform, especially when publishing houses are changing from public institutions into companies.

Importantly, in China's publishing industry, senior editors and junior editors are treated differently, leading to a growing tension between them. First, senior editors and junior editors sign contracts based on different time spans. In the Shanghai Science and Technology Publishing House, junior editors sign contracts once every year in the first three years. From their fourth year, only those "excellent" (well-behaved) editors are allowed to sign contracts once every three years. Maybe a few years later, they can sign contracts once every five years, depending on their performance. Meanwhile, senior editors initially sign their contracts once every three years according to the Labor Law effective in 1995. Afterward, they sign contracts that guarantee their lifetime employment. The contracts for senior editors are more symbolic in meaning than real in their effects. They sign contracts only to conform to the requirements of the Labor Law.

Second, senior editors are often given less demanding tasks by the leaders in the publishing houses. Since the beginning of media reform in the publishing industry, in most cases, senior editors have been assigned to edit textbooks because publishing textbooks is exceedingly profitable, and the incomes of editors are basically determined by the profit that is generated. On the other hand, leaders have always assigned more demanding tasks to junior editors. For example, in the Shanghai Science and Technology Publishing House, junior editors are mainly responsible for publishing books that introduce new science and technology. It is difficult to predict how many people will be interested in books of this kind. As the market is rather unpredictable, profit cannot be guaranteed. In the interview, Huang mentioned:

> In our publishing house, senior editors are always in charge of editing and publishing conference pamphlets and government guidebooks. They do not have to worry about the sales of those publications because most of them are purchased in advance, and substantial profit is guaranteed. Junior editors are assigned to edit books on very specific areas of science and technology. For example, the leader has assigned me to edit a book on contemporary scientific developments in diabetes research. Since such books have incredibly limited target groups, they are unlikely to generate a huge profit. I am not the only person who complains about the unfairness of giving "easy" tasks to senior editors and "challenging" tasks to junior editors. My colleagues, who are responsible for "seasonal" publications, such as books on knitting, are pressured to meet fixed deadlines so that the books can be published before they are in high demand. Very often, my colleagues have to work overtime, and sometimes they work seventeen hours a day. (Huang 2010)

Third, both the reward and punishment systems are different for senior and junior editors. In terms of the reward system, senior editors easily get promoted. In the publishing industry, senior editors are more respected due to their ages instead of their professional skills and abilities because seniority is widely honored according to the Chinese tradition. As for the punishment system, lacking marketing knowledge, senior workers can hardly make enough profit specified in their contracts. However, they are often excused by the leaders if they are working hard, and not making any trouble for the leaders' control and management of other editors. On the other hand, the profit that junior editors have generated for the publishing houses is carefully calculated, and mainly determines their incomes. That is to say, the monthly incomes of junior editors can be largely reduced if they fail to earn the amount of profit specified in their contracts. As such, there is no doubt that junior editors experience tremendous work pressure to ensure that their books sell well, and they need to be very sensitive about the demands of the readers.

In fact, the interviews reveal that in the Chinese publishing industry, both senior editors and junior editors are facing the same problems brought about by the media marketization process which has led to the precarious condition of editors. However, it is important to understand that even though senior editors are less competent than junior editors, precisely speaking, it is the junior editors who are in a more precarious situation. Junior editors are pressured to sign a contract based on shorter time periods, take more challenging work with intense work pressure, and obtain fewer chances to get promoted. Moreover, they receive more severe financial punishment if they fail to meet their monthly workload or generate the amount of profit specified in their contracts. Therefore, a broader fragmentation of employment has emerged when "differences and inequalities in terms and conditions are created between workers who were previously employed under the same conditions" (Flecker et al. 2009, 32). At the present time, both junior and senior editors feel continuously under pressure with the increasing insecurity of their jobs. More critically, however, dissatisfaction among junior editors and increasing conflicts between junior and senior editors have resulted in competing relations among editors in the publishing industry.

To conclude, since the beginning of a decisive transformation in the nature of China's economy, from one characterized by central planning and the operation of collective institutions and state-owned enterprises, to a market economy dominated by various types of non-state firms, the political-economic environment in which the Chinese working class lives and labors has dramatically deteriorated (Weeden and Grusky 2005; Li 2010). In response, in the Chinese publishing industry, editors are pushed to take different measures to protect their rights and get rid of the precarious condition in which they are situated. One of the most effective methods is through internal bargaining (Sargeson 1999). Editors, particularly junior editors, in most large publishing houses have established various channels to communicate with the leaders in order to increase their monthly incomes and pass regulations to limit their work hours and their monthly workload, with the help of worker organizations and trade unions in the publishing industry. For example, in the Shanghai Science and Technology Publishing House, union officials are not only responsible for organizing social activities to celebrate major holidays in China, including the Chinese New Year, Women's Day, and the Mid-autumn Festival, but also responsible for taking the initiative in participating in the daily management of the publishing house to fully represent and protect editors' interests. Union officials are playing an active role in the policy decision-making process, gaining access to both financial and administrative information that is not revealed in public, and obtaining the power to approve or deny the promotion of editors, particularly junior editors. This statement will be further elaborated and addressed when the roles and impacts of worker organizations and trade unions in the reform era are examined afterward.

It is also important to note that in contrast to industrial workers, Chinese editors, and media workers as a collective, are not responding in the form of massive social protests or demonstrations because the dissatisfaction of Chinese media workers has not yet developed into shared worker anger against the state. In other words, Chinese media workers (including editors) have not been mobilized to challenge the current political-economic system; neither have they been able to fully articulate their economic interests and translate these interests into political programs or changes in China's social distribution process (Ogden 2000).

CONCLUSION: SOCIAL CHANGES, CLASS RELATIONS, AND POWER DYNAMICS

By incorporating the ideas of human agency, social process, and social practice into the analysis of social structures, structuration provides valuable insight into the understanding of class relations and power dynamics. In my analysis of the structuration process of the Chinese publishing industry, I have addressed the challenges facing Chinese editors as a class, understanding their common problems, interests, prospects, and responses, as well as their relations to other parts of the working class. Also, in this chapter, I have argued that when media and communication are increasingly shaped by the social relations of communication as well as the wider institutional power structure, it becomes significantly important to scrutinize class relations and the struggles of Chinese editors in the process of their production, control, and distribution of information and communication.

Additionally, structuration is an entry point to examine the mutual constitution of *structure* and *agency* in the political economy of communication. On the one hand, it is important to understand that since the economic reform in the late 1970s, the Chinese publishing industry has experienced enormous changes in every aspect of editors' lives, ranging from employment and living conditions to social relations (Zhang and Li 1998). The fundamental social changes, including technological, political, and economic ones, and most importantly, the changes in class relations and power dynamics, have brought about five critical problems for Chinese editors. These are the following: the problems related to technological changes, the problems of how to follow the Party principle in the media marketization process, the problems associated with the marketization process in the social welfare system, the problems brought about by the smashing of the work-unit system, and the conflicts resulting from the inner division within the working class. From this vantage point, knowledge workers in China's publishing industry, mainly editors, are in a precarious employment situation.

On the other hand, it is equally important to examine how Chinese editors are responding to these problems. First, in association with the rapid technological changes, Chinese editors are pushed to attend different lectures, take short-term training classes, and even receive further education for either degrees or certificates to upgrade their knowledge structures and enhance their professional skills. Second, in pursuit of the economic interests and following the Party's leadership at the same time, Chinese media workers (including editors) are cultivating a new form of public/civic media, mainly characterized by the concentration on social conflicts and the problems of contemporary Chinese society when adhering to a politically correct standpoint in the observation, interview, analysis, and programming of such conflicts and problems. Third, as a response to the dramatic decrease in social security and health care benefits, most Chinese editors are pressured to save a large portion of their incomes and buy private medical insurance, which basically covers the increasing costs of their medicines and medical service. However, the enormous economic pressure has exacerbated the precarious situation in which Chinese editors are marginalized, and they are worried about their future lives. Fourth, with the smashing of the work-unit system, most of the university and college graduates do not choose editing as their ideal jobs. For those editors who have been working in the publishing industry, they are changing their jobs frequently, and moving to private and foreign companies which can offer higher salaries with even more intense work pressure. Last, but most importantly, editors, particularly junior editors, in most of the large publishing houses in China have established various channels to communicate with the leaders in order to increase their monthly incomes and pass regulations to limit their work hours and their monthly workload, with the help of worker organizations and trade unions in the publishing industry.

At this point it becomes noteworthy to ask when China further integrates into the global political economy, will there be more challenges or opportunities for editors in the Chinese publishing industry? The next chapter attempts to answer this question by specifically examining the spatialization process of the political economy of communication.

NOTES

1. In my research, I have conducted eleven semi-structured interviews with editors from numerous large publishing houses in China, for example, the Shanghai Science and Technology Publishing House and the Shanghai Education Publishing House.

2. All the participants in the interviews refused to be identified in my research. It is largely due to the fact that censorship, which is still strict in China, is likely to pose a risk to them, leading to the loss of employment, diminished self-esteem, or their high standings in the community might be compromised. Therefore, for ethical concerns, pseudonyms are given to protect each participant's identity in this book.

3. The Chinese Communist Youth League is a mass organization of advanced youth under the leadership of the CPC. The basic task of the CCYL is to equip youths with lofty ideals, moral integrity, and high sense of discipline for the socialist construction.

Chapter Four

The Spatialization Process

Globalization, Neoliberalism, and the Global Division of Labor

In this chapter, I will broaden my theoretical horizon by examining the impact of the *spatialization* process on the Chinese media industry, particularly the Chinese publishing industry. As defined by Henri Lefebvre (1979), *spatialization is the process of overcoming spatial and temporal constraints in social life*. In the age of globalization, developments in communication and information technologies have dramatically diminished the constraints placed by spatial distance on the expansion of capital. Due to capital expansion and the acceleration of corporate concentration, transnational corporations now play a crucial role in the global political economy (McChesney 1999; Winseck and Pike 2007). My exploration of the impact of the spatialization process on the Chinese publishing industry will be divided into the analysis of the three main contributing factors to the former: globalization, neoliberalism, and the global division of labor.

I will begin this chapter by examining globalization and its two substantial effects on the Chinese publishing industry. On the one hand, Chinese publishing houses have tried to establish tight connections with major transnational media corporations through joint ventures and other organizational and financial alliances. Both copyright trade and business cooperation between domestic publishing houses and their foreign counterparts have become common. On the other hand, the Chinese government has been forced to adopt an array of competitive strategies to ensure that its radio, television, and newspapers remain visible in the crowded global media sphere. For example, it has responded to the pressure from foreign publishing companies by merging existing domestic publishing outlets to form large-scale publishing conglomerates, thus achieving political control of, economic efficiency within, and international competitiveness for the Chinese publishing industry, and media industry as a whole (Lee 2003a).

I will continue by examining the effects of the rise of neoliberal ideologies on the Chinese publishing industry and its workers. Generally, the Chinese media system has undergone the processes of privatization, commercialization, trade liberalization, and deregulation due to the rapid expansion of neoliberal policies within the global media industry. The authoritarian government has, however, set many important limitations to the penetration of neoliberal policies in the Chinese media industry. According to Robison (2006, 4), even though the state attempts to "incorporate neoliberal elements to extend the values and relations of markets into a model for the broader organization of politics and society in China," the Party's leadership will not voluntarily limit its own powers. Thus, Chinese media workers are caught between the "twin modalities of the neoliberal governmentality" (Ong 2006, 3). On the one hand, they are faced with neoliberal policies designed to maximize entrepreneurial dynamism and facilitate interactions with the global market; on the other hand, they are tightly controlled by the authoritarian state. Also, in the publishing industry, Chinese editors are pressured to generate profit for their companies, as well as to expand democracy and promote political and social reforms, but only to the extent allowed by the political interests of the authoritarian state. These conflicting pressures have only intensified since China's official entry into the World Trade Organization (WTO) in December 2001.

Finally, I will explore the effects of the global division of labor on the Chinese publishing industry and its workers. The global division of labor occurs when the process of production is no longer confined to national economies. In this context, editors have been dramatically impacted by the global division of labor to cope with changes to both their value systems and their daily work process, as well as extremely intense work pressure. Based upon my interviews conducted in the Shanghai Science and Technology Publishing House and the Shanghai Education Publishing House, I have concluded that the changes accompanying the global division of labor—for example, the differentiation of work, the segmentation of workers, and the disaggregation of labor on a global scale—have led to the increasing specialization and depersonalization of labor.

In summary, the three main contributing factors to the spatialization process in the Chinese media industry, particularly the publishing industry, are the deepening of globalization, the accompanying expansion of neoliberalism, and the global division of labor. As a result of these influences, Chinese editors are forced to "dance with chains" (Zhao 1998, 161) within a market economy that precariously balances neoliberal elements and authoritarian centralized control (Harvey 2005). The latter has also led to the exploitation of Chinese editors, despite the fact that China is increasingly integrated into global networks of wealth, power, and symbols.

GLOBALIZATION AND THE
CHINESE PUBLISHING INDUSTRY

According to Elizabeth Perry and Mark Selden (2010), China has experienced one of the highest rates of economic growth since the late 1970s, and has benefited greatly from its integration into the global political economy. In their view, the main purposes of China's economic reform are not only to accelerate China's economic growth, to eliminate poverty, and to bolster Party authority, but to strengthen the country's international position in the world economy. During the past three decades, the central government has encouraged foreign investment, gained access to overseas consumer markets, and tried to maximize the benefits and minimize the costs of globalization.

Transnational Media Corporations in China

Chin-Chuan Lee (2003b) argues that globalization has led media organizations to adopt new varieties of organizational and economic restructuring, downsizing, technological improvements, managerial techniques, as well as an increased emphasis on flexibility. It is widely acknowledged, however, that the most significant effect of globalization on the global publishing industry has been the expansion of transnational media corporations, such as Time Warner, Disney, News Corporation, Bertelsmann AG, and Viacom (Mosco 2009). As Lee (2003b, 8) maintains, transnational corporations "comprise vertically and horizontally integrated layers of companies across the entire spectrum of media form—from film, radio, television, cable, sports, music, home video, publishing, magazines, to multimedia." As a result, not only have the lines between news and entertainment been blurred, so have the lines between traditional broadcast media, such as radio and television, and new media, such as computer networks (Bagdikian 2000).

The rise of transnational media corporations has increased the concentration of the world's communication and information systems, with the result that a handful of powerful media conglomerates are now dominating the global diffusion and utilization of telecommunications. In the global publishing industry, the control of publishing mergers, which have become increasingly necessary, is concentrated in a few transnational corporations (Mowlana 1997). For example, as one of the top ten book publishers in the United States in 2009, Simon and Schuster, a publishing merger that included Free Press, Pocket Books, Howard Books, and Scribner, among others, is now owned by Viacom (Hyatt 2010). In general, such publishing mergers provide great advantages, such as better inventory control, higher advertising budgets, wider distribution channels, newer technologies, and lower production costs. Furthermore, unit prices decrease due to the larger numbers of books produced at each printing. Given the advantages of merging with transnational corporations, it is no wonder that small, regional publishing houses are becoming less and less competitive in the global publishing market (Xin 2005).

In recent years, many transnational media corporations have established branches in China, and they are currently working with domestic publishing houses on various issues, including copyright trade and business cooperation. According to Zhou (2005b), since the Fifth National People's Congress in June 1980, the Chinese government has emphasized the importance of foreign copyright trade as a major component of national economic growth. Consequentially, China's copyright trade has enjoyed a steady boom. In 2002, the total trade volume of media products reached 127 million dollars: 107 million dollars for imported books, magazines and journals, newspapers, audiovisual products, and electronic publications, mainly from the United States, Britain, and Japan; and 20 million dollars for similar products exported to many countries and regions, including Taiwan, Korea, and the United States (The Book Publishing Management Department of the GAPP 2008). Table 4.1 tracks the changes in the total trade volume of imported and exported media products to/from China in the period extending from 1997 to 2002, and demonstrates that the imported trade volume of all media products far exceeds the exported volume.

Gerald Sussman and John Lent (1998) observe that foreign capital has widely circulated in the Chinese media market through strategic joint ventures and capital investments in information technologies, books and magazines, satellite television markets, and Internet portals and websites. There are many explicit examples of business cooperation between Chinese and foreign media organizations. For example, in 2001, the Chinese government allowed the Hong Kong-based channel, China Entertainment Television, whose parent company is Time Warner, to provide Mandarin signals to the cable channels in Guangdong province (Landler 2001). To take another example, Cable News Network (CNN), another outfit of Time Warner, has launched a regional production center in Hong Kong with the Chinese market in mind. As a fully integrated newsgathering and production hub, the latter provides network programming, newsgathering, and online production for all of CNN's television, radio, and new media services worldwide. It also operates as the logistical and planning center for the nine CNN bureaus located in Asia: Bangkok, Beijing, Hong Kong, Islamabad, Jakarta, New Delhi, Seoul, Sydney, and Tokyo (Network18 2007).

Specifically in the publishing industry, copyright trade with foreign media organizations has become increasingly extensive. Table 4.2 illustrates the total number of book titles imported and exported to/from China in the peri-

Table 4.1. Total Trade Volume of Imported and Exported Media Products, 1997–2002.

Total Trade Volume of Imported Media Products

Years	1997	1998	1999	2000	2001	2002
Books	11.02[a]	20.73	22.63	24.30	28.25	26.22
Magazines and Journals	22.94	25.72	24.95	27.34	32.11	61.20
Newspapers	2.53	3.29	8.96	6.27	8.67	7.45
Audio Products	2.08	0.36	0.75	1.17	3.96	3.28
Visual Products	0.187	0.003	0.001	0.001	0.169	0.001
Electronic Publications	1.85	2.63	2.83	3.83	6.59	8.94
Total	41.53	52.77	60.14	62.93	79.76	107.10

Total Trade Volume of Exported Media Products

	1997	1998	1999	2000	2001	2002
Books	9.27	11.16	12.48	12.33	13.70	13.63
Magazines and Journals	2.67	2.10	2.31	3.39	2.85	3.03
Newspapers	0.14	1.54	1.09	0.98	1.07	0.73
Audio Products	0.111	0.026	0.102	0.139	0.089	0.028
Visual Products	0.078	0.222	0.331	0.372	0.478	1.755
Electronic Publications	0.031	0.075	0.049	0.083	0.021	0.039
Total	12.31	15.13	16.36	17.31	18.41	19.58
Trade Deficit	29.21	37.64	43.78	45.62	61.36	87.53

Source: Zhou (2005b).

[a] Millions of dollars.

od extending from 1997 to 2002, together with the corresponding annual growth rates. The current transborder flow of books, journals, and magazines is immense, and over ten thousand different books were imported and 1,300 were exported in 2007 alone (Cao and Han 2008). It also indicates that both the production and trade of printed materials have grown at unprecedented rates in the past few years.

Business cooperation between domestic and foreign publishing companies has also been dynamic and fruitful. For example, as a joint venture with Egmont, the Children's Fun Publishing House published 424 new titles and achieved an annual output value of 84 million *yuan* in 2002, making it one of the top five children's book publishers in China (Xin 2005).[1] A growing number of transnational media corporations set up offices in many large cities in China, and thereafter become directly involved in the production of audiovisual and electronic publications. For example, since its launch in 1997, the German company Bertelsmann AG has strategically invested in

Table 4.2.   Total Number of Book Titles Imported and Exported with the Annual Growth Rates, 1997–2002.

Years	Number of Book Titles Imported	Annual Growth Rate	Number of Book Title Exported	Annual Growth Rate
1997	3,224	22.02%	353	41.20%
1998	5,469	69.63%	588	66.57%
1999	6,461	18.14%	418	-28.91%
2000	7,343	13.65%	638	52.63%
2001	8,250	12.35%	677	6.11%
2002	10,235	24.06%	1,297	91.58%

Source: Zhou (2005b).

printing, radio, television, and e-commerce, in cooperation with the Chinese central government. It also co-publishes books, journals, and magazines with local Chinese publishing houses, and has used its management expertise to expand its readers' clubs in most large Chinese cities. At present, there are more than 400,000 members in its readers' clubs nationwide. Most significantly, in December 2003, it successfully obtained partial ownership of the 21st Century Chain, which has become the first foreign-owned national chain-bookstore complex (Lee 2003c).

Chinese Publishing Exports in the Global Media Sphere

As the world's most populous country and a major power in the world economy, China plays an important role in the global media industry. Alongside the country's economic liberalization, the Chinese government has adopted various strategies, and employed new technological developments in communication to circulate its publications in the global media sphere. Such strategies include the launch of the English version of *The China Daily* and the promotion of the online version of *The People's Daily*.

To specify, known as "Voice of China" or "Window to China," the English version of *The China Daily* was launched in New York in 1982, thus becoming China's first national English-language newspaper. By 2005, it had reached a global circulation of more than 200,000, one-third of which was among business-oriented international readers, who use it as a guide to China's official policies. From 1996 to the present, the online edition of the newspaper has been read by around five million people daily (Thussu 2000).

As for *The People's Daily*, founded in 1948, it had a global circulation of three million in 2005, with its editorials regarded as authoritative statements of government policies by both foreign observers and Chinese readers. When the online edition was launched in 1998, it was available in Chinese, English,

Japanese, French, Spanish, Russian, and Arabic. Authoritative and semi-official, it disseminates both positive information about China and general news about the world at large (Xu 2008).

Chinese publishers have been actively participating in numerous international book fairs, such as the Frankfurt Book Fair, the Bologna Children's Book Fair, and BookExpo America. In the past ten years, five hundred to six hundred Chinese publishing professionals have attended the annual Frankfurt Book Fair. The Beijing International Book Fair (BIBF), sponsored by the General Administration of Press and Publication of China (GAPP), the State Council Information Office, the Beijing municipal government, has also drawn growing attention from both domestic and international publishing houses. In September 2011, the eighteenth BIBF was 53,600 square meters in size with 2,155 booths. Over two thousand publishers, coming from sixty countries and regions, participated in the exhibition, with more than 200,000 different book titles on display. Since its first exhibition in 1986, it has become the most important book copyright trade fair in Asia, as well as one of three major international book fairs held in China.[2] There is no denying that the Chinese publishing industry has become an indispensable component of the global media industry, and national boundaries are no longer major barriers for the global media industry.

Chinese Publishing Conglomerates

The pressure facing the Chinese publishing industry from foreign media companies is intense (Lynch 2000). Before China's media reform, its mass media served as propaganda machines, and its media organizations were heavily dependent on financial resources provided by the party-state. Thus, as He Zhou (2000) argues, the latter differed from major transnational media corporations in their mission, business models, values, and quality of their workforce. As a result, Chinese publishing organizations could not yet match the abilities and experience of their international counterparts in market competition, management, human resources, and the application of new technologies. Even after dramatic reform, Chinese publishing organizations are less competitive than their international counterparts in the global media market, and continue to confront significant challenges from foreign media organizations on the home front. Specifically, the media content imported by transnational media corporations may undermine China's official ideology (McCormick and Liu 2003). The imported business culture, with its less centralized but more commercialized institutional frameworks, may promote individual and enterprise autonomy beyond the limits set by the central government, and challenge existing Chinese political, economic, and social institutions. It is no wonder that Ding Guanggen, Minister of the Central Propaganda Department (CPD), warned that the good days of the Chinese publishing sector, and generally China's media industry, will be over when China fully integrates into the global political economy.

In response to the pressure and challenges and in an attempt to achieve political control, economic efficiency, and international competitiveness, the central government has merged existing domestic publishing outlets to form publishing conglomerates. He (2000) argues that, when competing with their foreign counterparts, these publishing conglomerates are more effective than individual publishing outlets in collecting resources, including political, social, and financial resources; upgrading their facilities, equipment, and other hardware; and applying sophisticated skills and techniques to the production of diverse publications.

In recent years, with the widespread expansion of economic deregulation and technological developments in the Chinese publishing industry, publishing houses are increasingly choosing to merge into publishing groups. Since 2002, when the media conglomeration process was initiated, large publishing groups have appeared in many provinces. It is important to emphasize that such publishing groups are the products of top-down policies. By establishing large publishing groups, the central government aimed to both strengthen its control over the domestic publishing industry, and to enhance the competence of China's publishing industry and its competitiveness in the global media market (Zhao 2001; Lee 2002). Some of the large and powerful publishing groups established by the central government include the Shanghai Century Publishing Group (Shanghai), the Beijing Publishing Group (Beijing), the Guangdong Publishing Group (Guangzhou, Guangdong province), and the Liaoning Publishing Group (Shenyang, Liaoning province). There were twenty-four registered publishing groups in China by the end of 2004. They have turned out to be highly important industrial organizations, integral to the development of China's publishing industry.[3]

To address, Chinese publishing conglomerates are subject to both economic and political pressure to attract a large audience by "softening their publicity messages and providing a wide range of information to respond to market demands" (He 2003, 210). In other words, turning themselves into "party-state publicity Inc.," Chinese publishing conglomerates are not only operating as business entities, but as the mouthpiece of the party-state because they are primarily responsible for publicizing the party-state's policies and interests (He 2003, 209). To better serve the interests of the state, Chinese publishing conglomerates are obliged to follow the Party principle, and this makes them somehow vulnerable to global competition. As He (2003, 209) argues, if foreign media corporations are allowed to "disseminate factual information (especially sensitive topics on domestic and international politics) that the Chinese publishing sector is not permitted to publish," there is no doubt that Chinese publishing conglomerates will be defeated by their competitors in the global media sphere.

In order to prevent this, the Chinese government has imposed restrictions on incoming foreign competitors in the entire media sector by limiting both their media content and the regions where their programs can be broadcast. Foreign programs can only be aired in some parts of China, and these programs must take either pro-China or moderate editorial stances. For example, more than thirty foreign television operators have aired their programs in Guangdong province, which is known as a "Special Media Zone" to selected overseas media corporations. In order to broadcast radio and television programs, these foreign media corporations are required to possess specific licenses, issued by the Chinese National Broadcasting, Film, and Television Department. These licenses are suspended immediately if the foreign corporations air any program critical of the Party's leadership. Specifically in the publishing industry, there are only forty Chinese publishing houses allowed in book copyright trade with foreign publishers, and they must obtain special business licenses from the central government. All of these publishing houses—of which the Beijing Publications Import and Export Corporation, the China National Publication International Trading Corporation, and the Shanghai Book Traders are the largest—are state-owned, and most of them are affiliated to either provincial press and publications administrations or with large publishing groups. These government measures ensure that, as Schlesinger (2000) claims, the introduction of transnational media corporations to the Chinese media industry (including the publishing industry), although related to the rising tide of neoliberalism on a global scale, does not challenge the Party's leadership in any circumstance.[4]

NEOLIBERALISM AND CHINESE EDITORS

The Twin Modalities of the Neoliberal Governmentality

Neoliberalism, which is intricately linked to the global economic restructuring that has occurred since the 1970s, views the free market as the solution to social justice and inequality issues, and dismisses the need for government intervention. This belief has resulted in significant changes to the roles of the government, corporations, and individuals (Adams and Welsh 2008). In the wake of the rapid global expansion of neoliberal policies, the past several decades has witnessed widespread privatization, commercialization, trade liberalization, and overall deregulation or market-based reregulation in national media systems. The role of the state has been greatly diminished on the global scale, both as a provider of media service and as a regulator of media ownership in broadcasting and telecommunications (Zhao and Hackett 2005).

However, according to Kai Hafez (2005), the infiltration of neoliberal concerns, especially of market-driven truths and calculations into government policies, has been highly uneven worldwide. David Harvey (2005, 13) also notes that both the "uneven geographical development of neoliberalism" and "the complex ways in which political forces, historical traditions, and existing institutional arrangements all shaped why and how the process of neoliberalization actually occurred." In China, there is no denying that neoliberal governmentality has made many contributions to China's accelerated post-1978 social transition from a centrally planned economy to a market economy, but there are many strict limitations on the penetration of neoliberal policies in China. This is especially true in the Chinese media industry, particularly in the publishing industry, because the role of the state has not been significantly challenged, and the mass media are still presumed to perform a propaganda function.

While the Chinese state has continually attempted to incorporate neoliberal elements, thus "extend[ing] the values and relations of markets into a model for the broader organization of politics and society" (Robison 2006, 4), these attempts have been self-limited by the need to comply with the state's authoritarian centralized control. Thus, Aihwa Ong (2006, 3) maintains that in the Chinese publishing industry, editors are trapped between the "twin modalities of the neoliberal governmentality" that include *"neoliberalism as exception"* and *"exceptions to neoliberalism."*

On the one hand, the main purpose of China's economic reform is to liberate the market from the state, thus accelerating capital accumulation. The Chinese government has adjusted the overall institutional framework to guarantee private property rights and to promote free markets as well as free trade, as it increasingly integrates into the world political economy (Hung 2009). Through these processes, China has been moving toward the model of "neoliberal" capitalism: the state is being downsized, its capacity is being weakened, and its role in the economy is significantly reduced. It has also actively offloaded its welfare and human service onto the market and society, leading its private sector and the various labor, capital, and finance markets to experience a rapid expansion. As Ong (2006, 3) suggests, the Chinese government has taken the initiative in embracing neoliberal calculations as an effective means of maximizing its entrepreneurial dynamism and facilitating its access to the global market. This modality is known as *"neoliberalism as exception,"* because neoliberal policies are exceptions under the otherwise tight control of the authoritarian state.

On the other hand, the state employs strategic *"exceptions to neoliberalism,"* excluding certain populations and places from neoliberal calculations, with the intention of thereby eliminating discrimination, promoting social equality, and maintaining political control (Ong 2006, 3). Even though the central government has tentatively stimulated market-oriented developments in the publishing sector, its control over the system is steady and ubiquitous. As Li (1997b, 58) puts it, Chinese editors should "advocate healthy, lofty ideology and culture under the Party's leadership, in order to create a good environment of public opinion for the modernization drive, and give a moral support to the modernization drive." Therefore, it is imperative for Chinese editors to take precautions against criticism of the Party, in order to maintain the advance of the modernization drive.

Basically, the concept of neoliberalism, derived from Western social science traditions, changes significantly when it is applied to the analysis of what is currently happening in the Chinese publishing industry. This point is echoed by Robison (2006, 4), who claims that neoliberalism in China is not "just a reincarnation of laissez-faire sentiment or a simple neo-classical attachment to the idea of the inherent efficiency of markets." Also, as Huang and Cui (2005) suggest, neoliberalism in China does not exclusively focus on the economic policies of market liberalization, deregulation, privatization, and fiscal austerity associated with the Washington Consensus, the shock therapy, and the structural adjustment programs applied to Russia and other transnational economies. In the Chinese context, neoliberalism must embrace the political interests of the party-state, the economic interests of transnational media corporations, and the general interests of the public in promoting democracy.

As I have remarked in previous chapters, one significant result of the widespread expansion of neoliberal policies is that Chinese publishing houses and newspaper agencies have been thrown out of the party-state budget and forced to survive on the market. He (2000) maintains that media organizations run by either the Communist Party of China (CPC) or by various state organizations are expected to be self-sufficient and earn their own revenue. At the same time, however, they have an unmistakable political mission: to serve as the party-state's voice, promoting its interests, policies, and ideology. Chinese editors are thus pressured to meet the demands of both market power and the Party principle. While market power is harnessed to stimulate the growth of the domestic publishing industry, the Party principle dominates publishing management and controls publishing infrastructure (Yu 2011).

China's Accession to the World Trade Organization

The implementation of neoliberal policies has been accelerated since China entered the WTO in December 2001. There is a general belief that China's official entry into the WTO marked a turning point in the country's decades-long efforts to be accepted into the international community, and constituted a historic landmark in the broader global neoliberal movement (He 2003). Martin Hart-Landsberg and Paul Burkett (2004) point out that China's entry into the WTO, and the related breakdown of trade barriers, have led to a further dismantling of the state, as evidenced in the removal of state subsidies, the reorientation of market strategies in favor of export, and the consolidation of foreign production as an important force in the Chinese economy.

As part of the conditions for its entrance into the WTO, the Chinese central government has made several substantive concessions to open up the domestic media market. Due to rapid developments in communication and information technologies, foreign investment in information infrastructures, service provision, and technological knowledge within China's media industry has been highly encouraged (Yu 2002). The WTO has opened the door for foreign capital to invest in media advertising and management. The Chinese government has also favored granting licenses to transnational corporations in the new media, such as telecommunications firms, which are well funded and run by large professional staff members (Li 2001; Zhou 2002). News media and television, however, continue to be largely sheltered from foreign competition. The central government has never relinquished its editorial authority over media content, and it has also taken various measures designed to protect the ideological power of the government.

According to Hart-Landsberg and Burkett (2004), in China's news media and television sectors, there is still little clarity on how regulations will be made to comply with the WTO agreements. Many mass media scholars in China believe, however, that ongoing technological developments will pressure the central government to make more and more changes to its regulatory policies, thereby pushing China's media reform toward greater liberalization, and thus making the media market much more open and transparent (Petras 2006). Nevertheless, Chinese media workers, particularly editors in the publishing industry, have suffered considerable losses resulting from the neoliberal policies already in place within the Chinese media industry. As addressed before, recent years have seen these workers face the problems of rising unemployment, growing economic insecurity, class polarization, intensified exploitation, and declining health and education conditions.

THE GLOBAL DIVISION OF
LABOR AND CHINESE EDITORS

The global division of labor is another social trend accompanying globalization. As Sussman and Lent (1998) point out, while profit rates in the central capitalist economies continue declining under the pressure of global competition, the motion of capital continues to expand and accelerate—overcoming spatial, temporal, and political constraints—due to the global division of labor, mainly organized by transnational corporations. This is accomplished by their searching for the cheapest locations to manufacture and assemble components, as well as taking advantage of transportation and communication technology.

Technological developments have greatly facilitated capital mobility, opening areas once remote from the geographical reach of the core industrial powers. Both Ong (2006) and Lai Si Tsui-Auch (1998) maintain that massive transfers of labor-intensive industries from these powers to developing countries have become feasible and profitable, due to the latter's low labor costs, favorable tax rates, and relaxed production restrictions. Thus, recent decades have witnessed a growing integration of world production on the basis of this new relationship between highly industrialized and less-developed countries. In this section of the chapter, I will focus on the emergence of the global division of labor with its widespread expansion in the world political economy, as well as explore three critical challenges facing Chinese editors in the publishing industry, due to the global division of labor: changes to their value systems, changes to their daily work process, and the intensification of work-related pressure.

The Emergence of the Global Division of Labor

As early as the 1970s, Stephen Hymer (1972) argued that the spatial division of labor—primarily under the control of transnational corporations—as well as organizational hierarchization and a structure of domination/subordination, has characterized the world political-economic system. In the past four decades, the geographical dispersion of production has accompanied the movement by transnational corporations toward more complex and efficient multiproduct, multidivisional structures (Mosco, McKercher, and Huws 2010). In other words, according to Taylor (2008), transnational corporations, by distributing their production activities throughout the world, as well as imposing a vertical integration that cuts across national, political, and ethnic lines, incorporate workers of economically less-developed countries into a new global division of labor.

With the rise of the global division of labor, the geographical dispersion of production has brought about significant changes in the relationship between capital and labor, as well as contributed to a new relationship between highly industrialized and less-developed countries. Top-level administrative activities, which require numerous knowledge workers and well-developed communication systems, are mainly located in large cities that are close to financial markets. Manufacturing and sales activities, however, are located throughout the world, depending entirely upon the availability of labor, markets, and raw materials. Therefore, there is an uneven expansion and development of capital, particularly of the global production of transnational corporations worldwide (Tsui-Auch 1998).

It is in this uneven context of transnational capital expansion and development that China has transformed itself into the "factory of the world" (Frank 2011). In tandem with the consolidation of transnational corporations and the increased fluidity of capital investment, many highly industrialized countries—acting as sources of technological expertise, design, and financial outflows—have selected China as an offshore production location of capital. Ngai, Chan, and Chan (2010) claim that, due to its specialized assembly operations, China has become the world's largest producer of garment and textile products, electronic products, toys, and household appliances. In 2010, China eclipsed Japan as the world's second largest economy based on GDP measurements (Hamlin 2010).

In addition to its huge domestic market, China's comparatively low production costs, and its vast pool of cheap labor, are major reasons for its economic success (Hong 2010; Qiu 2010). According to Hennock (2002), Chinese industrial workers receive an average of about forty US cents an hour, which is a mere fraction of the amount that their US counterparts receive, and six times less than the amount that factory workers in Mexico receive.[5] Apart from their low wages, Chinese industrial workers also receive fewer collective social welfare benefits than their counterparts elsewhere. Increasingly subjected to coercive modes of labor control and arbitrary managerial power, most Chinese industrial workers have fallen into the ranks of the urban poor (Zheng 2004).

The stunning growth in China's production of media-related products—including the computers, telecommunications devices, and other technologies essential for global media activities—has made the country central to the global division of labor. According to statistics released by the Ministry of Industry and Information Technology (2011), the total value of exported media products was 30.35 billion dollars in the first half of 2011, with the annual growth rate reaching 15.8 percent. The export of media products has constituted one third of the country's total export volume in the past few years. This rapid growth has been accompanied, however, by the deteriorating working and living conditions of factory workers, which were infamously brought to light by the Foxconn suicides.

Recently, twenty universities in Hong Kong, Taiwan, and the mainland jointly produced a research report on the Foxconn suicides entitled "Foxconn Factories Are Labor Camps," based on interviews with more than 1,800 workers from twelve Foxconn-owned factories in nine mainland cities. The report revealed that assembly line workers in Foxconn factories have to work double or triple the legal overtime limit under a Spartan management style.[6] The assembly lines run fast, and workers are required to finish every procedure in exactly two seconds. They are not allowed to talk, smile, sit down, walk around, or move unnecessarily during their long working hours, and are required to finish twenty thousand products every day (Students and Scholars against Corporate Misbehavior 2010). In addition, teenage students have been employed extensively by Foxconn, without the protection of labor contract or statutory industrial insurance. Under these conditions, at least seventeen Foxconn workers have attempted to commit suicide, fourteen successfully. Long working hours, discrimination against mainland Chinese workers by their Taiwanese coworkers, and heavy labor intensity have all been cited as potential causes for the suicides.

With its population of highly qualified skilled workers growing constantly, China is considered an attractive and cost-effective labor source, in contrast to knowledge-intensive developed countries. Alongside the sharp rise in the global production of communication and information technologies in the 1990s, transnational corporations began to set up subsidiaries in offshore regions, rather than migrating those highly qualified knowledge workers to the countries where their headquarters were located (Sahay, Nicholson, and Krishna 2003). Not only have low-skilled workers in the factories of traditional industries been affected by such offshore sourcing, but their highly qualified counterparts working in knowledge-intensive areas are also beginning to feel the negative impacts of the new patterns in world production and trade (Huws 2003; Blinder 2006). In the next section, I will examine the impact of the global division of labor on Chinese editors, who were once assumed to be both the "creative" protagonists and beneficiaries of globalization (Florida 2002; Huws, Lehndorff, and Grimshaw 2010).

The Impact of the Global Division of Labor on Chinese Editors

In the world media and communications industry, the global division of labor is also primarily based on "process specialization." As defined by Fröbel, Heinrichs, and Kreye (1980) in the early 1980s, "process specialization" refers to the strategic process whereby transnational media corporations have shifted the capital and technology intensive process of media production to developed countries, while simultaneously transferring the labor-intensive process of manufacturing media products to developing countries, such as China, India, and Malaysia.

As Karen Klein (2007) argues, China's large and relatively low-paid workforce has contributed to the substantial growth of its media industry, transforming it into a "world manufacturing center" that increasingly monopolizes worldwide media production. For example, many foreign media companies, including Disney, MTV, Cartoon Network, and Warner Bros. have outsourced most of their animated features to Chinese animation studios. These animation studios primarily produce Western-designed cartoon programs at an extraordinarily high quality with very low costs (Bennett 2006). The increasing number of Chinese animation studios has resulted in a boom in knowledge workers—including artists, animators, and technicians, trained in the use of SGCS, SFX, and other motion-capture software and facilities—in the Chinese animation industry.[7]

Chinese media workers—including knowledge workers in the animation industry; newspaper, television, and radio journalists; and editors in publishing houses—are facing critical changes to their value systems and everyday working procedures, as well as the intensification of work-related pressure, due to the increasing incorporation of the Chinese media industry into centrally coordinated "global factories" headquartered in the core capitalist states.

First, Chinese media workers, particularly editors, have largely changed their value systems. A survey on workers' political status and political relations conducted by the All-China Federation of Trade Unions (ACFTU) in 1993 revealed that Chinese editors continued to hold a value system informed by collectivist and/or nationalist ideologies, despite the fact that they were working in a post-state-socialist society. In my interview with Gao, he talked about this disjuncture between deep-seated values and the current socioeconomic structure:

> Our old value system completely denied that labor is a commodity. Therefore, we preferred to stay in the same publishing house until our retirement, because this was the most direct way to express our loyalty to publishing houses. In return, publishing houses used to guarantee every editor lifetime employment, together with a moderate monthly income and basic social welfare benefits. (Gao 2010)

This value system is fundamentally different from that informing the current global capitalist understanding of labor. In accordance with the value system informing the global capitalist market, labor is a commodity, tradable at a price set by existing labor markets (Mosco and McKercher 2008; Mosco 2009). Due to the commodification of labor, workers must compete for wages in the labor markets, which are driven by the capitalists' desire to secure the cheapest possible labor (Gang and Bandurski 2011). As the global division of labor deepens in the world media industry, Chinese editors, and media workers in general, must prepare for actual or potential layoffs, due to the fact that their labor is becoming increasingly exchangeable and replaceable.

Second, the emergence of the global division of labor in the Chinese publishing industry has led to crucial changes in the daily work process of many Chinese editors, such as their increasing limitation to the performance of simple tasks that require few technical and professional skills. For example, in the Shanghai Science and Technology Publishing House, most editors are only responsible for composing and printing the books, journals, and magazines that are edited by their foreign counterparts. This emphasis on foreign-edited publications partially explains why numerous publishing houses have been established in large cities along the country's eastern coastal sub-regions, from which it is most convenient to transport printed books, journals, and magazines abroad (The Book Publishing Management Department of the GAPP 2008). Located in Melbourne, the Australian firm of Tingleman Outsource Media is becoming one of the world's largest outsource print brokers, focusing on providing quality assurance and negotiation services for transnational publishers outsourcing printing in China. In 2005, while sourcing from thirteen large publishing houses in China, the company's total annual sales volume reached 2.5 million dollars (Cui 2010).

Third, for Chinese editors, the global division of labor has not mitigated the intense work-related pressure resulting from the media marketization process. On the contrary, it has only increased the pressure to compete for jobs and/or to plan for the future of their careers. Due to the country's large population, which offers a great amount of cheap labor for employers, competition for jobs has always been intense in China. In general, the extensive outsourcing of media production by transnational media corporations to the Chinese media industry does not necessarily guarantee increased job opportunities for every Chinese media worker. Chinese media workers are pushed to compete for jobs with their counterparts in other developing countries that have entered global capitalism, such as India and the former Soviet bloc countries (Yates 2003; Hong 2011).

Due to the increasingly fierce competition for jobs in the publishing industry, Chinese editors, particularly senior editors, are understandably worried about losing their current jobs. My interviews with editors in several large publishing houses in Shanghai reveal that this anxiety has become an inherent part of editors' everyday lives, rendering their futures even less certain. As a result, editors are pressured into continuing professional training and education, which is believed to be essential for moving up into the skilled levels of production (Sun and Yang 2002).

In addition to the immediate fear of losing their jobs, Chinese editors have had to deal with decreasing predictability in and control over their work and careers. As long as they feel powerless to cope with the changing "moods" of either the global market or of their own management, they will be less concerned about workplace reform than about simply "surviving" and "defending the positions they have already achieved" in their companies (Boes and Kampf 2010, 111). My surveys indicate that 62.5 percent of Chinese editors have never changed their jobs, and only 5 percent have changed their jobs three times or more. These editors do not complain about their work, because they are fearful of losing their jobs. Instead, they work harder than their colleagues, and try their best to achieve the profit levels set by the leaders.

CONCLUSION

In our digitally connected age, all kinds of information, including political discourse, scientific research, corporate data, personal communication, and media entertainment circulate around the world at incredible speed. As Thussu (2007) remarks, advances in digital networks and technologies have largely freed the production, consumption, and distribution of information from both temporal and spatial constraints. These innovations have contributed to China's increasing engagement in the global political economy—that is, the reshaping of its economy by broader transnational production networks, under the auspices of the central government—since the late 1970s. In short, mass-media communication processes, institutions, and technologies in China have both contributed to, and been affected by, the broader wave of globalization (Zhou and Chen 2010).

To come to terms with the problems experienced by Chinese editors as a result of the massive technological, political, and economic changes of recent decades, it is essential not only to examine the *structuration* process of the political economy of communication, but to analyze the media *spatialization* process, which has three main contributing factors: the deepening of globalization, the accompanying expansion of neoliberalism, and the global division of labor. The spatialization process has trapped Chinese editors between the "twin modalities of the neoliberal governmentality" (Ong 2006, 3), brought about crucial changes in their value systems and their daily work process, and intensified their work-related pressure.

What are the plausible solutions to the precarious situation in which Chinese media workers, specifically editors in the publishing industry, currently find themselves? In the next chapter, I will examine the benefits and limitations of labor convergence, and question the success of worker organizations and trade unions in protecting and safeguarding the rights and interests of Chinese media workers. In particular, I will analyze the role that the ACFTU is playing to help Chinese media workers, particularly editors, deal with the challenges stemming from current media reform.

NOTES

1. Egmont is one of the Europe's leading media entertainment companies and the largest publisher of children's books in Europe.

2. To note, the three major international book fairs in China are the Beijing International Book Fair, the Beijing Book Fair, and the National Book Fair.

3. As aforementioned, the publishing groups in China accounted for 31.3 percent of all published titles (65,129 different book titles), 37.8 percent of all copies of printed books (2,422.88 million), 31.4 percent of all copies of printed sheets (14,618.489 million), and 30.2 percent of all the revenue from books (17,932.47 million *yuan*) in 2004.

4. Transnational media corporations also face intense pressure when they attempt to open China's media market. They have to be very cautious about the limitations on media content,

and, at the same time, they need to satisfy the preferences and interests of the local audience. Together with their domestic co-producers, transnational media corporations are pushed to "take China's social, cultural and political mores, memories, and aesthetic currencies seriously, if they are to achieve deep purchase and a lasting profile in the markets" (Lee and Huang 2002, 108). In this sense, globalization and localization are not two opposed processes, but are mutually connected (Robertson 1995; Sreberny 2000).

5. As of July 24, 2009, the federal minimum wage in the United States was $7.31 per hour. Some states and municipalities set minimum wages higher than the federal level, with the highest state minimum wage being $8.67 in Washington.

6. Workers in Foxconn factories are forced to work eighty to one hundred hours of overtime per month. Under the Labor Law, the legal limit on overtime is forty-four hours a month.

7. SGCS stands for Silicon Graphics Computer Systems. SFX, shorthand for "special effects," is a leading live entertainment sound playback software application.

Chapter Five

Labor Convergence

Worker Organizations and Trade Unions

As mentioned in previous chapters, although it is perceived as an indispensable part of the continuing economic and social transformations in China, Chinese media reform has eliminated many of the privileges that Chinese media workers took for granted in the planned economy. Particularly in the Chinese publishing industry, editors are increasingly confronted with the problem of contingent employment, declining social welfare benefits, and intense work pressure. They are also caught in a double-bind: while they are responsible for serving and publicizing the party-state's policies and interests, they are also expected to adapt to the media marketization process and generate profit like private businesses (Cheek 1997; Zhao 2008). In other words, Chinese editors, operating within the new propaganda-commercial model, are enormously pressured by the competing factors of market competition and strict Party control. It is therefore unsurprising that China's increasing integration into the global political economy, particularly its gradual adaptation to the global division of labor, has necessitated great changes to most editors' value systems and everyday work practices. In this chapter, I will explore possible ways in which Chinese editors, and media workers in a broader sense, can begin to better their frustrating and precarious situation.

I will begin this chapter by introducing the concept of labor convergence and addressing its importance: in China, both worker organizations and trade unions, as the two main patterns of labor convergence, have gradually come to represent the concrete interests and legitimate rights of the working class, with particular attention to the regulation of employer-employee relationships, even though the state is still playing an important role in worker organization and trade union activities (Clarke 2005). I will examine the effectiveness of worker organizations and trade unions by analyzing the main duties and functions of several important worker organizations representing Chinese media workers, editors in particular, including the Publishers Association of China (PAC, established in 1979) at the national level, and the Publishers Association of Shanghai (PAS) at the regional level. I will also concentrate on the main duties and functions of China's trade unions, especially the ACFTU, which serves as the sole national trade union federation of China, leading all Chinese trade unions as their "union center" (Hong and Ip 2007, 65). My examination of the status of worker organizations and trade unions in contemporary China will allow me to address the reform of such organizations in the Chinese media industry, as well as the effects of media commodification, structuration, and spatialization.

Moreover, even though worker organizations and trade unions are effective in representing and safeguarding the rights and interests of the Chinese media workers, particularly editors, as I have argued above, I will outline their major limitations as both of them are under rapid transformation: they lack substantial political and economic power compared with the Party organs; their obligations to uphold the state's reform policies and the interests of the working class often conflict; and they are slow to reshape their guiding philosophies and promote personnel system reform in accordance with new imperatives accompanying the market economy (Wang 2001). As many Chinese and Western scholars, including Alvin So (2007), Chris White (2007), and Beverly Silver and Lu Zhang (2009) have observed, there has been a rising tide of labor unrest in China's reform era, even though the central government has emphasized a "new development model" aimed at reducing inequalities among classes and regions in pursuit of a "harmonious society" (The People's Daily 2005). Given the limitations of worker organizations and trade unions, and the volatility of the employer-employee relationship, it is essential to consider how new information technologies, changes inside the ACFTU, and the labor nongovernmental organizations can aid in improving representation of the legitimate rights and interests of the working class, including knowledge workers in the publishing industry.

LABOR CONVERGENCE

McKercher and Mosco (2007, 3–4) point out that converging technologies and converging companies have led workers to come together across various industries, seeking improved collective bargaining opportunities and successful political interventions: "one of the trends in the trade union movement in both the developed and developing world is the consolidation of small and narrowly focused unions into larger and more diverse organizations, representing not simply workers in a specific trade, or even within a single industry but in a broad sector of the economy, such as the converging communications, culture, and information sector."

In recent years, the Communications Workers of America, India's Union for ITES (IT-enabled Services) Professionals, and the Union Network International (the global union for skills and services) have succeeded in bringing together workers in different occupations, including both industrial and knowledge workers whose jobs are outsourced from other countries and regions, as well as those whose jobs are threatened due to outsourcing.

In China, labor is also converged in various forms to respond to the problems brought about by media reform and social transformation in the context of China's increasing integration into the global political economy. Worker organizations and trade unions are the two main patterns of labor convergence. In the pre-reform era, worker organizations and trade unions were parts of the state socialist system. As a result, there was no tension between workers' groups and the state, which regarded itself as the sole arbiter and protector of workers' rights and social stability (Hishida et al. 2010). As Feng (2003) remarks, in the pre-reform era, the paternalistic socialist state protected and ensured the workers' fundamental political and economic rights and interests, offering lifetime employment, comprehensive social security, and basic health care. With the advance of social and economic transformations in China, however, the state has gradually shifted from "socialist paternalism" to "market socialism," and enterprises have become independent economic entities, "responsible for their own production, management, employment, wages, welfare, insurance and so on" (Wu 2010, 10). The state has largely shifted the responsibility of administering labor relations to enterprises, but employers have often chosen to maximize their economic interests at the expense of the workers' job security. In response to these changes, both worker organizations and trade unions in China have evolved to represent the interests of the working class and draw attention to employment regulations.

In both the Shanghai Science and Technology Publishing House and the Shanghai Education Publishing House, worker organizations and trade unions have become more effective at communicating *directly* with the leaders, advancing the demands, opinions, and suggestions of editors, and pushing for the leaders' responses. They have also become more effective at communicating *indirectly* with various bureaus of the Shanghai municipal government, sending reports to and pressing their concerns upon the latter. For example, in 2004, the Shanghai Municipal Labor and Social Security Bureau stipulated that when editors revoke their labor contracts, the maximum economic compensation paid to their workplaces by the individual editors should not exceed 5,000 *yuan*. This decision was influenced by the results of surveys conducted by the Shanghai Federation of Trade Unions among workers in all professions, including editors, which indicated that workers had to pay a significant economic compensation, far beyond the acceptable range, to leave their enterprises. As a result, these workers had no choice but to stay in the same enterprises until their contracts expired. The limitations placed on compensation have granted editors, and generally the working class, more flexibility in choosing and changing their employers in the market economy.

While worker organizations and trade unions are becoming less and less dependent on the party-state, they are more reliant on higher-level worker organizations or trade unions, like the ACFTU, which helps to defend the rights and interests of the working class by applying legal and political pressure on employers. Wang (2008b) claims that the ACFTU possesses the expertise, resources, and connections to strengthen the influences of worker organizations and trade unions, and forge previously non-existent connections among different groups of workers. In the next two sections of this chapter, I will explore the basic duties and functions of worker organizations and trade unions, mainly in China's publishing industry, and the role that the ACFTU plays in helping Chinese media workers, particularly editors, adapt to the challenges related to current media reform.

WORKER ORGANIZATIONS

Worker organizations and trade unions in China are mass organizations of the working class, formed by workers on a voluntary basis, which coordinate the interests of three parties—the party-state, enterprises, and workers (Jiang 1996). As opposed to China's trade unions, which are generally organized by workers in different enterprises and institutions, China's worker organizations or associations—such as the China Translator Association (established in 1982), the China Chef Association (1987), the Chinese Institute of Certified Public Accountants (1988), the China Banking Association (2000), and the China Medical Doctor Association (2002)—are organized by workers in a single profession. The main purpose of China's worker organizations is to engage in professional training, assist workers in enforcing their legal rights, and help workers become more effective advocates in the workplace.

There are numerous worker organizations in the Chinese publishing industry, covering book, newspaper, journal and magazine, and audiovisual product publishing at both the national and the regional level. Major national worker organizations include the PAC, the China University Presses Association (1987), the China Periodicals Association (1992), and the China Editors' Association (1992). The following lists the most important Chinese worker organizations in the publishing industry with their years of establishment.

Name of Association (Year of Establishment)

China Paper Association (1964)
Publishers Association of China (1979)
Printing Technology Association of China (1980)
Printing and Printing Equipment Industries Association of China (1985)
China University Presses Association (1987)
China Copyright Protection Association (1990)
China Book and Periodical Issuing Association (1991)
China Periodicals Association (1992)
China Editors' Association (1992)
China Audio and Video Association (1994)

At the regional level, worker organizations—such as the Publishers Association of Beijing, and the PAS—are established in almost every province and in four municipalities (Beijing, Shanghai, Tianjin, and Chongqing). Both the Publishers Association of Beijing and the PAS rely on the vertical chain of command to receive instructions and orders from the PAC, which acts as their administrator. The former are mainly responsible for carrying out the concrete policies and regulations passed by the latter, as well as for fulfilling the tasks assigned by it.

The Publishers Association of China

This section and the next section will specifically look at worker organizations for editors at the national level and regional level, respectively. At the national level, established in December 1979, the PAC is a national autonomous organization of provincial and municipal publishers associations, primarily representing book and journal publishing. There are also thirty working committees affiliated to the PAC in various fields, such as science and technology, youth issues, women's issues, copyright, and proofreading. As a nonprofit and nongovernmental organization, the PAC aims to link publishers with governments at all levels. For example, the PAC has worked with the Books and Periodicals Distribution Association of China and the Xinhua Bookstore to draft the "Regulations on Importing Overseas Copyrights," which serves as the guideline for trading between Chinese and foreign publishers (The Publishers Association of China 2008). Moreover, the PAC promotes best practices in the publishing industry, most notably by offering several influential book awards, for example, the China National Book Award and the Taofen Publishing Award. At the same time, the PAC cooperates with the Taofen Foundation and a few large Chinese publishing conglomerates to produce an annual list of the Top 100 Chinese Publishers, the release of which has been one of the most significant yearly events in China's publishing industry since 1993 (Xin 2005).

The PAC has also arranged for Chinese publishing professionals to attend many international book fairs, such as the Frankfurt Book Fair, the Bologna Children's Book Fair, and BookExpo America. In the past ten years, five hundred to six hundred Chinese publishing professionals have attended the annual Frankfurt Book Fair, which has strongly promoted business cooperation between Chinese and foreign publishers. The PAC has also sponsored dozens of international copyright fairs and book fairs in China, as well as arranged international copyright cooperation symposiums and lectures designed to make Chinese-language publishing more accessible to the outside world. Among them, as mentioned in chapter 4, the Beijing International Book Fair (BIBF) has drawn growing attention from both Chinese and international publishing houses since its beginning in 1986.

The Publishers Association of Shanghai

In contrast to national worker organizations, such as the PAC, which are mainly engaged in drafting regulations, promoting best practices, and organizing copyright trades, regional worker organizations are mainly engaged in offering training for editors and protecting both the political and economic interests of the latter. In my interview with Ma, who works in the PAS, she mentioned that the PAS has become an indispensable source for those editors interested in continuing their professional training, offering various seminars and short-term training lectures since its establishment in 1981. Since 1993, it has held thirty-three professional training sessions attended by two thousand employees in Shanghai's publishing circle (Wang and Zhou 2009). More importantly, with the guidance of the PAC, the General Administration of Press and Publication of China (GAPP), and the Shanghai Municipal Education Commission, the PAS has collaborated with many universities and colleges in Shanghai, including Shanghai Normal University, Shanghai University, University of Shanghai for Science and Technology, and Shanghai Publishing and Printing College—in order to set up publishing-related majors, such as editing, publishing, and distribution. More and more employees in the Shanghai publishing industry, particularly those who do not have adequate professional education, have been receiving continuing professional training in these universities or colleges on a full-time or part-time basis (Tian 2010). Such training usually lasts for one and a half to two years, and an official degree is granted when the training is completed.[1]

Several other worker organizations in Shanghai—including the Shanghai Women Editors' Association, the Shanghai Interpreters' Association, the Shanghai Books and Periodicals Distribution Association, and the Shanghai News and Publishing Association—conduct training sessions for editors at irregular intervals, focusing on book market research, book advertising and promotion, book distribution, publishing management and strategies, and other topics relevant to the fundamental changes that are occurring in the marketplace (Baensch 2003).

The PAS performs some other duties in order to support its members. First, in order to strengthen the connection between publishers in Taiwan and those in Shanghai, the PAS sponsored the First Cross-Straits Book Fair in August 2011. Over one hundred Taiwan publishing houses set up booths to take orders from libraries, bookstores, and readers in Shanghai. The Cross-Straits Book Fair has not only offered a legal venue for the publishers in Shanghai and Taiwan to do business face to face, but it has also been a significant cultural event for most of the editors in these publishing houses. Second, the PAS has long encouraged junior editors in Shanghai to actively participate in many national exhibitions, competitions, and events organized by the PAC, including the Annual National Book Design Exhibition, the National Editing and Proofreading Competition for Junior Editors, and the China's Publishers' Picture Exhibition and Publishing Materials Fair. Third, since its establishment, the PAS has also helped the PAC edit the "Publishing in Shanghai" section in the *China Publishers' Yearbook*, which records China's reform of the publishing industry, including changes in publishing policies; the reform of publishing houses; and the growth of publishing output in every province, municipality, and autonomous region in China. In these ways, the PAS strives to enhance both the competency and competitiveness of most editors in Shanghai, as well as to enrich their daily lives outside of their work.

TRADE UNIONS

Different from worker organizations which are organized by workers in a single profession, trade unions in China are working-class mass organizations led by the Communist Party of China (CPC) and formed voluntarily by workers and staff members in various enterprises, institutions, and government agencies (Lee 1986). According to the Trade Union Law (effective in 1992), industrial and knowledge workers in enterprises, institutions, and government agencies, who rely on wages or salaries as their main sources of income—irrespective of their nationality, race, gender, occupation, religious belief, or educational background—have the right to organize or join trade unions (article 3).[2] That is to say, trade unions are composed of members from a large number of different enterprises: state-owned, foreign-owned, privately owned, and joint-ventures. The basic duty of trade unions is to safeguard the legitimate rights and interests of the working class, as stipulated by the Labor Law (1995) and the Constitution (revised in 1992), under the organizational umbrella of the nation's mainstream and most comprehensive trade union center, the ACFTU. Compared with Western trade unions, Chinese trade unions carry out a wider range of functions, such as organizing social events, providing professional training, taking care of workers' social welfare benefits, helping management to implement operational decisions, coordinating relations between management and workers, and assisting laid-off workers in regaining employment and coping with the ongoing social transformation (Verma and Yan 1995; Cooke 2005).

Trade Unions as "Transmission Belts"

Chinese trade unions act as "transmission belts" between the party-state and workers (Ishii 2010, 1). On the one hand, trade unions serve the "top-down" function of mobilizing workers for labor production on behalf of the state. Taylor, Kai, and Qi (2003, 40) suggest that, although trade unions are theoretically autonomous public organs formed by the Chinese working class, they are, in practice, under the monopolistic control of the party-state, effectively functioning as an "arm of the Party." Significantly, according to the Trade Union Law, trade unions in enterprises, institutions, and government agencies should "abide by the leadership of the Communist Party of China, and conduct their work independently and voluntarily in accordance with the Trade Union Charter" (article 4).[3] In the Chinese publishing industry, trade unions are committed to transmitting the state's policies to editors, and supporting publishing houses to meet their production targets, thereby promoting the nationwide economic development and maintaining long-term social stability under the Party's leadership (Zhang 1994; Chen 2003).

On the other hand, trade unions also serve the "bottom-up" function of communicating workers' demands for improved working conditions and benefits to the state (Taylor, Kai, and Qi 2003). As Lee and Warner (2007, 65) remark, one of the guiding principles of trade unions is to harmonize the state's policies with the workers' need for better protection of their interests at a time when the majority of Chinese workers are losing their previously privileged political and economic status due to "marketization" and "desocialization."

Judging from my interviews, in both the Shanghai Science and Technology Publishing House and the Shanghai Education Publishing House, trade unions are actively organizing many social activities to celebrate traditional Chinese holidays—such as the Chinese New Year, the Mid-autumn Festival, and the Double Ninth Festival—as well as distributing gift cards and transportation subsidies to both senior and junior editors in the publishing house. More importantly, according to Jin (2010), who has worked as a union official in the Shanghai Science and Technology Publishing House for more than thirty years, trade unions have performed four other major social functions in addition to organizing social activities and distributing social welfare benefits:

In accordance with the regulations of both the Labor Law (effective in 1995) and the Trade Union Law, trade unions in the publishing industry are currently organized around four major social functions designed to unite editors. These four major social functions are: protecting the legitimate interests, both material and cultural, and the political rights of editors, particularly their rights to work; mobilizing and organizing editors to take part in the country's social construction and reform, as well as to accomplish economic and social achievements; representing and organizing editors to enroll in the administration of the state and social affairs, and to participate in the democratic management of publishing houses; and educating editors to conform to socialist ideologies, as well as to expand their knowledge and enrich their cultural experiences. To conclude, the ultimate purpose of trade unions in the publishing industry is to protect the overall interests of the editors, promote the development of a socialist market economy, and strive for the realization of China's socialist modernization. (Jin 2010)

In recent years, Chinese trade unions have made progress in fulfilling their basic duty to safeguard the legitimate rights and interests of the working class under the Party's leadership, principally through their *direct* communications with employers and *indirect* communications with government officials at all levels, particularly in the Chinese publishing industry.

In their *direct* communications with employers, many trade unions in China's publishing industry have put forward the demands, opinions, and suggestions of editors and pushed for responses. As mentioned in chapter 3, editors are responsible for a large proportion of their own medical expenses, due to increasing marketization in the health care system, which helps the publishing houses alleviate their heavy social burdens (Du and Zhang 1995). According to the World Health Organization (2002), the state's withdrawal from providing free medicines and medical service to individuals caused the proportion of the medical expenses paid by individuals in China to grow from 53.3 percent in 1995 to 63.4 percent in 2000. In the Shanghai Science and Technology Publishing House, however, union officials engaged in *direct* communications with the leaders, and presented a petition signed by the editors, with the result that the leaders agreed to purchase supplementary health insurance from the China Life Insurance Company for every editor. The insurance covers 90 percent of the editors' total medical expenses, with a maximum reimbursement of 20,000 *yuan* annually. This reimbursement significantly relieves the economic pressure on editors at a time when the costs of medicines and medical service keep rising. As a result of such negotiations between the leaders and trade unions, many publishing houses in Shanghai are now buying supplementary health insurance for most of their editors.

When facing critical labor disputes, trade unions usually send reports to related government agencies, thus *indirectly* pressing them to take up their concerns. Even though government officials ultimately determine whether or not to accept the demands, opinions, and suggestions of trade unions, they are usually pressured to respond favorably. Trade unions at the regional level often assist local government agencies in drafting regulations and policies favorable to their own members' interests, and seek various forms of assistance from the local Party organs (Taylor, Kai, and Qi 2003). For instance, in the last three decades, a growing number of workers in many privately owned and some state-owned enterprises have been faced with the problems of delayed payment and nonpayment, due to bankruptcies, operational losses, and corrupted employers in their enterprises (Chan 1993). The problems of delayed payment and nonpayment are exacerbated due to the fact that employers unilaterally decide the wage levels, wage forms, and methods of payment, to the great disadvantage of the working class. According to the ACFTU (2000, 136), wages arrears in 1999 amounted to 36.37 billion *yuan* and were owed to 13.82 million workers, leading to massive labor disputes nationwide. In response, union officials at the regional level have sent reports and survey results on wages arrears among their members to the local government officials, pressuring the latter to issue regulations fixing acceptable wage-payment periods. Constant pressure from local trade unions led to the adoptions of the "Shanghai Enterprise Wage Payment Measure in 2003" and "Regulations of the Beijing Municipality on the Payment of Wages in 2004," both of which helped to secure the rights of employees to obtain remunerations and regulate wage payments (Zhao 2010).

In short, as public organs, trade unions in the publishing industry are bound to promulgate socialist ideology and follow the Party's leadership. At the same time, as representative organizations of editors, they are obliged to communicate the editors' concerns to powerful bureaucracies that make crucial economic decisions within publishing houses, as well as to government officials at all levels. Based on my analysis of both worker organizations and trade unions in the Chinese publishing industry, I conclude that they have gradually gained importance in the daily management of publishing houses, and have successfully represented editors' interests within a once heavily centralized planned economy. In the next section, I will concentrate on the duties and activities of the ACFTU, the sole national trade union federation of China, which leads all the Chinese trade unions as their "union center" (Hong and Ip 2007, 65).

The All-China Federation of Trade Unions

Founded on May 1, 1925, the ACFTU is a mass public organ formed by the Chinese working class on a voluntary basis, as a pro-communist trade union organization representing China's massive labor force. The ACFTU is the largest trade union in the world, claiming a total membership of more than 169.94 million workers at the end of 2006 (The International Center for Trade Union Rights 2005). Among them, 61.778 million of its members were women (36.4 percent of the total membership), and 40.978 million of its members were migrant workers (24.1 percent of the total membership). By 2006, 73.6 percent of Chinese workers belonged to the ACFTU. The ACFTU also seeks to strengthen and extend friendly and cooperative relations with trade union organizations from other countries, based on principles of independence, equality, mutual respect, and non-interference in each other's internal affairs.

According to the ACFTU charter, not only should trade union members in the same enterprise or institution be grouped under one umbrella organization, but trade union members in the same industrial branch of the national economy should be grouped under the same national industrial union (ACFTU 1953). As a result, the ACFTU is divided into ten national industrial unions, thirty-one provincial trade union federations, and 1.324 million grassroots trade union organizations. Ng and Warner (2000, 102) emphasize that "industrial unionism" is not only doctrinally consistent with Marxist-Leninist "socialist unionism," but it has become indispensable to the ACFTU leadership's attempts to consolidate the organization and solidarity of Chinese workers in the "grassroots" unit of the workplace.[4]

Since its establishment, the ACFTU, like other trade unions in China, has acted as a "transmission belt" between the party-state and workers (Ishii 2010, 1). On the one hand, to serve the "top-down" function of achieving the Party's goal of socialist construction, the ACFTU endeavors to mobilize workers' enthusiasm and encourage their efforts to take an active part in economic development, thus promoting nationwide economic growth. In addition to promoting economic construction on behalf of the Chinese working class, the ACFTU aims to "build a contingent team of well-educated and self-disciplined workers" who would constitute the main force in the development of socialist material and cultural civilization (Ng and Warner 1998). Accordingly, the ACFTU revised its constitution at the Twelfth People's National People's Congress in 1993, explicitly making both its structure and activities commensurate with the nation's goal of building "socialism with Chinese characteristics."

On the other hand, the ACFTU serves the "bottom-up" function of safeguarding the legitimate rights and interests of the working class, particularly those of laid-off workers. Since the state began economic reform of the public sector, both industrial and knowledge workers have been challenged by the problem of lay-offs (The Ministry of Labor and Social Security 2001). According to the State Council Information Office, this problem became more serious after China's entry into the World Trade Organization in 2001.

In response to the proposals initiated by the ACFTU, minimum wage and minimum living expense systems have been implemented by the central government, in order to provide laid-off workers unemployment compensation and guarantee them a basic living standard. When these two systems were first established, however, many laid-off workers were not able to gain access to the funds due to implementation problems (Tang 2001). In 2000, according to the National Bureau of Statistics and the Ministry of Labor and Social Security (2001, 67, 443), only 55 percent of unemployed workers received unemployment compensation, while the total number of unemployed workers reached 5.95 million. To solve these problems, the ACFTU has set up a nationwide network of service centers to offer advice to the jobless. It has also been very active in collaborating with Chinese trade unions at all levels, with the aim of offering laid-off workers with new employment opportunities. In its attempt to protect the interests of laid-off workers, the ACFTU has greatly improved its ability to:

1. integrate the re-employment of laid-off workers into the overall plan for national economic and social development;
2. improve the working body for re-employment and promoting re-employment work;
3. boost the reform of the social security system, thus guaranteeing the basic needs of laid-off workers;
4. intensify the supervision and combat the infringement of the workers' right to work. (Hong and Ip 2007, 68)

Through the protracted and unremitting efforts of the ACFTU, the re-employment rate of laid-off workers in some regions rose from 40 percent to 70 percent in the period between 2006 and 2008, even though sometimes the ACFTU served the interests of the state by fighting against workers who oppose state policies and practices.

The Labor Law

With the deepening of the social and economic reforms launched at the beginning of the 1980s, the ACFTU's top leadership has increasingly turned to legislative means to further its members' interests. The most far-reaching success was the implementation of China's first Labor Law in January 1995, after many years of heated debates and negotiations between the ACFTU and various political institutions, including the National People's Congress, the State Council, and the Central Committee of the CPC.

The Labor Law concentrates on the protection of workers' rights, regulating the number of work hours per week, the maximum amount of overtime work, the standard lay-off procedures, and the social welfare benefits of both the unemployed and retired (Li 2000). According to the Labor Law, workers' rights include both *individual* and *collective* rights. The *individual* rights of the working class include "the rights to be employed on an equal basis, choose occupations, obtain remunerations for labor, take rests, have holidays and leaves, receive labor safety and sanitation protection, get training in professional skills, enjoy social insurance and welfare treatment, and submit applications for settlement of labor disputes" (article 3).[5] The *collective* rights of the working class include the rights to participate in and organize trade unions; to take part in democratic management through workers' congresses and workers' representative assemblies in enterprises, institutions, or government agencies; and to negotiate and conclude collective contracts protecting the legitimate rights and interests of laborers on an equal footing with employers (Taylor, Kai, and Qi 2003). It is the provisions of the Labor Law that allow trade unions, especially the ACFTU, to safeguard the rights of workers and staff members.

At its core, the Labor Law promotes a clearly defined power balance between employers and workers, so as to ensure stable industrial relations, specifically concentrating on the handling of labor disputes (article 1).[6] It stipulates that both employers and laborers can appeal to *mediation* or *arbitration* in case of labor disputes (article 77).[7] Once a labor dispute occurs, the parties involved can appeal to the labor dispute *mediation* committee of their units for *mediation*. If the dispute cannot be settled through *mediation*, and one of the parties asks for *arbitration*, an application can be filed to a labor dispute *arbitration* committee for *arbitration*. According to articles 80 and 81 of the Labor Law, a labor dispute *mediation* committee is composed of the representatives of workers, employers, and trade unions.[8] According to the same articles, a labor dispute *arbitration* committee is composed of the representatives of labor administration departments, trade unions at the same level, and the employers. The chairmanship of the labor dispute *mediation* committee is held by a trade union representative, and that of the labor dispute *arbitration* committee is held by a representative of a labor administrative department. Through the implementation of the Labor Law, trade unions are playing an important role in labor disputes (Hong 2010).[9]

The Labor Law is a significant reform that offers workers great employment security and income protection. As Wang et al. (2009) argue, the Labor Law has energized many workers, who are now using the courts and the CPC-controlled trade unions to press their claims; however, it has not been implemented without problems. With its increasing autonomy, the local government has retained the power to adjust central policies and laws to local conditions; therefore, labor policies from the central government, laws promulgated by the National People's Congress, and regulations emanating from the ACFTU are easily thwarted and superseded at the regional level. For example, even though the Labor Law sets maximum working hours, at eight hours a day and forty-four hours a week, it is an open secret that many export-oriented enterprises violate this rule, often with the acquiescence of the local government (Benson and Zhu 2000).

It is important to note that despite the energy the ACFTU expends on crafting labor-related legislations, it does not possess the constitutional right to enact laws. Both in the processes of enacting and monitoring new laws, the ACFTU must subordinate itself to the Ministry of Labor and Social Security, which has the power to put legislative programs into effect within governmental systems (Perry 1995). As an autonomous organization formed by the working class and directly linked with the Central Committee of the CPC, the ACFTU has played an active role in protecting the interests of both the party-state and the working class. Due to its subordination to the Ministry of Labor and Social Security, however, the ACFTU is obliged to accommodate the interests of a variety of stakeholders, including the central government, large state-owned enterprises, and international corporations that sustain very strong economic ties to the central government (Cooke 2004). These obligations hinder its ability to safeguard and defend the interests of the working class, including knowledge workers in the publishing industry.

RETHINKING OF WORKER ORGANIZATIONS AND TRADE UNIONS

Worker organizations and trade unions in China have raised workers' educational levels, mediated labor disputes, and united the labor movement, thus representing and forwarding the rights and interests of the working class. Nevertheless, in the last section of this chapter, I will rethink the duties and functions that both worker organizations and trade unions perform in the reform era as their functions have also been under rapid and dramatic transformation since the beginning of current social reform. I will begin by examining the three major weaknesses of worker organizations and trade unions: their lack of substantial political and economic power, their conflicting obligations to uphold the interests of both the state and the workers, and their reluctance to reshape their guiding philosophies and promote personnel system reform. Due to these limitations, labor unrest in China has been on the rise. In this context, I will suggest that new information technologies, changes inside the ACFTU, and the emergence of labor nongovernmental organizations may aid the working class in its attempts to better represent its legitimate rights and interests.

Limitations of Worker Organizations and Trade Unions

Three major limitations of worker organizations and trade unions are addressed in this section.

First, due to the fact that they lack substantial political and economic power, neither worker organizations nor trade unions are the workers' first choice for assistance in times of trouble. The workers doubt that these organizations can function autonomously, protecting and expanding the political and economic interests of the working class independent of state and/or employer control (Wang 2001). On the contrary, these organizations have been accused of being unrepresentative and powerless, both in their relations with large state-owned enterprises and private or foreign enterprises (Guan 2001).

In the pre-reform era, the state played a decisive role in worker organization and trade union activities. Malcolm Warner (1995) argues that the state was virtually omnipotent in the planned economy, because it implemented important rules and regulations on changes in the workplace, such as wage reform, bonus distribution, working conditions, and social welfare benefits. Officials in both worker organizations and trade unions at various levels were appointed by the state, and both their promotion and demotion were managed by the leading administrative cadres in the Party organs. At the same time, the Central Committee of the CPC also ensured that each worker organization or trade union was under the tight surveillance and control of the Party organs at the corresponding bureaucratic level (Chan 2006). In short, the "top-down" function of transmitting Party's directives had substantially suppressed the "bottom-up" function of bettering working conditions and workers' benefits.

In response to the difficulties experienced by workers in current social reform, the Trade Union Law was amended in 2001, thus replacing the law enacted in the early 1950s, in order to better oversee and advance the interests of the working class. Nevertheless, worker organizations and trade unions have become increasingly dependent on employers in the market economy, particularly in China's publishing industry (Warner 2001). In his interview, Yu, a union official working in the Shanghai Education Publishing House, remarked that:

> In our publishing house, leaders (employers) rather than editors (workers) are gaining growing power in organizing and allocating personnel; dominating and controlling the process of industrial relations; and distributing wages, bonuses, and social welfare benefits among editors. These changes have been accompanied by the ascending social status of the leaders in the publishing house. As a consequence, not only are worker organizations and trade unions predominantly regulated by the leaders, but the social and political organizations of the leaders, for example management and employer associations, have become more influential than those of the editors. (Yu 2010)

The second problem is that officials in both worker organizations and trade unions have realized that, in the market economy, they are greatly

hampered by conflicting obligations to uphold both the state's reform policies and workers' interests (Chan 2000b), and their access to the workforce
has declined in proportion to the shrinking importance of the state-owned
sector in the economy—even though they still possess a strong presence in
some traditional state-owned industries, such as the railway industry (Cooke
2000). Besides, Liu and Li (2001) state that employers in the private sector,
where the functions of worker organizations and trade unions are not clearly
defined according to the Labor Law, have unilaterally determined labor standards, work rules, employment conditions, and the management and settlement of labor disputes.[10] This unilateralism has seriously disadvantaged
workers and undermined the mutual interests of employers and employees in
the private sector.

In the Chinese publishing industry, it is observed that worker organizations and trade unions in some publishing houses and newspaper agencies
have been increasingly organized around the interests of leaders instead of
around those of editors (Ding et al. 2002). Over the past few decades, some
union officials have established closer relationships with leaders, even admit-
ting them to membership in trade unions. As Sheehan (1999) suggests, some
union officials take pride in representing the interests of the leaders rather
than those of the editors, with some even going so far as to charge editors on
behalf of the leaders in labor disputes.

Third, according to Ng and Warner (1998), despite the pressure to harmonize with ongoing social marketization and privatization processes, both
worker organizations and trade unions are reluctant to reshape their guiding
philosophies and promote personnel system reform.

Reshaping the Guiding Philosophies

Worker organizations and trade unions maintain "democratic centralism" as
their guiding philosophy, thus functioning as the Party's popular organs for
organizing the masses (Hong 2010, 67). Officials in both worker organizations and trade unions are often in their posts not because they are the best
candidates for their jobs, but because they have been "unsuccessful" in their
previous managerial posts. Based on my surveys and interviews, most chief
officials of worker organizations and trade unions in the Chinese publishing
industry are elected from party secretaries, enterprise managers, or other
senior managerial staff. As a result, the independence and effectiveness of
worker organizations and trade unions remain highly questionable (Chan
1998).

Promoting Personnel System Reform

The vertical command structure of worker organizations, which linked those
at the national level with those at the regional level in the pre-reform era, has

been weakened by the processes of economic decentralization and privatization. In the publishing sector, for example, the PAS has been active in offering professional training sessions for editors in Shanghai's publishing circle, as well as sponsoring book fairs to enhance the communication between local publishers and those from other countries and regions, rather than focusing on implementing the policies and regulations passed by the PAC. While the publishing industry in Shanghai is developing rapidly due to the efforts of the PAS, the latter's decreasing dependence on the PAC has loosened the vertical command structure of worker organizations.

In addition to the three weaknesses aforementioned, both worker organizations and trade unions are also criticized by acting as welfare relief agents in order to mitigate worker discontent. This change of focus is strongly promoted by the party-state, especially when a growing number of petitions have been presented directly in front of the central government. Besides, in many enterprises and institutions, trade unions are no longer formed on a completely voluntary basis. Instead, workers are urged to join trade unions as part of routine workplace procedure, which violates the nature of trade unions, as stipulated in the Trade Union Law. Finally, demand from workers in the private sector to establish trade unions remains comparatively low. Many privately owned enterprises, without union organizations, themselves carry out the functions usually performed by trade unions. Migrant workers in these privately owned enterprises are not familiar with the concept of workplace representation, and they frequently stereotype trade unions as ineffective and redundant organizations compared to the Party organs (Cooke 2002).

Labor Unrest

Generally, in the planned economy, the state owned and operated massive enterprises that were its primary source of revenue, and it controlled both labor standards and daily work process. At the same time, however, it offered the working class lifetime employment, pensions, health care benefits, and subsidized housing (Perry and Selden 2010). As a result, collective labor actions were not common. So (2009) asserts that the welfare role of the state has largely disappeared with the implementation of social reform. In other words, for both industrial and knowledge workers, with the declining political and economic power of the state, their incomes, social security and welfare benefits, and the prestige that was once offered by the state, have been jeopardized. According to Naughton (2007, 35), the seemingly harmonious management-labor relationship in the planned economy has been replaced with one that is characterized by "conflicting interests, rising disputes, and increasing inequality in contractual arrangements between management and labor." As the state places increasing emphasis on improving efficiency and less on social justice and equality, the interests of the workers are sacrificed to those of capital and management. In this sense, Chinese workers collectively are enduring a dramatic decline in their political and social status, as well as significant weakening of their economic interests, resulting in major alternations in their class consciousness.

Meanwhile, workers also have difficulties protecting their rights and interests as "an independent social class or by collective force" (Taylor, Chang, and Qi 2003, 89) due to the pressure and limitations placed on worker organizations and trade unions by both government officials and enterprise employers. There is a growing feeling among many Chinese workers that they have no effective institutional channels through which to express discontent or complain about unfair treatment. In response, the Chinese working class, particularly industrial workers, has actively engaged in many types of collective labor action, including group petitions, slowdowns, strikes (illegal since 1982), acts of sabotage, and physical violence against managerial personnel, all of which is reported to have increased at a rapid pace over the past three decades.[11]

The deepening commodification of labor in the reform era has been accompanied by three rising tides of labor unrest in China. The first wave of large-scale collective labor actions was carried out at the beginning of the 1990s, primarily by workers laid off from state-owned enterprises (Silver and Zhang 2009). During that period, state-owned enterprises abandoned the previous work-unit system, and carried out massive lay-offs as part of an effort to promoting production effectiveness and competing with their international counterparts; both of these decisions led to widespread protests in "China's rustbelt" (Lee 2007c). As Pringle (2002) remarks, in the early 1990s, newspapers published almost weekly reports of collective labor actions, such as a demonstration demanding pensions; a railway line being blocked by angry, unpaid workers; and collective legal action against illegal employer behavior, such as body searches. According to the Ministry of Labor and Social Security, collective labor actions peaked in 1993, with ten thousand collective labor actions, frequently in the form of strikes, involving 730,000 protestors. These figures represented an increase of 900 percent in collective actions from those of the early 1980s (Ding and Warner 1999), and led to the enactment of the Company Law in 1994, which prohibits massive lay-offs in state-owned enterprises.

The second wave of collective labor actions was mainly organized by young migrant factory workers drawn to the coastal areas from the countryside (Silver 2003) after China's entry into the WTO. As China has become more integrated into the global political economy, its own economy boomed with the constant influx of capital from foreign countries. Unfortunately, this boom was achieved at the expense of serious deterioration of working conditions for the Chinese working class, particularly for migrant workers in the private sector. Considered a cheap and flexible source of labor in the new free market, migrant workers are faced with violations of shop-floor labor, occupational safety, and health standards, as well as threats to their rights to work (Chan 2001). Moreover, factories dictate their terms of employment, and require "deposits" from migrant workers beginning work in the factories. If workers quit without the permission of management before their contracts expire, or if they are fired, they forfeit the "deposits." Therefore, most migrant workers are bound to their factories because they cannot afford to lose the "deposits," which are normally between half a month to a month's wage, even though the working conditions in these factories are terrible. As a result of these deplorable conditions, "unprecedented series of [strikes] and walk-outs" have hit factories in China: there were 6,767 collective labor actions, involving 251,268 workers in 2000; and 8,247 collective labor actions, involving 259,445 workers in 2003 (Cody 2004). In 2004, millions of migrant workers went on strike in many factories in China's Pearl River Delta, protesting against their wages and working conditions. White (2007) remarks that the number of cases brought by workers before the official labor *arbitration* committees has increased steadily, from 78,000 per year in 1994 to more than 800,000 per year in 2003.

The third wave of collective labor actions occurred in the aftermath of recent global economic turndown. At least twenty million Chinese workers are facing job losses after the closures of tens of thousands of labor-intensive, export-oriented factories due to the global financial crisis, accompanied by a surge of collective labor disputes, with each case on average involving twenty-three people (Xinhua News 2008). Even a large number of industrial workers in profitable enterprises, such as electronics and manufacturing factories, were subject to low pay, grueling hours, and sometimes martial workplace rules. For example, seventeen workers have attempted to commit suicide at the Foxconn Technology Group in Shenzhen, due to intense work pressure, and fourteen of them died. Workers at this factory have to work twelve hours a day, six days a week. They must wear a uniform and a badge in the factory to be easily identified, as they are not allowed to walk outside of the authorized areas within the factory. Also, they must live in dormitory compounds watched by guards (Blanch 2010).

A typical case of collective labor actions in this period was the strike at Honda's Foshan Factory in 2010 (Chatterjee 2010; Tabuchi 2010). About two thousand workers called a strike to demand better pay and better working conditions. The military-style administration and harsh working conditions at Honda's Foshan Factory has made its workers, most of whom are in their early twenties with little or no social support, work on highly repetitive assembly line tasks for up to twelve hours without a break. In addition, the wages of the company's Japanese employees in China were fifty times those of the striking Chinese workers. After nearly two weeks of intense negotiations, workers agreed to resume work after they were assured that their basic wages would increase by 366 *yuan*—a typical Honda industrial worker earns 1,000 *yuan* a month—in addition to receiving other allowances and concessions, and fair chances to get promoted. The increasing costs of labor in China reflect the growing tension between workers and foreign companies, which rely on China to provide both a source of cheap labor and a fast-growing market.

Identifying labor problems as the biggest threat to social and political stability, the central government started to move away from a single-minded emphasis on attracting foreign capital and fostering economic growth at all costs to the idea of a "new development mode" aimed at reducing inequalities among classes and regions in pursuit of a "harmonious society" (The People's Daily 2005). In 2007, President Hu Jintao made an important speech on safeguarding the legitimate rights and interests of workers in the reform era (Xinhua News 2008). The new Labor Law was enacted in 2008, in an attempt to achieve a new balance between workers and employers by enhancing job security, putting significant restrictions on employers' rights to hire and fire workers without causes, and strengthening the roles of both worker organizations and trade unions. Particularly in the Chinese publishing industry, the new Labor Contract Law has shifted bargaining power in favor of editors, raised awareness of rights among editors, and ushered in a new era of higher costs of production. In addition, the ACFTU amended its constitution in 2003 to make the protection of workers' rights (including editors) a priority, in an attempt to halt and reduce rising labor unrest and maintain social stability (Chan and Kwan 2003).

Prospects: How to Better Represent Workers' Rights and Interests

In this section, I will concentrate on three approaches, through which workers' rights and interests, including those of editors, can be better represented. First, the latest technological developments, particularly the expansion of the Internet, have allowed the working class to become more tightly connected to trade unions (Lucore 2004). Workers are not only able to access a large amount of online information about trade unions, workers' activities, and labor disputes, but can bond with workers in different professions by sharing common problems, interests, and prospects, thereby promoting solidarity among different groups of workers. Second, recent changes have been taking place inside the ACFTU, including the expansion of union branches at the local level (Zheng 2004), direct elections for local union officials (Howell 2006), and the enforcement of the *tripartite consultative procedure* in the workplace (Shen and Benson 2008). Third, many labor nongovernmental organizations have emerged in China, such as the Chinese Working Women

Network (CWWN) and the China Labor Bulletin (CLB). In practice, these organizations have improved communication among "progressive domestic social forces, global labor and civil society organizations, and Chinese workers" (Zhao and Duffy 2007, 40), further empowering workers in labor relations with employers and the state.

Technological Developments

New information technologies have made unions much more approachable for the working class. With rapid technological developments, particularly with the widespread expansion of the Internet, workers are able to gather different kinds of information, communicate horizontally across official structures, and easily post their comments and publish their own information about labor-related happenings on their blogs (Lucore 2004). For example, at the time of writing, 65,801,602 visitors have launched the homepage of the ACFTU, which offers the latest news and updates important published files of the ACFTU. Specifically, the "Statistics" section under the "Document" column covers a broad spectrum of topics, including the construction of trade union organizations, education and training among trade union cadres, labor contracts and collective contracts, trade unions' legal work, and international exchanges conducted by trade unions every year (ACFTU 2007). Additionally, workers are welcome to post their feedback on the current activities organized by the ACFTU to the "Window on Workers" column, which has substantially strengthened the interaction between workers and the ACFTU.

New information technologies have also promoted solidarity among different groups of workers. Perry (1995) argues that internal differences within the working class have often provoked the resentment of one group of workers against another, such as contract workers against permanent workers, migrant workers against local workers in the cities, and workers from one locality against those from another. The differences between workers cannot be easily eliminated, and it is difficult to convince them that they share common problems, interests, and prospects. With the introduction of new information technologies, however, workers in all professions can be connected by participating in online labor issue discussions, joining in the same QQ cluster to share their work experiences, and logging on various labor forums to respond to the current labor disputes (Qiu 2010). For example, "Editors Online," a popular online labor forum launched in 1996, has successfully offered a platform for editors to post their problems and seek assistance, report breaking news on domestic and foreign labor issues, and update information on labor disputes nationwide. Thanks to "Editors Online" and other online labor forums mainly serving the interests of knowledge workers in China's publishing industry, the class consciousness of editors is steadily being built.

Changes Inside the All-China Federation of Trade Unions

The rising tides of labor disputes have provided the ACFTU with more direct incentives to expand union branches (Zheng 2004). One of the most significant signs of progress is the ACFTU's requirement that any basic-level trade union committee with a membership of twenty-five or more should be registered under the district trade union (The Workers' Daily 2009). Meanwhile, as Sun (2009a) remarks, lower-level trade unions continue to expand their membership by targeting migrant workers in small-scale and privately owned enterprises. Essentially, the ACFTU has issued an urgent directive to prevent the loss of membership in the face of large numbers of jobless and returning migrant workers. As a result, nearly 50 percent of China's migrant workers had become union numbers by 2009 (Coolloud News 2009).

In addition to the expansion of local union branches, the ACFTU also promotes holding direct elections for union officials at the regional level. For example, the ACFTU in Guangdong province began holding direct elections for local union officials in 1986. Howell (2006) claims that by early 2004, one-third of all trade unions in foreign-invested and privately owned enterprises in Guangdong province had chairs and committees directly elected by workers. My interviews with both editors and union officials in the Shanghai Science and Technology Publishing House suggest that union officials directly elected by the editors are playing an important role in the daily management of the publishing house, by participating in policy decisions; jointly approving the editors' promotions; and obtaining access to all its financial, administrative, and political information. As Jin, a union official in the Shanghai Science and Technology Publishing House, mentioned in her interview:

> There is one chief union official and seven other union officials in the publishing house. Every union official is responsible for contacting eight to ten editors, and sending regular reports to chief union official. We, as both union officials and editors, work together with other editors. Only chief union official deals with union administrative affairs on a full-time basis. Directly elected once every two years by editors and staff members, we enjoy a very high reputation inside the publishing house because, as union officials, we have dedicated ourselves to making editors' voices heard in high-rank administrative meetings. It is critical to mention that, at the present time, the suggestions proposed by chief union official, in most cases, are taken seriously by the leaders. Also, any policy regarding editors and staff members in the publishing house should be approved by chief union official before its implementation. In a nutshell, as union officials, we endeavor to represent and safeguard the rights and interests of the employed—editors rather than the leaders, in a most extensive way. (Jin 2010)

Although it is difficult to determine how much impact the direct election of union officials has had in building an independent trade union movement in China, there is no doubt that it has created an opening for changes in the union structure, and potentially in the relationship between trade unions and the party-state.

Warner and Ng (1999, 307) argue that Chinese union officials have drawn very limited attention to collective bargaining, due to "their serious lack of the necessary back-up bargaining resources, skills, and capacities." However, in 2002, the ACFTU issued a directive, addressing invigorating efforts to the establishment of a nationwide *tripartite consultative procedure*, referred to as "collective bargaining" by the central government and the ACFTU, to handle labor disputes (Shen and Benson 2008, 231). In the Chinese publishing sector, the *tripartite consultative procedure* involves trade unions, leaders, and the government, with all parties contributing to the development of labor standards and the protection of editors' rights and interests through voluntary interaction and dialogue. As Hong Yu (2011) observes, over the past few years, the *tripartite consultative procedure* has been playing an active role in the settlement of labor disputes, the formation of labor regulations, and collective bargaining among editors. For example, the ACFTU demanded that either publishing houses or newspaper agencies should avoid job cuts and wage cuts, and follow the procedure of collective consultation before making job reduction decisions. Leaders are also required to obtain consent from trade unions through the *tripartite consultative procedure* before hammering out any emergency plan. In order to improve editors' abilities to undertake collective bargaining on wages, under the current *tripartite consultative procedure*, trade unions have:

1. set up an office for wage negotiations, thus providing an institutional framework for such work;
2. formulated policies for wage negotiations;
3. provided grassroots trade unions and enterprises with information about relevant laws and policies, guidelines for annual wage increases, and labor costs;
4. extended specific assistance to enterprises, setting good examples and providing guidance. (Fang 2004, 8–9)

As a response to both the growing incidence of labor disputes and the ongoing social and economic transformations within China, the *tripartite consultative procedure* serves as the cornerstone of collective bargaining, and has the potential to incite a new wave of working-class solidarity, particularly among editors.

The Emergence of Labor Nongovernmental Organizations

With the help of international academic institutions, as well as labor and human rights organizations, many labor nongovernmental organizations have emerged in China. Zhao and Duffy (2007, 40) claim that these organizations are actively promoting communication between "progressive domestic social forces, global labor and civil society organizations, and Chinese workers," thereby empowering workers in their labor relations with employers and the state. Among these nongovernmental organizations, the CWWN and the CLB are the two most influential ones.

The CWWN was set up in 1996, as a nongovernmental organization with the mission of promoting betterment for the lives of Chinese migrant women workers and developing feminist awareness of workers' empowerment. In other words, it attempts to defend labor rights; build feminist consciousness; strengthen occupational health and safety; and offer alternative socioeconomic life for labor organizers, feminists, university professors, researchers, social workers, cultural activists, workers, and students. Ngai and Chan (2004) claim that the Cultural Women Workers' Center, affiliated to the CWWN, is one of its most important projects in China. Located in Shenzhen, the center provides migrant women workers, including female workers in the publishing industry, with a cultural and physical space, apart from their workplaces and dormitories, through reading groups, singing and dancing groups, movie sharing networks, poem writing groups, handicraft making networks, and other activities. The CWWN also strives to cooperate with concerned organizations to facilitate self-empowerment among Chinese women knowledge workers. To that end, the CWWN has been participating in a great number of conferences and workshops at both the local and the international level, such as the Chinese Labor Seminar, the Fifth East Asian Women's Forum, and the Ethical Trading Initiative Conference.

Another influential labor nongovernmental organization is the CLB, which was founded in Hong Kong in 1994. Having grown from a small monitoring and research group into a proactive outreach organization, the CLB seeks to defend and promote the rights of workers in China through extensive links and wide-ranging cooperative programs with labor groups, law firms, and academics throughout China, as well as with the international labor movement. Additionally, the CLB has produced an extensive series of research reports in both Chinese and English that provide an in-depth analysis and overview of some of the most important labor issues in China, including the workers' movement, migrant workers, child labor, and coal mining accidents. In 2003, according to Caryl (2010), the CLB launched a Labor Rights Litigation Program, with the purpose of identifying cases of labor rights abuse, providing legal advice and support to the workers concerned, and helping workers seek justice through the court system. There is no denying that this program has offered valuable legal assistance to the working class, including editors in the Chinese publishing industry when they meet different kinds of difficulties.

CONCLUSION

Along with the transition from a socialist planned economy to a reformed liberalized market economy, both industrial workers and knowledge workers, employed in state-owned enterprises, private or foreign firms, and joint ventures, have been stripped of the privileged political and economic status that they used to enjoy under the state socialist system. As Sargeson (2001) argues, the Chinese population has been increasingly polarized into winners and losers. Most workers have been the losers of the ongoing social reform, becoming more vulnerable to material insecurities and productivity pressure due to the rise of the contingent employment. Therefore, in this chapter, it is not only essential to examine how Chinese media workers, particularly editors, have benefited from labor convergence—worker organizations and trade unions as its two main patterns—but more importantly, to understand how the working class, including both industrial workers and knowledge workers, is organized to protect and expand its rights and interests when workers are increasingly subject to strict directives and productivity demands, as well as tight control of the labor process, at a time when their wages, social welfare benefits, and pensions have considerably declined.

In accordance with labor convergence worldwide, Chinese workers have formed both worker organizations and trade unions to represent their rights and interests and regulate the employer-employee relationship. As mass organizations of the working class formed by workers and staff members on a voluntary basis, both worker organizations and trade unions coordinate the interests of three parties—the party-state, enterprises, and workers. In the Chinese media industry, based on the findings from my interviews with editors, leaders, government officials, and union officials, I conclude that both worker organizations and trade unions have been engaged in representing the legitimate rights and interests of the working class through various means under the Party's leadership. In China's publishing sector, not only have trade unions (as state apparatuses) taken different measures to adapt editors to the labor and economic policies of the state, but they have also (as labor organizations) greatly improved their ability to conduct *direct* communications with editors and *indirect* communications with government officials at all levels, thus offering workers better working conditions and benefits (Chen 2003).

There are, however, several major weaknesses of worker organizations and trade unions in China as both of them are changing their structures, functions, and modes of management along with the current social transformation. According to social critics, such as Elizabeth Perry (1995), Martin Whyte (1999), and Sally Sargeson (2001), both worker organizations and trade unions have failed to fully represent workers' interests because they serve the interests of the state more than those of the workers. In most cases, their obligations to uphold the state's reform policies and the interests of the working class largely contradict. In the private sector in particular, the employers have unilaterally determined the labor standards, workplace rules and regulations, employment conditions, and the procedures for management and settlement of labor disputes, thereby severely disadvantaging workers and undermining the mutual interests of employers and employees. As a result, labor movements are on the rise.

This leads one to ask how the legitimate rights and interests of the working class could be further protected in such a way that workers could better deal with the challenges brought about by government officials, state-owned enterprise managers, and/or employers in the private sector. Based on my surveys and interviews in China's publishing industry, I argue that there are three plausible approaches: opportunities brought about by the latest technological developments, the changes inside the ACFTU, and the growth of labor nongovernment organizations. The next chapter, the concluding chapter, will summarize the basic findings of this book, with a summary of its theoretical, methodological, and substantive findings followed by a discussion of suggestions for future research.

NOTES

1. It is worth pointing out that even though worker organizations are public organs autonomously formed by Chinese workers, their training sessions are guided by a number of laws and regulations issued by the state. Such laws and regulations include the Labor Law (1995), the Education Law (1995), the Enterprise Law (1998), the Higher Education Law of China (1998), and the Enterprise Employee Training Regulations (1996). These laws and regulations are supplemented by regional and local training regulations of the government, as well as by the training policies of the corresponding worker organizations.

2. According to the Trade Union Law, "All manual and mental workers in enterprises, institutions, and government departments within the territory of China who rely on wages or salaries as their main sources of incomes, irrespective of their nationality, race, gender, occupation, religious belief or educational background, have the right to organize or join trade unions according to law. No organizations or individuals shall obstruct or restrict them" (article 3).

3. According to the Trade Union Law, "Trade unions shall observe and safeguard the Constitution, take it as the fundamental criterion for their activities, take economic development as the central task, uphold the socialist road, the people's democratic dictatorship, leadership by the Communist Party of China, and Marxist-Leninism, Mao Zedong Thought and Deng Xiaoping Theory, persevere in reform and the open policy, and conduct their work independently in accordance with the Constitution of trade unions. The National Congress of Trade Unions formulates or amends the Constitution of Trade Unions of the People's Republic of China, which shall not contravene the Constitution of the People's Republic of China or other laws. The State protects the legitimate rights and interests of trade unions from violation" (article 4).

4. The ten national industrial unions are: the National Committee of the Chinese Educational, Scientific, Cultural, Medical, and Sports Workers' Union; the National Committee of the Chinese Seamen and Construction Workers' Union; the National Committee of the Chinese Energy and Chemical Workers' Union; the National Committee of the Chinese Machinery, Metallurgical, and Building Material Workers' Union; the National Committee of the Chinese Defense Industry, Postal, and Telecommunications Workers' Union; the National Committee of the Chinese Financial, Commercial, Light Industry, Textile, and Tobacco Workers' Union; the National Committee of the Chinese Agricultural, Forestry, and Water Conservancy Workers' Union; the All-China Federation of Railway Workers' Unions; the National Committee of the Chinese Aviation Workers' Union; and the National Committee of the Chinese Banking Workers' Union.

5. According to the Labor Law, "Laborers have the right to be employed on an equal basis, choose occupations, obtain remunerations for labor, take rests, have holidays and leaves, receive labor safety and sanitation protection, get training in professional skills, enjoy social insurance and welfare treatment, and submit applications for settlement of labor disputes, and other labor rights stipulated by law. Laborers shall fulfill their tasks of labor, improve their professional skills, follow rules on labor safety and sanitation, observe labor discipline and professional ethics" (article 3).

6. According to the Labor Law, "This Law is hereby formulated in accordance with the Constitution in order to protect the legitimate rights and interests of laborers, readjust labor relationship, establish and safeguard the labor system suiting the socialist market economy, and promote economic development and social progress" (article 1).

7. According to the Labor Law, "In case of labor disputes between the employer and laborers, the parties concerned can apply for *mediation* or *arbitration*, bring the case to courts, or settle them through consultation. The principle of *mediation* is applicable to *arbitration* and court procedures" (article 77).

8. According to the Labor Law, "A labor dispute *mediation* committee can be set up inside the employer. This committee shall be composed of workers' representatives, the representatives of the employer, and trade union representatives. The chairmanship of this committee shall be held by a trade union representative. Agreements reached on labor disputes through *mediations* shall be implemented by the parties involved" (article 80). Also, "Labor dispute *arbitration* committees shall be composed of the representatives of labor administrative departments, representatives from trade unions at the same level, and the employer's representatives. The chairmanship of such a committee shall be held by the representative of a labor administrative department" (article 81).

9. Both the "Regulations on the Settlement of Labor Disputes in Enterprises," effective in 1993, and "Labor Dispute Mediation and Arbitration Law," effective in 2008, comprehensively explain both the *mediation* and *arbitration* procedures for labor disputes. Both of them are considered as effective ways to adjust capital-labor relationships in China.

10. Levine (1997) argues that in the private sector, union membership levels are extremely low, and union activities are less popular—only about 30 percent of private organizations have established unions to offer workers better working conditions and benefits. It is also worth pointing out that even state laws and regulations designed to protect workers are often ignored or violated in the private sector. Therefore, industrial conflicts in the private sector have multiplied in recent years.

11. Critically, Chinese workers do not have the right to strike according to the current Constitution. Such right, which had originally been granted to workers, was removed in the 1982 Constitution. Therefore, neither the Labor Law nor the Trade Union Law allows workers to go on strike.

Conclusion

Throughout this book, I have examined the challenges confronting knowledge workers in China's publishing industry—challenges brought about by current media reform and social transformation, resulting (in turn) from the technological developments of the information age and China's increasing integration into the global political economy—using a critical political economic approach. This project was informed by my original case studies of the Shanghai Science and Technology Publishing House and the Shanghai Education Publishing House, which provided primary insight into the interrelated processes of *commodification, structuration,* and *spatialization* in the Chinese publishing industry.

SUMMARY OF THE BOOK

I began by exploring the media *commodification* process—characterized by the transformation of publishing houses from public institutions to companies, the formation of publishing conglomerates, and the widespread expansion of private and foreign investment in the Chinese publishing industry—which has left Chinese editors torn between the need to conform to the political restrictions and propaganda functions of the state, and the obligation to generate profit for their companies. In other words, these workers are expected to serve the political interests of the state, while also expanding democracy and promoting political and social reforms. In addition to negotiating this double-bind, Chinese editors must also deal with a range of problems springing from the *commodification* process, including contingent employment, deteriorating working conditions, declining social welfare benefits, and intense work pressure (e.g., changes in their work hours, locations, duties, and their monthly incomes).

155

I then turned to explore the *structuration* process—characterized by the many technological, political, and economic transformations that have accompanied the *commodification* process—which has led to radical changes in class relations and power dynamics, thus resulting in five critical problems for Chinese editors. First, the rise of new technologies has resulted in the devaluation of professional knowledge and skills upon which editors had once prided themselves, leading many to upgrade their qualifications and enhance their professional skills by pursuing continuing education. Second, the media marketization process has proved difficult to reconcile with the Party principle, and editors, as well as other knowledge workers in China's media industry, have been forced to cultivate new forms of public/civic media that walk the fine line between serving the interests of the party-state and generating profit. Third, the application of market principle to the social welfare system has led to the decline of state- and employer-provided protections, including both pensions and health care, for Chinese editors, resulting in pressure for those workers to buy private medical insurance and to save a large portion of their incomes for the future. Fourth, the dismantling of the work-unit system has left editors increasingly dependent on market forces and decreasingly assured of job security, subject to contingent employment rather than lifetime employment contracts and uncertain performance evaluations to which their salaries and promotions are tied. Fifth, social stratification within the publishing industry has produced problematic and often exploitative power relationships. Leaders in the publishing industry have separated from the mass of editors, thus forming an independent social stratum that holds decision-making power over the distribution of bonuses, the allocation of social welfare benefits, and the management of human resources. Therefore, Chinese editors have been forced to establish intimate personal connections with the leaders, if they hope to be successful in the recruitment process or in their applications for Party membership. In addition, divisions have developed between editors, with junior editors being pressured to sign shorter-term contracts, receiving more challenging work assignments, enduring intense work pressure, and getting fewer chances for promotion than senior editors. As a result, junior editors in large publishing houses have joined with worker organizations and trade unions to negotiate increases in their monthly incomes and limits on their work hours and monthly workload from the leaders.

I then turned from the structural changes within Chinese society to examine the global trends that have contributed to the media *spatialization* process: globalization, neoliberalism, and the global division of labor. With China's integration into the global political economy, Chinese editors have been forced to accept that their labor has become a commodity, tradable at a price set by existing labor markets, and increasingly exchangeable and replaceable (McKercher and Mosco 2010; Mosco 2009). Instead of staying in the same publishing houses, Chinese editors must now prepare for actual or potential layoffs. In addition, they are finding themselves trapped between the "twin modalities of the neoliberal governmentality" (Ong 2006, 3), and subject to the growing tension within a propaganda-commercial model split between the forces of market competition and strict party control. Furthermore, the global division of labor has meant that many Chinese editors have been marginalized to perform simple tasks that require few technical and professional skills. Thus, they have lost their privileged positions as "master" of the country, and must deal with decreasing predictability in and control over their work and careers (Rocca 2003).

After examining the impacts of the *commodification*, *structuration*, and *spatialization* processes in the Chinese publishing industry, I then explored the ways in which Chinese editors are responding to them. I found that both worker organizations and trade unions, under the Party's leadership, have been engaged in representing the legitimate rights and interests of the working class, including both industrial and knowledge workers. Although, as state apparatuses, trade unions are responsible for adapting workers to the labor and economic policies of the state, they have been successful in defending workers' interests by engaging in *direct* communications with employers and *indirect* communications with government officials at all levels. While trade unions serve the "top-down" function of mobilizing workers for labor production on behalf of the state, they also serve the "bottom-up" function of communicating workers' demands for improved working conditions and benefits to the state (Taylor, Kai, and Qi 2003). As Lee and Warner (2007, 65) remark, one of the guiding principles of trade unions is to harmonize the state's policies with the workers' need for better protection of their interests at a time when the majority of Chinese workers are losing their previous political and economic status due to "marketization" and "de-socialization." In the past three decades, however, labor unrest has been on the rise due to their failure to do this effectively, as well as their lack of substantial political and economic power, and their reluctance to reshape their guiding philosophies and promote personnel system reform (Wang 2001).

I then suggested plausible solutions to the problems of Chinese editors, and generally of media workers, arguing that new information technologies, changes inside the All-China Federation of Trade Unions (ACFTU), and the emergence of labor nongovernmental organizations may aid the working class (including editors) in its attempts to better represent its legitimate rights and interests. First, the latest technological developments, particularly the expansion of the Internet, have led to tighter connections between working class individuals and trade unions, as well as between workers in different organizations and professions (Lucore 2004). Workers are not only able to access a large amount of online information about trade unions, workers' activities, and labor disputes, but can bond with workers in different organizations and professions by sharing common problems, interests, and prospects. Second, recent changes inside the ACFTU, including the expansion of union branches at the local level (Zheng 2004), direct elections for local union officials (Howell 2006), and the enforcement of the *tripartite consultative procedure* in the workplace (Shen and Benson 2008) have created an opening for further reform in the union structure, and potentially in the relationship between trade unions and the party-state to better represent workers' rights and interests. Third, many labor nongovernmental organizations have emerged in China, such as the Chinese Working Women Network (CWWN) and the China Labor Bulletin (CLB), improving communication among "progressive domestic social forces, global labor and civil society organizations, and Chinese workers" (Zhao and Duffy 2007, 40), and thereby empowering workers in labor relations with employers and the state.

As a conclusion, the acceleration of commercialization in the Chinese publishing industry has led to the transformation of the Chinese publishing sector from a state-subsidized and single-minded propaganda organ into a state-controlled, advertising-supported, and self-interested economic entity. This transformation has only been partial, and the publishing sector is still treated as the party's political propaganda organs (Zhao 2005, 2008). In general, while the Chinese public's need for entertainment, social, and business information, and its participation in economic and cultural life are acknowledged and partially fulfilled through the media, the latter's ties to the state have placed great limitations on its effectiveness (Lee 1994a; Zhao and Duffy 2007; Qiu 2010; Hong 2008, 2011). The Party hinders and sometimes even prohibits the media's access to political information, their meaningful participation in political life, and any significant role they might seek to play in making key economic decisions. Such restrictions within the media system simply mirror the broader social policy, dictating that the Party principle must not be directly challenged under any circumstance, and Chinese media workers, particularly editors, could only survive by softening, rather than challenging, the prescribed political propaganda by broadening its content to include social and personal issues. As a result, the mass media often serve as a supplement, rather than an opposition, to the more conventional Party organs. In other words, Chinese media workers, including knowledge workers in China's publishing industry, must put on a good show while "dancing with chains" (Zhao 1998, 161).

CONTRIBUTIONS OF THE BOOK

Theoretical Significance

Zhao and Duffy (2007, 230) argue that, with the development of "authoritarian capitalism," the reconfiguration of class power has played a constitutive role in China's market reform, and as a consequence, it is impossible to fully understand the characteristics of China's socioeconomic changes without clarifying the distinctions between China's social classes and conceptualizing their relations. In contemporary China, the working class, including both industrial and knowledge workers, whose wages represent their sole or main source of livelihood, is the largest class group (Wood 1994; Hassard et al. 2007). In my book, I contributed to the project of elucidating the situation of China's working class by strategically focusing on one subgroup—knowledge workers in the Chinese publishing industry, mainly editors—and applying a political economic approach to the macro-triangle framework of power relations among the state, capital, and civil society; the propaganda-commercial model; the global division of labor; and the rise of worker organizations and trade unions. In an age when Chinese society is increasingly shaped by the social relations of communication, and the institutional power structure of the society is undergoing a fundamental transition from a socialist planned economy to a reformed liberalized market, an analysis of the dramatic changes in the labor process of Chinese editors—by focusing on their common problems, interests, prospects, and responses as a class—is vitally important. My study also explored the relations between Chinese editors, as well as their relations to, other working class groups, which will largely determine both whether the Communist Party of China (CPC) can successfully construct a harmonious society and the possibilities of China's further economic and political reforms.

Methodological Significance

I organized my book around two original case studies of the Shanghai Science and Technology Publishing House and the Shanghai Education Publishing House—which allowed me to produce a more accurate picture of the factors contributing to the current condition of Chinese editors (media workers in general), and their responses to it than what is available through statistical analyses that deal with situations where behavior is homogeneous and routine. By allowing researchers to compare their firsthand observations with the results obtained through other methods of research, the "deep data" or "thick description" provided by case studies can help bridge the gap between abstract research and concrete practice (Stake 2000, 437). In addition, case studies allow for not only the examination of the particular complexities of a case, but they also enable the researcher to gain insight into larger systematic issues, allowing the researcher to look at an issue using both close- and long-focus lenses.

In order to avoid sample and measurement biases that are associated with subjective decisions in data collection and analysis used in case studies, I have adopted a mixed-methods research approach, also known as *triangula-*

tion. Berg (2007) maintains that subjective decisions can influence how the research is conducted, what alternative research methods are used, and how surveys and questionnaires are prepared. In other words, subjective decisions are involved in every step of the case study: from deciding which case to examine to the final hours of writing up the findings. *Triangulation*—examining the same research questions and collecting data by using multiple sources (e.g., documents, observations, surveys, and interviews)—helps to spell out the choices the researcher has made and the direction that he or she has taken.

Substantive Significance

This book expands our understanding of the working conditions and life experience of millions of knowledge workers in the Chinese publishing industry, shedding light on an important dimension of the rise of the information society. For example, in order to better understand the massive impacts of the global division of labor on the Chinese publishing industry, I not only concentrated on the two primary factors that have facilitated the global division of labor—the decomposition of complex media production process into separate and simple units of production, and the technological and telecommunications convergence, which frees media production from the constraints of geographical location—but I also highlighted the development of a world-wide reservoir of tens of thousands of knowledge workers in the media industry who are both politically and financially repressed and subjugated. Thus, in chapter 4, I addressed the critical changes facing Chinese media workers, particularly editors when the Chinese publishing industry is increasingly incorporated into the centrally coordinated "global factories" headquartered in the core capitalist states.

As Mosco (2009, 493) remarks, despite a number of outstanding exceptions, "media labour and class formation is a blind spot in communication studies." The growth of employment in the communication industry, and the technological and institutional changes unleashed by corporate concentration and informationalized capitalism, have raised the importance of examining the changing nature of work and worker organizations, so as to advance our understanding of the broader transformative historical process that both shapes and is carried out through media and communications. In this book, I have emphasized how Chinese editors, like industrial workers, have suffered from the problem of contingent employment, the decline of social welfare benefits, and intense work pressure, which most scholars and policymakers have ignored (Qiu 2010; Hung 2011). Labor analysis is important because, even though the Constitution still labels them as the "master" of the country, Chinese workers have largely lost their power due to current social reform.

SUGGESTIONS FOR FUTURE RESEARCH

I propose three suggestions for future research. First, while my book is based on surveys and semi-structured interviews with editors from most of the large publishing houses in Shanghai, further research could focus on editors in publishing houses in other big cities in China—for example, Beijing, Guangzhou, and Shenzhen—where market principle has also been largely applied to the local publishing industry. Second, while my book is focused on editors, future research could produce a more detailed description of the status of Chinese media workers by focusing on journalists, photographers, broadcasters, and publication distributors. Third, while my book revealed unequal treatment of junior and senior editors, future research could examine the distinct (and relative) treatment of permanent, temporary, and contract editors; unionized and non-unionized editors; and male and female editors.

It is said that "the squeaky wheel gets the grease," but Chinese media workers, particularly editors, have functioned as the all-too-silent cogwheels of the social machine. By looking at their labor process transformation; their social, economic, political, and cultural dynamics; and their dilemma, challenges, and opportunities, I intend to give a voice to their situations and open up new possibilities for the improvement of both their working conditions and social welfare benefits, as well as to better understand the broader social and economic transformations that have been taking place in China since the late 1970s.

Appendixes

APPENDIX A: ORIGINAL SURVEY QUESTIONS

The questions of my survey are divided into four parts: personal information, the changes in the working conditions, the changes in the social welfare benefits, and the comments on China's media reform.

Section One: Personal Information

1. What is your age?
2. What is your gender?
3. What is your marital status?
4. What is your final degree? From which university are you graduated?
5. Are you a permanent resident of Shanghai?

Section Two: The Changes in the Working Conditions

6. When were you enrolled in the publishing house?
7. How much is your monthly income? How much is your annual income?
8. How much do you expect to earn, considering the increase in the living cost of Shanghai?
9. Have you ever compared your income with other media workers in Shanghai, for example, journalists? Or editors either in other publishing houses in Shanghai or those in publishing houses of other provinces?
10. Do you take any part-time job?
11. Do you have to work overtime? If yes, how many extra hours do you have to work? Where do you work?
12. How often do you sign your contract?

13. Is your everyday attendance strictly recorded?
14. Have you ever changed your job? If yes, how often?
15. What are your main tasks as an editor?
16. Is being an editor your first choice as your lifetime career?
17. What are the results of the implementation of the contingent employment in the publishing house? Is your quality of life affected? If yes, in what kind of ways?
18. What are the problems of the evaluation system in the publishing house?
19. Are you satisfied with your current job? If yes, why? If no, what are the reasons?
20. What is the major pressure for you as an editor? Where does it come from?

Section Three: The Changes in the Social Welfare Benefits

21. Do you have a child? If yes, have you ever taken a maternity leave?
22. Have you received any subsidy for your housing? Do you have to pay a mortgage every month? If yes, how much do you have to pay?
23. Do you receive medical insurance and unemployment benefits?

Section Four: The Comments on China's Media Reform

24. What do you think of current media reform? What is the positive influence exerted on you as a result of the implementation of current media reform? On the contrary, what are the negative effects? In association with current media reform, what do you think of the media conglomeration process in the publishing industry?
25. How effective are unions in the publishing house to protect your rights?

APPENDIX B: INTERVIEW OUTLINE

1. As an editor, how would you define the changes in your social status over the past few decades? What do you perceive to be the reasons for these changes?
2. How would you understand the changes in your work process?

    a. Specify the differences in the work process, if possible.
    b. How do you understand the Party principle as the governing rule in the previous years?
    c. To what extent do you recognize the challenges toward the propaganda function of the publishing sector by commodification?

    d. What is the role that technology has been playing in chang-
ing your work process? To what degree have you been
aware of both the opportunities and challenges brought
about by the rapid development of information and communication technologies?

3. How would you define your social role?

    a. How do you cope with your personal dilemma—namely, on
the one hand, to serve political and ideological interests of
the state; on the other hand, to pursue economic interests—
within the propaganda-commercial model of journalism?

    b. How do you understand media democratization? What are
your thoughts about how to make it come true in contemporary China?

    c. What is the impact of direct or indirect impact of neoliberal
policies on your work, or your social role as an editor? To
be more specific, how would you describe your work in a
global context, particularly from the perspective of the global division of labor?

    d. What are your responses to the above changes? How popu-
lar is unionization in the publishing house? Otherwise, is
there any other resource or organization that you can turn to
if you are faced with difficulties?

APPENDIX C: INTERVIEW QUESTIONS
FOR EDITORS AND UNION OFFICIALS

Interview Questions for Editors

My questions for editors mainly focus on their *changing labor process* as
well as the decline of their *social welfare benefits*. For the questions of the
changing labor process, they include, but are not limited to:

1. How many hours do you work per day? How many days do you work
per week? When do you start working and when does your work end
every day? Do you have fixed or flexible work hours? Is your attendance officially recorded?

2. What is your main work as an editor? What was your main work
before media reform? Are they different? What are the abilities that
are required for your job? How do they differ before and after media
reform?

3. What are the criteria of assessment? How do these criteria relate to your monthly income? How about the workload every month? In term of the intensity of your work, is it easy to finish all the required work? Do you have to work overtime?
4. What are the procedures for promotion? What are the qualifications for promotion? How do you understand the pressure to get yourself promoted?

At the same time, the questions to understand the decline of editors' *social welfare benefits* include:

1. What are the compositions of your monthly income?
2. How often do you sign your contract? Do you know how often other editors sign their contracts? Is there any difference? More importantly, how do you understand these differences?
3. Who is paying for your unemployment benefits and medical insurance? What is the amount? Is there any extra insurance that has been purchased for you by the publishing house?
4. Is there any subsidy provided to help with housing? If yes, what are the forms, and what is the amount? Do you think it is sufficient?
5. Is training popular and institutionalized? What are the forms of training? Is training accessible to all the editors?
6. Is there any other benefit in the publishing house, for example, travelling grants, new year gifts, birthday cakes, moon cake tickets for the mid-autumn festival, food expenses subsidies, and so on?

Interview Questions for Union Officials

My questions for union officials are mainly about the *main functions of unions* in publishing houses and the *practical problems* facing them to better organize workers. The questions that I have addressed include:

1. How popular is unionization in the publishing house?
2. How unions are financially supported? If their financial resources come from administrative units, how can unions be independent from representing the interests of the employers?
3. What is the organizational structure of unions? Are union officials performing their duties on a part-time or a full-time basis? What are the responsibilities for chief union official(s) and union officials, respectively?
4. How are union officials elected? Who are qualified to be elected? What are the restrictions on their terms of service?

5. What are the main functions of unions? Are union members satisfied with what they have achieved?
6. Do you think unions can play a more active and profound role in the publishing house? If yes, what are the problems, political and social, internal and external, that are now facing unions? What are the opportunities for the growth of unions with further publishing reform?

APPENDIX D: INTERVIEW PARTICIPANTS

	Gender	Age	Educational Background	Category	Affiliation
1	M	46	Bachelor	Editor	Shanghai Science and Technology Publishing House
2	F	37	Master	Editor	Shanghai Science and Technology Publishing House
3	F	55	College	Editor	Shanghai Science and Technology Publishing House
4	F	33	Master	Editor	Shanghai Science and Technology Publishing House
5	M	25	Bachelor	Editor	Shanghai Education Publishing House
6	F	31	Master	Editor	Shanghai Education Publishing House
7	M	32	Master	Editor	Shanghai Education Publishing House
8	M	55	Bachelor	Editor	Shanghai Education Publishing House
9	F	34	Doctoral	Editor	Fudan University Press
10	M	58	Bachelor	Chief Editor	Shanghai Art and Literature Publishing House
11	M	59	Doctoral	Chief Editor	Shanghai Lexicographical Publishing House
12	F	45	Bachelor	Union Official	Shanghai Science and Technology Publishing House
13	F	33	Master	Union Official	Shanghai Science and Technology Publishing House
14	F	42	Bachelor	Union Official	Shanghai Education Publishing House
15	M	32	Master	Union Official	Shanghai Education Publishing House
16	M	44	Bachelor	Chief Union Official	Shanghai Art and Literature Publishing House

17	M	53	Bachelor	Chief Union Official	Fudan University Press
18	M	48	Master	Government Official	Shanghai Publication Bureau
19	F	43	Bachelor	Government Official	Shanghai Publishers Association

References

Abplanalp, Alex. 2009. "China Media Market Growth Drivers." Retrieved May 1, 2011 (www. chinamediaconsulting.com/china/.../chinabusinessreview-media.pdf).

ACFTU. 1953. *Proceedings of Seventh All-China Congress of Trade Unions.* Beijing: China Legal Publishing House.

———. 1997. *Chinese Trade Unions Statistics Yearbook 1997.* Beijing: China Statistics Press.

———. 2000. *Chinese Trade Unions Statistics Yearbook 2000.* Beijing: China Statistics Press.

———. 2007. "Work Statistics of the Chinese Trade Unions in 2006." November 27. Retrieved December 9, 2011 (www.acftu.org.cn/template/10002/file.jsp?cid=68&aid=239).

Adams, Tracey and Sandy Welsh. 2008. *The Organization and Experience of Work.* Toronto: Thomson and Nelson.

Adler, Roy. 2008. "Counting on the Middle Class." Retrieved December 3, 2009 (www.miller-mccune.com/article/counting-on-the-middle-class).

Akhavan-Majid, Roya. 2004. "Mass Media Reform in China: Toward a New Analytical Framework." *Gazette* 66(6): 553–565.

Aronowitz, Stanley and William DiFazio. 1994. *The Jobless Future: Sci-Tech and the Dogma of Work.* Minneapolis: University of Minnesota Press.

Artz, Lee, Steve Macek, and Dana Cloud. 2006. *Marxism and Communication Studies: The Point Is to Change It.* New York: Peter Lang.

Baensch, Robert. 2003. *Book Publishing in China.* New Brunswick and London: Transaction Publishers.

Bagdikian, Ben. 2000. *Media Monopoly.* 6th ed. Boston: Beacon.

Bahr, Mort. 1998. *From the Telegraph to the Internet.* Washington, DC: National Press Books.

Barnett, Doak. 1986. "Ten Years after Mao." *Foreign Affairs* 40: 37–65.

Bell, Daniel. 1999. *The Coming of Post-Industrial Society.* New York: Basic Books.

Bennett, Lowell. 2006. "To Capture the Cartoon Cash: China Reanimates an Industry." *Economy* 6: 53–57.

Benson, John and Ying Zhu. 2000. "A Case Study Analysis of Human Resource Management in China's Manufacturing Industry." *China Industrial Economy* 4: 62–65.

Berg, Bruce. 2007. *Qualitative Research Methods for the Social Sciences.* 6th ed. Boston: Allyn and Bacon.

Bi, Xiangyang. 2005. "Institution and Participation: A Research on the Behavior of the Unemployed to Pay for a Pension." *Sociological Studies* 2: 103–131.

Bian, Yanjie. 1994. *Work and Inequality in Urban China.* Albany: State University of New York Press.

Bie, Biliang. 2007. "The Organization and Management of Editorial Department in Publishing Houses." *Journal of Yangtze Normal University* 23(4): 156–158.

Blanch, Bruce. 2010. "Foxconn Suicides: 'Workers Feel Quite Lonely.'" *BBC News*, May 28. Retrieved December 13, 2011 (www.bbc.co.uk/news/10182824).

Blinder, Alan. 2006. "Offshoring: The Next Industrial Revolution." *Foreign Affairs* 85(2): 112–128.

Boes, Andreas and Tobias Kampf. 2010. "Offshoring and the New Insecurities: Toward New Types of 'White Collar Consciousness' in Germany in Globalized Working Environments.'" In *Between a Rock and a Hard Place: The Shaping of Employment in a Global Economy*, edited by Ursula Huws, Steffen Lehndorff, and Damian Grimshaw, 104–119. London: Analytica Publications.

Bonnin, Michel. 2000. "Perspectives on Social Stability after the Fifteenth Congress." In *China under Jiang Zemin*, edited by Hung-mao Tien and Yun-han Chu, 153–161. Boulder and London: Lynne Rienner Publishers.

Braverman, Harry. 1974. *Labor and Monopoly Capital*. New York: Monthly Review Press.

Burawoy, Michael. 1979. *Manufacturing Consent: Changes in the Labor Process under Monopoly Capitalism*. Chicago: The University of Chicago Press.

Cao, Guangzhe. 1998. "The Dialectical Thinking about Publishing Groups." *China Publishing Journal* 9: 14–16.

Cao, Jin and Shaowei Han. 2008. "The Analysis of the Copyright Trade of Science Books in the Context of Globalization." *China Publishing Journal* 6: 31–35.

Caryl, Christian. 2010. "Beijing's Labor Pains." *Foreign Policy*, February 28. Retrieved December 15, 2011 (www.foreignpolicy.com/articles/2010/02/28/beijings_labor_pains).

Castells, Manuel. 1996. *The Rise of the Network Society*. Cambridge: Blackwell.

———. 1997. *The Power of Identity*. 2nd ed. Cambridge: Blackwell.

Chakravartty, Paul and Yuezhi Zhao. 2008. *Global Communication: Toward a Transcultural Political Economy*. Lanham, MD: Rowman and Littlefield.

Chan, Anita. 1998. "Labour Relations in Foreign-funded Ventures." In *Adjusting to Capitalism: Chinese Workers and their State*, edited by Greg O'Leary, 122–149. Armonk, NY: M. E. Sharpe.

———. 2000a. "Chinese Trade Unions and Workplace Relations in State-owned and Joint-venture Enterprises." In *Changing Workplace Relations in the Chinese Economy*, edited by Malcolm Warner, 34–56. Hampshire and London: Macmillan Press.

———. 2000b. "Globalization, China's Free Labour Market, and the Chinese Trade Unions." In *Globalization and Labour in the Asia Pacific Region*, edited by Chris Rowley and John Benson, 260–281. London: Frank Cass Publishers.

———. 2001. *China's Workers under Assault: The Exploitation of Labour in a Globalizing Economy*. New York and London: M. E. Sharpe.

———. 2006. "Realities and Possibilities for Chinese Trade Unionism." In *The Future of Organized Labor: Global Perspective*, edited by Craig Phelan, 275–304. New York: Lang.

Chan, Joseph. 1993. "Commercialization without Independence: Trends and Tensions of Media Development in China." In *China Review 1993*, edited by Joseph Cheng Yu-shek, and Maurice Brosseau, 25.1–25.21. Hong Kong: Chinese University Press.

———. 2003. "Administrative Boundaries and Media Marketization: A Comparative Analysis of the Newspaper, TV and Internet Markets in China." In *Chinese Media, Global Contexts*, edited by Chin-Chuan Lee, 159–176. London and New York: RoutledgeCurzon.

Chan, Siu-sin and Daniel Kwan. 2003. "Union's New Approach Puts Workers' Rights First." *South China Morning Post*, September 12. Retrieved December 10, 2011 (www. zhongguogongren.org/clw20100810/oldwebsite/Union%27s%20New%20Approach.htm?article_id=50046).

Chang, Kai. 1995. *Labour Relations, Labourers and Labour Rights: Labour Issues in Contemporary China*. Beijing: China Labor and Social Security Publishing House.

———. 1998. "Globalization and China's Labour Legislation." *Asian Labour* (September/ December): 33–45.

Chatterjee, Surojit. 2010. "Honda Hit by Another Strike in China." *International Business Times*, June 8. Retrieved December 12, 2011 (www.ibtimes.com/articles/27435/20100608/honda-workers-in-china-call-strike-again.htm).

Cheek, Timothy. 1997. *Propaganda and Culture in Mao's China: Deng Tuo and the Intelligentsia.* Oxford: Clarendon Press.

Chen, Feng. 2003. "Between the State and Labour: The Conflicts of Chinese Trade Unions' Double Identity in Market Reform." *The China Quarterly* 176: 1006–1028.

Chen, Xin. 2008. "The Challenges Facing China's Book Publishing Industry." *Information on Publishing* 3: 1.

Chen, Yiming. 2004. "*Focused Interview*: Retrospect on the Past Decade." *The Southern Weekend*, May 6.

Chen, Zhiwu. 2008. "The Savings Rate is Up to 46 Percent in China: Why Chinese People Love to Save Money." *China Securities Journal*, October 8. Retrieved September 8, 2011 (www.chinanews.com/cj/jrlc/news/2008/10-08/1404313.shtml).

China Statistical Yearbook Editorial Department. 2005. *China Statistical Yearbook 2005.* Beijing: China Statistics Press.

———. 2008. *China Statistical Yearbook 2008.* Beijing: China Statistics Press.

Chu, Godwin and Yanan Ju. 1993. *The Great Wall in Ruins: Communication and Cultural Change in China.* Albany: State University of New York Press.

Chu, Leonard. 1994. "Continuity and Change in China's Media Reform." *Journal of Communication* 44(3): 12–14.

Clarke, Simon. 2005. "Post-Socialist Trade Unions: China and Russia." *Industrial Relations Journal* 36(1): 2–18.

Cody, Edward. 2004. "In China, Workers Turn Tough: Spate of Walkouts May Signal New Era." *Washington Post*, November 27.

Cooke, Fang Lee. 2000. "Manpower Restructuring in the State-owned Railway Industry of China: The Role of the State in Human Resource Strategy." *International Journal of Human Resource Management* 11(5): 904–924.

———. 2002. "Ownership Change and the Reshaping of Employment Relations in China: A Study of Two Manufacturing Companies." *Journal of Industrial Relations* 44(1): 19–39.

———. 2004. "Foreign Firms in China: Modelling HRM in a Toy Manufacturing Corporation." *Human Resource Management Journal* 14(3): 31–52.

———. 2005. *HRM, Work and Employment in China.* London and New York: Routledge.

Coolloud News. 2009. "The ACFTU: Prevent Overseas Antagonistic Forces from Infiltrating Migrant Workers." *Coolloud News*, February 18. Retrieved December 10, 2011 (www.coolloud.org.tw/node/35461).

Cui, Baoguo. 2010. *The General Report on the Development of China's Media Industry 2010.* Beijing: Social Sciences Academic Press.

Datamonitor. 2010. "Advertising in China." Retrieved May 10, 2011 (www.datamonitor.com/store/product/advertising_in_china?productid=FE4471D7-E3EF-4EBB-BB02-77DD8886D759).

Davis, Deborah. 2000. "Introduction: A Revolution in Consumption." In *The Consumer Revolution in Urban China*, edited by Deborah Davis, 1–22. Berkeley: University of California Press.

Deng, Dayu and Tianfang Huang. 2001. "How to Learn Computers and Network for Editors of Science and Technology Journals." *Journal of Guangxi Teachers' College* (Natural Science) 18(3): 69–71.

Denzin, Norman and Yvonna Lincoln. 2008. *The Landscape of Qualitative Research.* 3rd ed. Los Angeles: Sage.

Ding, Daniel, Keith Goodall, and Malcolm Warner. 2002. "The Impact of Economic Reform on the Role of Trade Unions in Chinese Enterprises." *International Journal of Human Resource Management* 15(4/5): 836–852.

Ding, Daniel and Malcolm Warner. 1999. "'Re-inventing' China's Industrial Relations at Enterprise-level: An Empirical Field-study in Four Major Cities." *Industrial Relations Journal* 30(3): 243–260.

Dirlik, Arif. 1989. "Postsocialism? Reflections on 'Socialism with Chinese Characteristics.'" *Bulletin of Concerned Asian Scholars* 21(1): 33–44.

———. 2005. *Marxism in the Chinese Revolution.* Lanham, MD: Rowman and Littlefield.

Donald, Stephanie, Michael Keane, and Yin Hong. 2002. *Media in China: Consumption, Content and Crisis.* New York: RoutledgeCurzon.

Dong, Steve Guanpeng and Anbin Shi. 2007. "Chinese News in Transition: Facing the Challenge of Global Competition." In *Media on the Move: Global Flow and Contra-flow,* edited by Daya Kishan Thussu, 182–197. London and New York: Routledge.

Du, Jian and Weizhen Zhang. 1995. *Reform of the Social Security System.* Shanghai: Lixin Accounting Publishing House.

Duckett, Jane. 2004. "State, Collectivism and Worker Privilege: A Study of Urban Health Insurance Reform." *The China Quarterly* 177: 174–189.

Fang, Dan. 2004. "Research Report on Wage Determination and Workplace Management in China." Geneva: International Labor Organization. Retrieved December 8, 2011 (www.ilo.org/beijing/whatwedo/publications/lang--en/docName--WCMS_158642/index.htm).

Feng, Chen. 2003. "Between the State and Labour: The Conflict of Chinese Trade Unions' Double Identity in Market Reform." *The China Quarterly* 176: 1006–1028.

Flecker, Jörg, Ursula Holtgrewe, Annika Schönauer, and Stavros Gavroglou. 2009. *Value Chain Restructuring and Company Strategies to Reach Flexibility.* Leuven: HIVA.

Florida, Richard. 2002. *The Rise of the Creative Class and How It's Transforming Work, Leisure and Everyday Life.* New York: Basic Books.

Frank, Robert. 2011. "China Becomes 'Billionaire Factory To the World.'" *The Wall Street Journal,* March 9. Retrieved October 12, 2011 (blogs.wsj.com/wealth/2011/03/09/china-becomes-billionaire-factory-to-the-world/).

Fröbel, Folker, Jörgen Heinrichs, and Otto Kreye. 1980. *The New International Division of Labor.* London: Cambridge University Press.

Fursich, Elfriede and Elli Roushanzamir. 2004. "Corporate Expansion, Textual Expansion: Commodification Model of Communication." *Journal of Communication Inquiry* 25(4): 375–395.

Gallagher, Mary. 2004. "Times Is Money, Efficiency Is Life: The Transformation of Labor Relations in China." *Studies in Comparative International Development* (Summer): 11–44.

Gan, Xifen. 1994. "Debates of Journalism Development in China." *Journal of Communication* 44(3): 45.

Gang, Qian and David Bandurski. 2011. "China's Emerging Public Sphere: The Impact of Media Commercialization, Professionalism, and the Internet in an Era of Transition." In *Changing Media, Changing China,* edited by Susan Shirk, 38–76. New York: Oxford University Press.

Gao, Feng. 2000. "The Labour of Editors under the Condition of a Market-based Economy." *Journal of China's Women's University* 6: 70–72.

Garnham, Nicholas. 2000. *Emancipation, the Media, and Modernity: Arguments about the Media and Social Theory.* New York: Oxford University Press.

Garrison, Bruce. 2000. "Journalists' Perceptions of Online Information-gathering Problems." *Journalism and Mass Communication Quarterly* 77(3): 500–514.

Ge, Liyuan. 2010. "The Cooperation of State-owned and Private Publishers in China: A Case Study of the Hubei Changjiang Publishing Group." *Publishing Research* 7: 15–18.

Ge, Yanfeng. 1998. "The Problem of Construction of a System of Social Protection in the Process of Development and Reform." *Journal of Sociological Studies* 1: 98–109.

Gibson, Timothy. 2003. *Securing the Spectacular City: The Politics of Revitalization and Homeless in Downtown Seattle.* Lanham, MD: Lexington Books.

Giddens, Anthony. 1984. *The Constitution of Society: Outline of a Theory of Structuration.* Berkeley: University of California Press.

Golding, Peter and Graham Murdock. 2005. "Culture, Communication, and Political Economy." In *Mass Media and Society.* 4th ed., edited by James Curran and Michael Gurevitch, 15–32. London: Edward Arnold.

Goldman, Merle and Roderick Macfarquhar. 1999. *The Paradox of China's Post-Mao Reforms.* Cambridge and London: Harvard University Press.

Gordon, Kim. 1997. "Government Allows a New Public Sphere to Evolve in China." *Media Development* 4: 30–34.

Greenberg, Bradley and Tuen-yu Lau. 1990. "The Revolution in Journalism and Communication Education in the People's Republic of China." *Gazette* 45: 19–31.

Guan, Binfeng. 2001. "On Labor Law and the Protection of Human Rights of Labor." *Trade Union Tribune* 8(1): 51–54.

Guo, Minggang. 1994. "Reflections on the Nature of Publishing." *Jianghuai Forum* 3: 83–87.

Gurevitch, Michael and Jay Blumler. 1990. "Political Communication Systems and Democratic Values." In *Democracy and the Mass Media*, edited by Judith Lichtenberg, 269–287. Cambridge: Cambridge University Press.

Habermas, Jurgen. 1991. *The Structural Transformation of the Public Sphere: An Inquiry into a Category of Bourgeois Society*. Cambridge, MA: MIT Press.

Hackett, Robert and William Carroll. 2006. *Remaking Media: The Struggle to Democratize Public Communication*. London and New York: Routledge.

Hackett, Robert and Yuezhi Zhao. 1997. *Sustaining Democracy? Journalism and the Politics of Objectivity*. Toronto: Garamond Press.

Hafez, Kai. 2005. "Globalization, Regionalization, and Democratization: The Interaction of Three Paradigms in the Field of Mass Communication." In *Democratizing Global Media: One World, Many Struggles*, edited by Robert Hackett and Yuezhi Zhao, 145–164. Lanham, MD: Rowman and Littlefield.

Halford, Susan and Mike Savage. 1995. "Restructuring Organizations, Changing People: Gender and Restructuring in Banking and Local Government." *Employment and Society* 9(1): 97–122.

Hamlin, Kevin. 2010. "China Overtakes Japan as World's Second-Biggest Economy." August 16. Retrieved February 28, 2012 (www.bloomberg.com/news/2010-08-16/china-economy-passes-japan-s-in-second-quarter-capping-three-decade-rise.html).

Hao, Zhidong. 2003. *Intellectuals at a Crossroads: The Changing Politics of China's Knowledge Workers*. Albany: State University of New York Press.

Hart-Landsberg, Martin and Paul Burkett. 2004. "China and Socialism: Market Reforms and Class Struggle." *Monthly Review* 56: 1–116.

Harvey, David. 2005. *A Brief History of Neoliberalism*. New York: Oxford University Press.

Hassard, John, Jonathan Morris, Jackie Sheehan, and Yuxin Xiao. 2007. "Steeling for Reform: State-enterprise Restructuring and the Surplus Labour Question." In *Unemployment in China: Economy, Human Resources and Labour Markets*, edited by Grace Lee and Malcolm Warner, 203–228. London and New York: Routledge.

He, Zhou. 2000. "Chinese Communist Party Press in a Tug of War: A Political Economy Analysis of the Shenzhen Special Zone Daily." In *Power, Money, and Media: Communication Patterns and Bureaucratic Control in Cultural China*, edited by Chin-Chuan Lee, 112–151. Evanston: Northwestern University Press.

———. 2003. "How Do the Chinese Media Reduce Organizational Incongruence? Bureaucratic Capitalism in the Name of Communism." In *Chinese Media, Global Contexts*, edited by Chin-Chuan Lee, 196–214. London and New York: RoutledgeCurzon.

He, Zhou and Hualin Chen. 1998. *The Chinese Media: A New Perspective*. Hong Kong: The Pacific Century Press.

Hennock, Mary. 2002. "China: The World's Factory Floor." *BBC News*, November 11. Retrieved October 12, 2011 (news.bbc.co.uk/2/hi/business/2415241.stm).

Herman, Edward. 1998. "The Propaganda Model Revisited." In *Capitalism and the Information Age: The Political Economy of the Global Communication Revolution*, edited by Robert McChesney, Ellen Wood, and John Foster, 191–206. New York: Monthly Review Press.

———. 2000. "The Propaganda Model: A Retrospective." *Journalism Studies* 1(1): 101–112.

Herman, Edward and Noam Chomsky. 1988. *Manufacturing Consent: The Political Economy of the Mass Media*. New York: Pantheon Books.

Hishida, Masaharu, Kazuk Kojima, Tomoaki Ishii, and Jian Qiao. 2010. *China's Trade Unions—How Autonomous Are They? A Survey of 1,811 Enterprise Union Chairpersons*. London and New York: Routledge.

Ho, Virginia Harper. 2003. *Labor Dispute Resolution in China: Implications for Labor Rights and Legal Reform*. Berkeley: Institute of East Asian Studies.

Hobsbawn, Eric. 1973. "Karl Marx's Contribution to Historicography." In *Ideology in Social Sciences*, edited by Robin Blackburn, 265–283. New York: Vintage.

Hong, Ng Sek and Olivia Ip. 2007. "Unemployment in China and the All-China Federation of Trade Unions." In *Unemployment in China: Economy, Human Resources and Labour Markets*, edited by Grace Lee and Malcolm Warner, 65–86. London and New York: Routledge.

Hong, Yu. 2008. "Class Formation in High-tech Information and Communications as an Aspect of China's Reintegration into Transnational Capitalism." PhD dissertation, Department of Communication, University of Illinois at Urbana-Champaign.

———. 2010. "Will Chinese ICT Workers Unite? New Signs of Change in the Aftermaths of the Global Economic Crisis." In *Getting the Message: Communications Workers and Global Value Chain*, edited by Vincent Mosco, Catherine McKercher, and Ursula Huws, 69–70. London: Analytica Publications.

———. 2011. *Labor, Class Formation and China's Informationized Policy of Economic Development*. Lanham, MD: Lexington Books.

Howell, Jude. 2006. "New Democratic Trends in China: Reforming the All-China Federation of Trade Unions." IDS Working Paper 263. Sussex: Institute of Development Studies.

Hu, Jun. 2000. "A Sociological Thinking of the Evaluation of Status of Working Class during the Adjustment of Interests." *Journal of the Party School of the CPC Ningbo Municipal Committee* 22(6): 40–42.

Hua, Guofeng. 1980. "Speech on the Third Session of the Eleventh Central Committee of the CPC." *The People's Daily*, September 15.

Huang, Ping and Ziyuan Cui. 2005. *China and Globalization: The Washington Consensus or the Beijing Consensus*. Beijing: Social Sciences Academic Press.

Huang, Yu and Xu Yu. 1997. "Toward Media Democratization: The Chinese Experience and a Critique of the Neo-Authoritarian Model." *China Report* 33: 313–333.

Hung, Chen-Ling. 2011. "Book Review: Labor, Class Formation, and China's Informationized Policy of Economic Development." *Journal of Information Policy* 1: 174–178.

Hung, Ho-Fung. 2009. "A Caveat: Is the Rise of China Sustainable?" In *China and the Transformation of Global Capitalism*, edited by Ho-Fung Hung, 188–206. Baltimore: The Johns Hopkins University Press.

Hung, Kineta, Flora Fang Gu, and Davis Tse. 2005. "Improving Media Decisions in China: A Targetability and Cost-Benefit Analysis." *Journal of Advertising* 34(1): 50.

Huws, Ursula. 2003. *The Making of a Cybertariat: Virtual Work in a Real World*. New York: Monthly Review Press.

Huws, Ursula, Steffen Lehndorff, and Damian Grimshaw. 2010. *Between a Rock and a Hard Place: The Shaping of Employment in a Global Economy*. London: Analytica Publications.

Hyatt, Michael. 2010. "Top Ten U.S. Book Publishers for 2009." Retrieved October 1, 2011 (michaelhyatt.com/top-ten-u-s-book-publishers-for-2009.html).

Hymer, Stephen. 1972. "The Multinational Corporation and the Law of Uneven Development." In *Economics and World Order*, edited by Jagdish Bhagwati, 332–345. Albany: State University of New York Press.

Im, Yung-Ho. 1997. "Towards a Labour-process History of Newsworkers." *The Public/Javnost* 4(1): 31–48.

Ip, Olivia. 1995. "Changing Employment System in China: Some Evidence from the Shenzhen Special Economic Zone." *Work, Employment and Society* 9(2): 269–285.

Ishii, Tomoaki. 2010. "Trade Unions and Corporatism under the Socialist Market Economy in China." In *China's Trade Unions—How Autonomous Are They? A Survey of 1,811 Enterprise Union Chairpersons*, edited by Masaharu Hishida, Kazuk Kojima, Tomoaki Ishii, and Jian Qiao, 1–24. London and New York: Routledge.

Jiang, Kaiven. 1996. "The Conflicts between Trade Unions and the Party-state: The Reform of Chinese Trade Unions in the 1980s." *Hong Kong Journal of Social Sciences* 8: 121–158.

Jin, Ye. 1998. *The Corruption in Various Social Strata*. Zhuhai: Zhuhai Press.

Johnston, Paul. 2001. "Organize for What? The Resurgence of Labor as a Citizenship Movement" In *Rethinking the Movement: Labor's Quest for Relevance in the 21st Century*, edited by Lowell Turner, Harry Katz, and Richard Hued, 27–58. Ithaca, NY: Cornell University Press.

Ke, Guo. 2010. "Newspapers: Changing Roles." In *New Media for a New China*, edited by James Scotton and William Hachten, 61–73. West Sussex: Wiley-Blackwell.

Keane, Michael. 2006. "From Made in China to Created in China." *International Journal of Cultural Studies* 9: 285–296.

Keane, Michael and Stephanie Donald. 2002. "Responses to Crisis: Convergence, Content Industries and Media Governance." In *Media in China: Consumption, Content and Crisis*, edited by Stephanie Hemelryk Donald, Michael Keane, and Yin Hong, 200–211. New York: RoutledgeCurzon.

Khiabany, Gholam. 2006. "Religion and Media in Iran: The Imperative of the Market and the Straightjacket of Islamism." *Westminster Papers in Communication* 3(2): 3–21.

King, Ambrose. 1991. "Kuan-hsi and Network Building: A Sociological Interpretation." *Daedalus* 120(2): 63–84.

Klein, Karen. 2007. "Outsourcing in China Today." *Bloomberg Businessweek*, October 15. Retrieved October 12, 2011 (www.businessweek.com/smallbiz/content/oct2007/sb200710 15_563438.htm).

Landler, Mark. 2001. "AOL Gains Cable Rights in China by Omitting News, Sex, and Violence." *The New York Times*, October 29.

Lee, Chin-Chuan. 1994a. *China's Media, Media's China*. Oxford: Westview Press.

———. 1994b. "Ambiguities and Contradiction: Issues in China's Changing Political Communication." *Gazette* 53: 7–21.

———. 2000. *Power, Money, and Media: Communication Patterns and Bureaucratic Control in Cultural China*. Evanston, IL: Northwestern University Press.

———. 2003a. "Established Pluralism: U.S. Elite Media Discourse on China Policy." In *Chinese Media, Global Contexts*, edited by Chin-Chuan Lee, 76–96. London and New York: RoutledgeCurzon.

———. 2003b. "The Global and the National of the Chinese Media: Discourses, Market, Technology, and Ideology." In *Chinese Media, Global Contexts*, edited by Chin-Chuan Lee, 1–31. London and New York: RoutledgeCurzon.

———. 2003c. *Chinese Media, Global Contexts*. London and New York: RoutledgeCurzon.

Lee, Ching-Kwan. 1999. "From Organized Dependence to Disorganized Despotism: Changing Labour Regimes in Chinese Factories." *The China Quarterly* 157(3): 44–71.

———. 2002. "From the Specter of Mao to the Spirit of Law: Labor Insurgency in China." *Theory and Society* 31(2): 189–228.

———. 2007a. *Working in China: Ethnographies of Labor and Workplace Transformation*. London and New York: Routledge.

———. 2007b. "Pathways of Labor Activism." In *Chinese Society: Change, Conflict and Resistance*. 3rd ed., edited by Elizabeth Perry and Mark Selden, 57–79. London and New York: Routledge.

———. 2007c. *Against the Law: Labor Protests in China's Rustbelt and Sunbelt*. Berkeley: University of California Press.

Lee, Grace and Malcolm Warner. 2007. *Unemployment in China: Economy, Human Resources and Labour Markets*. London and New York: Routledge.

Lee, Lai To. 1986. *Trade Unions in China: 1949 to the Present*. Singapore: Singapore University Press.

Lee, Tain-Dow and Yingfen Huang. 2002. "We Are Chinese—Music and Identity in Cultural China." In *Media in China: Consumption, Content and Crisis*, edited by Stephanie Donald, Michael Keane, and Yin Hong, 105–115. New York: RoutledgeCurzon.

Lefebvre, Henri. 1979. "Space: Social Product and Use Value." In *Critical Sociology: European International Perspective*, edited by J. W. Freiberg, 285–296. New York: Houghton Mifflin.

Levine, Marvin. 1997. *Worker Rights and Labour Standards in Asian's Four New Tigers: A Comparative Perspective*. New York: Plenum Press.

Li, Cheng. 2010. *China's Emerging Middle Class: Beyond Economic Transformation*. Washington, DC: Brooking Institution Press.

Li, Hongsong. 2003. "A Study on the Relation between Economic Growth and Employment Elasticity." *Journal of Finance and Economics* 29(4): 23–27.

Li, Jiangfan. 2001. "On the Impact of Joining the WTO and Responses to It." In *A Political-Economic Analysis of Economic Globalization*, edited by Zhenzhong Wen, 284–296. Beijing: Social Sciences Documentation Press.

Li, Jing. 2004. "Ten Years of *Focused Interview*." *Sanlian Lifeweek Magazine*, April 12. Retrieved July 5, 2011 (lifeweek.com.cn/2004-04-26/000538468.shtml).

Li, Liangrong. 1995. "The Retrospect and Outlook of the Media Reform within Fifteen Years." *Journal of News and University* (Spring): 3–8.

Li, Lulu. 1999. "On Studies of Social Stratification." *Journal of Sociological Studies* 1: 101–109.

Li, Qi. 2000. *Transition of Labour Relations in Chinese State-owned Enterprises: Case Studies of a Process Dominated by Government*. Hong Kong: City University of Hong Kong.

Li, Qixian. 1997a. "Characteristics of the Labor of Editors." *Journal of Guangxi Normal University* 33(3): 101–104.

Li, Xiaofeng and Chaoying Zhang. 2008. "Problems and Solutions to the Current Social Welfare System in China." *Public Finance Research* 11: 54–56.

Li, Wenbing. 1997b. "Chinese Publisher's Social Responsibility Consciousness." Presented at the English International Forum on Publishing Studies. Tokyo: Japan Society of Publishing Studies.

Lin, Teh-chang. 2001. "The Reform of State-owned Enterprises in Mainland China: A Societal Perspective." In *Remaking the Chinese State: Strategies, Society, and Security*, edited by Chien-min Chao and Bruce Dickson, 157–168. London and New York: Routledge.

Liu, Chang-de. 2006. "Deskilling Effects on Journalists: ICTs and the Labour Process of Taiwanese Newspaper Reporters." *Canadian Journal of Communication* 31: 695–714.

Liu, Hainian and Lin Li. 2001. *Governing the Country According to Laws and Establishing the System of Laws*. Beijing: China Legal Publishing House.

Liu, Yufang. 2001. "On the Changes Occurred within the Structure of Working Class." *The Workers' Daily*, December 26.

Lu, Xiaobo and Elizabeth Perry. 1997. *Danwei: The Changing Workplace in Historical and Comparative Perspective*. New York and London: M. E. Sharpe.

Lu, Xueyi. 2002. *Studying Report on the Stratum in Contemporary China*. Beijing: Social Science Press.

Lucore, Robert. 2004. "Challenges and Opportunities: Unions Confront the New Information Technologies." In *Information, Technology and the World of Work*, edited by Daphne Taras, James Bennett, and Anthony Townsend, 41–54. New Brunswick and London: Transaction Publishers.

Luo, Hansen. 1995. "The Five Problems Facing Unions to Adjust Labor Relations." *Theoretical Study and Exploration* 6: 84–85.

Lynch, Daniel. 2000. "The Nature and Consequences of China's Unique Pattern of Telecommunications Development." In *Power, Money, and Media: Communication Patterns and Bureaucratic Control in Cultural China*, edited by Chin-Chuan Lee, 179–207. Evanston, IL: Northwestern University Press.

Ma, Qingying. 1998. "Functions and Characteristics of the Labor of Editors." *Journal of Liaoning University* 4: 76–77.

Macpherson, Crawford. 1977. *The Life and Times of Liberal Democracy*. New York: Oxford University Press.

Mansell, Robin. 2004. "Political Economy, Power and New Media." *New Media and Society* 6(1): 74–83.

Mao, Zedong. 1991. *Selected Works 5: 1961–1977*. Beijing: Foreign Languages Press.

Markus, Francis. 2004. "China's Ailing Health Care." *BBC News*, December 6. Retrieved September 8, 2011 (news.bbc.co.uk/2/hi/asia-pacific/4062523.stm).

McChesney, Robert. 1999. *Rich Media, Poor Democracy*. New York: The New Press.

———. 2000. "The Political Economy of Communication and the Future of the Field." *Media, Culture and Society* 22(1): 109–116.

———. 2007. *Communication Revolution*. New York: The Free Press.

McCormick, Barrett and Qing Liu. 2003. "Globalization and the Chinese Media: Technologies, Content, Commerce and the Prospects for the Public Sphere." In *Chinese Media, Global Contexts*, edited by Chin-Chuan Lee, 139–158. London and New York: Routledge.

McGowan, Ian. 2003. "Book Publishing in China." In *The Publishing Industry in China*, edited by Robert Baensch, 51–66. New Brunswick and London: Transaction Publishers.

McKercher, Catherine. 2002. *Newsworkers Unite: Labor, Convergence and North American Newspapers*. Lanham, MD: Rowman and Littlefield.

McKercher, Catherine and Vincent Mosco. 2007. *Knowledge Workers in the Information Society*. Lanham, MD: Lexington Books.

———. 2010. "Getting the Message: Communications Workers and Global Value Chain." In *Getting the Message: Communications Workers and Global Value Chain*, edited by Vincent Mosco, Catherine McKercher, and Ursula Huws, 1–9. London: Analytica Publications.

McLaughlin, Lisa and Helen Johnson. 2007. "Women and Knowledge Work in the Asia-Pacific: Complicating Technological Empowerment." In *Knowledge Workers in the Information Society*, edited by Catherine McKercher and Vincent Mosco, 249–266. Lanham, MD: Lexington Books.

Meehan, Eileen. 2002. "Gendering the Commodity Audience: Critical Media Research, Feminism, and Political Economy." In *Sex and Money: Feminism and Political Economy in the Media*, edited by Eileen Meehan and Ellen Riordan, 209–222. Minneapolis: University of Minnesota Press.

Melody, William. 1994. "The Information Society: Implications for Economic Institutions and Market Theory." In *The Global Political Economy of Communication*, edited by Edward Comor, 21–36. London: St. Martin's Press.

Miller, Toby, Nitin Govil, John McMurria, and Richard Maxwell. 2001. *Global Hollywood*. London: British Film Institute.

Mosco, Vincent. 1998. "Political Economy, Communication, and Labor." In *Global Productions: Labor in the Making of the Information Society*, edited by Gerald Sussman and John Lent, 13–38. Cresskill, NY: Hampton Press.

———. 2004. *The Digital Sublime*. Cambridge, MA: MIT Press.

———. 2006. "The Laboring of Communication." *Canadian Journal of Communication* 31: 494–497.

———. 2008. "Knowledge Workers of the World! Unite?" *Canadian Journal of Communication* 33: 121–125.

———. 2009. *The Political Economy of Communication*. 2nd ed. London: Sage.

Mosco, Vincent and Catherine McKercher. 2006. "Convergence Bites Back: Labour Struggles in the Canadian Communication Industry." *Canadian Journal of Communication* 31(3): 733–751.

———. 2008. *The Laboring of Communication: Will Knowledge Workers of the World Unite?* Lanham, MD: Lexington Books.

Mosco, Vincent, Catherine McKercher, and Ursula Huws. 2010. *Getting the Message: Communications Workers and Global Value Chains*. London: Analytica Publications.

Mosco, Vincent and Janet Wasko. 1983. *The Critical Communications Review: Labor, the Working Class, and the Media*. Norwood: Ablex Publishing Corporation.

Mowlana, Hamid. 1997. *Global Information and World Communication*. 2nd ed. London: Sage.

Murphy, David. 2003. "A Shot in the Arm." *Far Eastern Economic Review* 166(22): 24–25.

MyCOS. 2009. "The Annual Report of Chinese University and College Graduates' Employment 2009." Retrieved September 9, 2011 (wenku.baidu.com/view/eea94d94dd88d0d23 3d46a47.html).

———. 2010. "The Ranking of University and College Graduates' Employment Ability 2010." Retrieved September 9, 2011 (edu.sina.com.cn/j/qzzk07/index.shtml).

Naughton, Barry. 2007. *The Chinese Economy: Transitions and Growth*. Cambridge and London: MIT Press.

Network18. 2007. "Partners." Retrieved October 1, 2011 (www.network18online.com/partners.html).

Ng, Sek Hong and Malcolm Warner. 1998. *China's Trade Unions and Management.* New York: St. Martin's Press.

———. 2000. "Industrial Relations versus Human Resource Management in the PRC: Collective Bargaining with Chinese Characteristics." In *Changing Workplace Relations in the Chinese Economy,* edited by Malcolm Warner, 100–116. New York: St. Martin's Press.

Ngai, Pun and Wailing Chan. 2004. "Community Based Labor Organizing." *International Union Rights* 11(4): 10–11.

Ngai, Pun, King Chi Chan, and Jenny Chan. 2010. "The Role of the State, Labour Policy and Migrant: Workers' Struggles in Globalized China." *Global Labour Journal* 1(1): 132–151.

Ogden, Suzanne. 2000. "China's Developing Civil Society: Interest Groups, Trade Unions and Associational Pluralism." In *Changing Workplace Relations in the Chinese Economy,* edited by Malcolm Warner, 263–298. New York: St. Martin's Press.

———. 2004. "From Patronage to Profits: The Changing Relationship of Chinese Intellectuals with the Party-State." In *Chinese Intellectuals between State and Market,* edited by Edward Gu and Merle Goldman, 111–137. London and New York: RoutledgeCurzon.

O'Leary, Greg and Andrew Watson. 1985. "Economic Co-operation Revisited: New Directions in Chinese Agriculture." In *China: Dilemmas of Modernization,* edited by Graham Young, 1–17. London: Croomhelm.

Ong, Aihwa. 2006. *Neoliberalism as Exception: Mutations in Citizenship and Sovereignty.* Durham, NC: Duke University Press.

Pan, Zhongdang. 2000. "Improvising Reform Activities: The Changing Reality of Journalistic Practice in China." In *Power, Money, and Media: Communication Patterns and Bureaucratic Control in Cultural China,* edited by Chin-Chuan Lee, 68–111. Evanston, IL: Northwestern University Press.

Pan, Zhongdang and Ye Lu. 2003. "Localizing Professionalism: Discursive Practices in China's Media Reforms." In *Chinese Media, Global Contexts,* edited by Chin-Chuan Lee, 215–236. London and New York: RoutledgeCurzon.

Pei, Minxin. 1994. *From Reform to Revolution: The Demise of Communism in China and the Soviet Union.* Cambridge, MA: Harvard University Press.

Pendakur, Manjunath. 1993. "Political Economy and Ethnography: Transformations in an Indian Village." In *Illuminating the Blindspots: Essays Honoring of Dallas W. Smythe,* edited by Janet Wasko, Vincent Mosco, and Manjunath Pendakur, 82–108. Norwood, NJ: Ablex Publishing Corporation.

Perry, Elizabeth. 1995. "Labor's Battle for Political Space: The Role of Worker Associations in Contemporary China." In *Urban Spaces in Contemporary China: The Potential for Autonomy and Community in Post-Mao China,* edited by Deborah Davis, Richard Kraus, Barry Naughton, and Elizabeth Perry, 302–325. Cambridge: Cambridge University Press.

Perry, Elizabeth and Mark Selden. 2010. *Chinese Society: Change, Conflict and Resistance.* 3rd ed. New York: Routledge.

Petras, James. 2006. "Past, Present, and Future of China: From Semi-Colony to World Power?" *Journal of Contemporary Asia* 36: 423–441.

Pressly, Linda. 2011. "Middle Class China Turns to Private Health Insurance." *BBC News,* July 18. Retrieved September 8, 2011 (www.bbc.co.uk/news/business-14141740).

Pringle, Tim. 2002. "Industrial Unrest in China: A Labour Movement in the Making?" *The China Labour Bulletin,* January 31. Retrieved December 20, 2008 (www.hartford-hwp.com/achives/55/294.html).

Qi, Zhirong and Xiaohou Xu. 1995. *The Introduction of Chinese Labor Relationship.* Hangzhou: Zhejiang People's Publishing House.

Qin, Yan. 1999. *China's Middle Class: The Future Mainstream of the Social Structure.* Beijing: China Planning Press.

Qiu, Jack Linchuan. 2010. "Across the Great Wall We Can Reach Every Corner in the World: Network Labour in China." In *Getting the Message: Communications Workers and Global Value Chain,* edited by Vincent Mosco, Catherine McKercher, and Ursula Huws, 83–95. London: Analytica Publications.

Redl, Anke and Rowan Simons. 2002. "Chinese Media: One Channel, Two Systems." In *Media in China: Consumption, Content and Crisis*, edited by Stephanie Donald, Michael Keane, and Yin Hong, 18–27. London and New York: Routledge.

Riordan, Ellen. 2002. "Intersections and New Directions: On Feminism and Political Economy." In *Sex and Money: Feminism and Political Economy in the Media*, edited by Eileen Meeham and Ellen Riordan, 3–15. Minneapolis: University of Minnesota Press.

Robertson, Roland. 1995. "Globalization: Time-space Homogeneity-heterogeneity." In *Global Modernities*, edited by Mike Featherstone, Scott Lash, and Roland Robertson, 25–44. London: Sage.

Robison, Richard. 2006. *The Neo-liberal Revolution: Forgoing the Market State*. New York: Palgrave Macmillan.

Rocca, Jean-Louis. 2003. "Old Working Class, New Working Class: Reforms, Labour Crisis and the Two Faces of Conflicts in Chinese Urban Areas." In *China Today: Economic Reforms, Social Cohesion and Collective Identities*, edited by Taciana Fisac and Leila Fernandez-Stembridge, 77–104. London and New York: RoutledgeCurzon.

Ross, Andrew. 2009. *Nice Work If You Can Get It: Life and Labor in Precarious Times*. New York: New York University Press.

Rothschild, Kurt. 2002. "The Absence of Power in Contemporary Economic Theory." *Journal of Socioeconomics* 31: 433–442.

Sahay, Sundeep, Brian Nicholson, and Swamy Krishna. 2003. *Global IT Outsourcing: Software Development across Borders*. Cambridge: Cambridge University Press.

Sargeson, Sally. 1999. *Reworking China's Proletariat*. New York: St. Martin's Press.

———. 2001. "Assembling Class in a Chinese Joint Venture Factory." In *Organizing Labor in Globalizing Asia*, edited by Andrew Brown and Jane Hutchison, 48–70. New York: Routledge.

Schiller, Dan. 2007. *How to Think about Information*. Urbana and Chicago: University of Illinois Press.

Schiller, Herbert. 1973. *The Mind Managers*. Boston: Beacon Press.

Schlesinger, Philip. 2000. "The Nation and Communicative Space." In *Media Power, Professional and Policy*, edited by Howard Tumber, 99–115. London: Routledge.

Scotton, James and William Hachten. 2010. *New Media for a New China*. Malden, MA: Wiley-Blackwell.

Sheehan, Jackie. 1999. *Chinese Workers: A New History*. London: Routledge.

Shen, Jie and John Benson. 2008. "Tripartite Consultation in China: A First Step towards Collective Bargaining?" *International Labour Review* 147(2–3): 231–248.

Shen, Qinqin. 2003. "The Transformation of Industrial Relations and Major Goals of Trade Unions in China." *Theory and Practice of Trade Unions* 17(6): 1–6.

Shi, Donghui, Liming Wang, and Baosheng Dong. 2008. *The Analysis of the Organizations of China's Publishing Industry*. Nanning: Guangxi People's Publishing House.

Shirk, Susan. 2011. *Changing Media, Changing China*. New York: Oxford University Press.

Silver, Beverly. 2003. *Forces of Labor: Workers' Movements and Globalization since 1870*. New York: Cambridge University Press.

Silver, Beverly and Lu Zhang. 2009. "China as an Emerging Epicenter of World Labor Unrest" In *China and the Transformation of Global Capitalism*, edited by Ho-Fung Hung, 174–187. Baltimore: Johns Hopkins University Press.

Smythe, Dallas. 1977. "Communications: Blindspot of Western Marxism." *Canadian Journal of Political and Social Theory* 1(3): 1–27.

So, Alvin. 2007. "The State and Labor Insurgency in Post-Socialist China." In *China's Challenges in the Twenty-First Century*, edited by Joseph Cheng, 475–501. Hong Kong: City University of Hong Kong Press.

———. 2009. "Rethinking the Chinese Developmental Miracle." In *China and the Transformation of Global Capitalism*, edited by Ho-Fung Hung, 50–64. Baltimore: The Johns Hopkins University Press.

Sreberny, Annabelle. 2000. "The Global and the Local in International Communications." In *Mass Media and Society*, edited by James Curran and Michael Gurevitch, 93–119. London: Edward Arnold.

———. 2001. "Mediated Culture in the Middle East: Diffusion, Democracy, Difficulties." *International Communication Gazette* 63(2/3): 101–119.

Stake, Robert. 2000. "Case Studies." In *Handbook of Qualitative Research*. 2nd ed., edited by Norman Denzin and Yvonna Lincoln, 435–454. Thousand Oaks: Sage.

Stepanek, James. 1992. "China's Enduring State Factories: Why the Years of Reform Have Left China's Big State Factories Unchanged." In *China's Economic Dilemmas in the 1990s: The Problems of Reforms, Modernization and Interdependence*, edited by Joint Economic Committee, Congress of the United States, 440–453. Armonk, NY: M. E. Sharpe.

Stockmann, Daniela. 2011. "What Kind of Information Does the Public Demand? Getting the News during the 2005 Anti-Japanese Protests." In *Changing Media, Changing China*, edited by Susan Shirk, 175–201. New York: Oxford University Press.

Students and Scholars against Corporate Misbehavior. 2010. "Foxconn Factories Are Labor Camps." *South China Morning Post*, October 11. Retrieved January 4, 2012 (fr-fr.facebook.com/note.php?note_id=156848724349172).

Sun, Chunlan. 2009a. "Catch Up with Time and Grow with the Country." *All-China Federation of Trade Unions*, October 10. Retrieved December 8, 211 (www.acftu.net/template/10004/file.jsp?cid=853&aid=82678).

Sun, Lizhi. 2006. "Creativity of Editorial Work." *Journal of Hulunbeier College* 14(6): 10–11.

Sun, Xupei. 1994. *New Theories of Journalism*. Beijing: Contemporary China Press.

Sun, Yafei. 2009b. "The Growth and Success of Focused Interview." *Southern Weekly*, July 30. Retrieved on June 12, 2011 (www.dzwww.com/2009/2009jy/xxjy/200907/t20090730_4963800.htm).

Sun, Yihong and Junyan Yang. 2002. "On Nurturing Young Editors of Science and Technology Journals." *Metallurgical Information Review* 2: 41–42.

Sun, Yuseng. 2003. *A Decade: Starting from Changing Television Mode of Expression*. Shanghai: Sanlian Bookstore.

Sussman, Gerald and John Lent. 1998. "Global Production." In *Global Productions: Labor in the Making of the "Information Society,"* edited by Gerald Sussman and John Lent, 1–11. Cresskill, NY: Hampton Press.

Tabuchi, Hiroko. 2010. "Chinese Honda Strike a Wake-Up Call for Japan." *New York Times*, June 1. Retrieved December 12, 2011 (www.nytimes.com/2010/06/02/business/global/02honda.html).

Tang, Jun. 2001. *WTO, Unemployment and Employment Policies*. Beijing: China Worker Press.

Taylor, Bill, Kai, Chang and Li Qi. 2003. *Industrial Relations in China*. Cheltenham and Northampton, UK: Edward Elgar.

Taylor, Marcus. 2008. *Global Economy Contested: Power and Conflict across the International Division of Labor*. London and New York: Routledge.

The Book Publishing Management Department of the GAPP. 2008. *The China Book Publishing Industry Report 2005–2006*. Beijing: China Renmin University Press.

The Central Organization Department of the CPC. 2009. *The Dictionary of the Organization of the CPC*. Beijing: Party Building Books Publishing House.

The Chinese Academy of Social Sciences. 1998. *The Social Blue Paper: The Analysis and Prediction of Chinese Societal Situation in 1998*. Beijing: Social Science Academic Press.

The International Center for Trade Union Rights. 2005. *Trade Unions of the World*. London: John Harper Publishing.

The International Labor Organization. 2000. *Symposium on Information Technologies in the Media and Entertainment Industries: Their Impact on Employment, Working Conditions and Labor-Management Relations*. Geneva: International Labor Organization.

The Ministry of Industry and Information Technology. 2011. "The Growth Rate of the Total Value of Media Products Exports Reached 15.6 Percent." *Sina Finance and Economics*, June 25. Retrieved January 3, 2012 (finance.sina.com.cn/roll/20110725/111110201927.shtml).

The Ministry of Labor and Social Security. 2001. "Statistics Bulletin of Labor and Social Security: First Half of 2001." Retrieved December 7, 2011 (www.molss.gov.cn/index_tongji.htm).

The National Bureau of Statistics and the Ministry of Labor and Social Security. 2001. *China Labor Statistical Yearbook*. Beijing: China's Statistics Publishing House.

The People's Daily. 2005. "Building Harmonious Society Crucial for China's Progress." June 27. Retrieved November 15, 2008 (english.peopledaily.com.cn/200506/27/eng20050627_192495.html).

The Publishers Association of China. 2008. *China Publishers' Yearbook*. Beijing: China Publishers' Yearbook Press.

The Shanghai Municipal Human Resources and Social Security Bureau. 2011. "Amount both Employees and Employers Paid for Social Welfare Benefits." Retrieved May 10, 2011 (www.12333sh.gov.cn/).

The Shanghai Municipal Statistics Bureau. 2009a. "The Average Annual Income of Knowledge Workers in Different Professions in China." Retrieved May 11, 2011 (www.stats-sh.gov.cn/2004shtj/tjnj/tjnj2009.htm).

————. 2009b. "The Average Annual Income of Industrial Workers in Different Professions in China." Retrieved May 11, 2011 (www.stats-sh.gov.cn/2004shtj/tjnj/tjnj2009.htm).

————. 2009c. "Major Expenses for Editors in Their Daily Lives in Shanghai." Retrieved March 3, 2011 (www.stats-sh.gov.cn/2004shtj/tjnj/tjnj2009.htm).

The State Administration of Radio, Film, and Television. 2006. *Report on Development of China's Radio, Film, and Television*. Beijing: Social Sciences Academics Press.

The Workers' Daily. 2009. "Positive Trends in the Establishment of Lower-level Trade Unions." June 8. Retrieved December 9, 2011 (www.gov.cn/jrzg/2009-07/08/content_1359867.htm).

The World Health Organization. 2002. *The World Health Report 2002, Reducing Risks, Promoting Healthy Life*. Geneva: World Health Organization.

Thussu, Daya Kishan. 2000. *International Communication*. 2nd ed. New York: Oxford University Press.

————. 2007. *Media on the Move: Global Flow and Contra-flow*. London and New York: Routledge.

Tian, Zhongyu. 2010. "On the Quality and Training of Editors in the Knowledge Economy Era." *Journal of Qiqihar Junior Teachers' College* 114(2): 71–72.

Tong, Bin. 2003. "Political Civilization: A New Topic for Journalism Studies." *Journalism and Communication Studies* 10(3): 13–20.

Tong, Bin and Mei Cheng. 1993. *A Teaching Program for Journalism Theory*. Beijing: Chinese People's University Press.

Tsui-Auch, Lai Si. 1998. "Regional Subcontracting and Labor: Information/Communication Technology Production in Hong Kong and Shenzhen." In *Labor in the Making of the Information Society*, edited by Gerald Sussman and John Lent, 145–172. Cresskill, NY: Hampton Press.

Vallas, Steven, William Finlay, and Amy Wharton. 2009. *The Sociology of Work: Structures and Inequalities*. New York: Oxford University Press.

Verma, Anil and Zhiming Yan. 1995. "The Changing Face of Human Resource Management in China: Opportunities, Problems and Strategies." In *Employment Relations in the Growing Asian Economies*, edited by Anil Verma, Thomas Kochan, and Russell Lansbury, 315–335. London: Routledge.

Wang, Haiyan, Richard Appelbaum, Francesca Degiuli, and Nelson Lichtenstein. 2009. "China's New Labour Contract Law: Is China Moving towards Increased Power for Workers?" *Third World Quarterly* 30(3): 485–501.

Wang, Jing. 2008a. *Brand New China*. Cambridge and London: Harvard University Press.

Wang, Lilong and Jinsong Wang. 1999. "The Knowledge Renewal of Editors of Science and Technology Journals." *Journal of Hefei University of Technology* (Social Sciences) 13(3): 73–75.

Wang, Limin. 1994. "Assessments of the Quality and Quantity of Editorial Work." *Journal of Fuzhou University* (Social Sciences) 8(4): 51–54.

Wang, Shaoguang. 1995. "Learning by Debating: The Changing Role of the State in China's Economy and Economic Theories." *Policy Studies Journal* 23: 11–26.

Wang, Shitao. 2001. "Infringement of Labor Rights and Legal Compensation." *Journal of the North-eastern University of Finance and Economics* 4: 89–91.

Wang, Xiansen. 2003. "The Study of Collective Bargaining of Trade Unions in Western Countries." *Theory and Practice of Trade Unions* 17(6): 54–57.

Wang, Zhaoguo. 2008b. "The Social Roles of China's Trade Unions." *Contemporary Workers* 12: 20–22.

Wang, Zhen and Haiwang Zhou. 2009. *The Report on Human Resources Development in Shanghai (2008–2009)*. Shanghai: Shanghai Academy of Social Sciences.

Warner, Malcolm. 1995. *The Management of Human Resources in Chinese Industry*. New York: St. Martin's Press.

———. 2000. *Changing Workplace Relations in the Chinese Economy*. London and New York: St. Martin's Press.

———. 2001. "Human Resources Management in the People's Republic of China." In *Human Resource Management in Developing Countries*, edited by Pawan Budhwar and Yaw Debrah, 19–33. London: Routledge.

Warner, Malcolm and Sek-Hong Ng. 1999. "Collective Contracts in Chinese Enterprises: A New Brand of Collective Bargaining under 'Market Socialism.'" *British Journal of Industrial Relations* 21(2): 258–316.

Warner, Malcolm and Ying Zhu. 2000. "The Origins of Chinese Industrial Relations." In *Changing Workplace Relations in the Chinese Economy*, edited by Malcolm Warner, 15–33. New York: St. Martin's Press.

Weeden, Kim and David Grusky. 2005. "The Case for a New Class Map." *American Journal of Sociology* 111(1): 141–212.

West, Loraine. 1999. "Pension Reform in China: Preparing for the Future." *Journal of Development Studies* 35(3): 153–183.

White, Chris. 2007. "China's New Labour Law: The Challenges of Regulating Employment Contracts." Evatt Foundation Papers. Retrieved November 15, 2008 (evatt.org.au/publications/papers/193.html).

White, Lynn. 1990. "All the News: Structure and Politics in Shanghai's Media Reform." In *Voices of China: The Interplay of Politics and Journalism*, edited by Chin-Chuan Lee, 88–110. New York: Guilford.

Whyte, Martin. 1999. "The Changing Role of Workers." In *The Paradox of China's Post-Mao Reforms*, edited by Merle Goldman and Roderick Macfarquhar, 173–196. Cambridge: Harvard University Press.

———. 2010. *Myth of the Social Volcano: Perceptions of Inequality and Distributive Injustice in Contemporary China*. Stanford: Stanford University Press.

Winseck, Drwayne. 1998. *Reconvergence: A Political Economy of Telecommunications in Canada*. Creskill, NY: Hampton Press.

Winseck, Dwayne and Robert Pike. 2007. *Communication and Empire: Media, Markets, and Globalization, 1860–1930*. Durham, NC: Duke University Press.

Wong, Linda and Susan MacPherson. 1995. *Social Change and Social Policy in Contemporary China*. Aldershot, UK: Avebury.

Wood, Ellen Meiksins. 1994. "From Opportunity to Imperative: The History of the Market." *Monthly Review* (July/August): 14–40.

Wortzel, Larry. 1987. *Class in China: Stratification in a Classless Society*. Westport, CT: Greenwood Press.

Wu, Friedrich. 1985. "Socialist Development of Self-Reliance within the Capitalist World Economy: The Chinese View in the Post-Mao Era." In *The End of An Isolation: China after Mao*, edited by Kapur Harish, 234–263. Dordrecht: Martinus Nijhoff Publishers.

Wu, Guoguang. 2000. "One Head, Many Mouths: Diversifying Press Structures in Reform China." In *Power, Money, and Media: Communication Patterns and Bureaucratic Control in Cultural China*, edited by Chin-Chuan Lee, 45–67. Evanston, IL: Northwestern University Press.

Wu, Yaping. 2010. "China's Trade Unions in the Social Transformation: Challenges and Main Responsibilities." *Journal of Zhejiang Provincial Party School* 4: 8–12.

Xin, Guangwei. 2005. *Publishing in China: An Essential Guide*. Singapore: Thomson.

Xinhua News. 2008. "Hu: China to Promote Sustainable Development, Protect Workers' Rights and Interests." *Xinhua News,* January 7. Retrieved December 11, 2011 (us.china-embassy.org/eng/zt/zgrq/t397367.htm).

Xu, Dejiang. 2008. "The Outstanding Contributions of the Overseas Edition of the People's Daily." *Chinese Character Culture* 81: 81–82.

Yates, Michael. 2003. *Naming the System: Inequality and Work in the Global Economy.* New York: Monthly Review Press.

Yi, Tuqiang. 2011. "Private Publishing in China. Contributions, Cruxes, and Reform Suggestions." *Journal of Henan University* 2: 149–156.

Yin, Jie. 2008. "China's Book Publishing Industry: Current Situation and Reform Proposals." *Pioneering with Science and Technology Monthly* 5: 52–53.

Yin, Robert. 2009. *Case Study Research: Design and Methods.* 4th ed. Beverly Hills: Sage.

Yu, Haiqing. 2011. "*Dwelling Narrowness*: Chinese Media and Their Disingenuous Neoliberal Logic." *Journal of Media and Cultural Studies* 25(1): 33–46.

Yu, Xu. 2002. "The WTO Impact on China's Media Will be Limited." *Ming Pao Monthly* (April): 20–22.

Ze, David. 1995. "China." In *International Book Publishing: An Encyclopedia,* edited by Philip Altbach and Edith Hoshino, 447–460. New and London: Garland.

———. 1996. "The Future of State Publishing in China." *Ballagio Newsletter* 16: 15–17.

Zhang, Dinghua. 1994. "A Work Report to the 12th National Congress of All-China Federation of Trade Unions." In *The Twelfth National Congress of China Trade Unions,* October 1993, 11–57. Beijing: All-China Federation of Trade Unions.

Zhang, Jie and Xiaobin Li. 1998. *Social Transition in China.* Lanham, MD: University Press of America.

Zhang, Peibin. 2001. "The Transformation of Trade Unions in the New Era." *Trade Unions' Tribune* 7(6): 19–22.

Zhang, Wangjun and Jianfeng Peng. 2001a. "The Trends of Human Resources Management in the Information Age." *China's Talent* 8: 21–23.

———. 2001b. "Motivation System in Chinese Knowledge Enterprises." *Science Research Management* 22(6): 90–96.

Zhang, Yunqiu. 1997. "An Intermediary: The Chinese Perception of Trade Unions since the 1980s." *Journal of Contemporary China* 6(14): 139–152.

Zhang, Zihui. 2004. "To Advance the Publication Reform from Both Institutional and Techno-logical Perspectives." *Journal of China Publishing* 12: 37–39.

Zhao, Xiaoshi. 2010. *Research on the Adjustment of the Labor Relations in the Chinese Social Transformation.* Beijing: Economic Science Press.

Zhao, Yuezhi. 1998. *Media, Market, and Democracy in China: Between the Party Line and the Bottom Line.* Urbana and Chicago: University of Illinois Press.

———. 2000. "From Commercialization to Conglomeration: The Transformation of the Chinese Press within the Orbit of the Party State." *Journal of Communication* 50(2): 3–26.

———. 2001. "Media and Elusive Democracy in China." *The Public/Javnost* 8(2): 21–44.

———. 2003. "'Enter the World': Neo-liberal Globalization, the Dream for a Strong Nation, and Chinese Press Discourses on the WTO." In *Chinese Media, Global Contexts,* edited by Chin-Chuan Lee, 32–56. London and New York: RoutledgeCurzon.

———. 2005. "Who Wants Democracy and Does It Deliver Food? Communication and Power in a Globally Integrated China." In *Democratizing Global Media: One World, Many Struggles,* edited by Robert Hackett and Yuezhi Zhao, 57–80. Lanham, MD: Rowman and Littlefield Publishers.

———. 2008. *Communication in China: Political Economy, Power, and Conflict.* Lanham, MD: Rowman and Littlefield.

Zhao, Yuezhi and Rob Duffy. 2007. "Shorted-Circuited? The Communication of Labor Struggles in China." In *Knowledge Workers in the Information Society,* edited by Catherine McKercher and Vincent Mosco, 229–266. Lanham, MD: Lexington Books.

Zhao, Yuezhi and Robert Hackett. 2005. "Media Globalization, Media Democratization: Challenges, Issues, and Paradoxes." In *Democratizing Global Media: One World, Many Struggles,* edited by Robert Hackett and Yuezhi Zhao, 1–33. New York: Rowman and Littlefield.

Zheng, Yongnian. 2004. *Globalization and State Transformation in China*. Cambridge: Cambridge University Press.

Zhou, Wei. 2002. *Media Update*. Beijing: Guangming Daily Press.

Zhou, Weihua. 2005a. "The Problems of Publishing Reform: From the Perspective of Industrial Organization Theory." *China Publishing Journal* 4: 14–19.

———. 2005b. "The Report on the Chinese Publishing Industry." Beijing: China Renmin University Press.

Zhou, Xiaohong and Qin Chen. 2010. "Globalization, Social Transformation, and the Construction of China's Middle Class." In *China's Emerging Middle Class: Beyond Economic Transformation*, edited by Cheng Li, 84–103. Washington, DC: Brookings Institution Press.

Zhu, Guanglei. 1994. *Great Division Breeds New Organization: An Analysis of Social Stratification in Contemporary China*. Tianjin: Tianjin People's Press.

Zhu, Qingfang. 1998. "Characteristics of Urban Poverty, Poverty Reasons and Anti-Poverty Policies." *Social Science Research* 1: 62–66.

Zhu, Xixi and Changzhen Dai. 2009. "Knowledge Workers in the Socialist Market Economy." *China Economic and Trade Herald* 24: 103–104.

Zhu, Ying. 1995. "Major Changes under Way in China's Industrial Relations." *International Labour Review* 124: 37–49.

Index

About the Author

Dr. Jianhua Yao received his doctoral degree in sociology from Queen's University, Canada, in 2012. Before that, he majored in public administration, and obtained both his bachelor's and master's degrees from Fudan University in 2004 and 2007, respectively. Dr. Yao's research mainly focuses on political economy, media and communications, and labor issues, and he has been the co-translator of a few books, including *The Moral Foundations of Politics* (2006), *Critical Communication Theory* (2007), and *The Political Economy of Communication* (2013).

CPSIA information can be obtained at www.ICGtesting.com
Printed in the USA
BVOW03*0400070714

358213BV00002B/3/P

9 780739 186640